Fundamentals of Marketing

Fundamentals of Marketing

W. G. LEADER
N. KYRITSIS

Series created by W. G. Leader,
Principal of London City College and Joint Managing
Director of Business Expansion Consultancy Services Ltd

Edited by F. Roberts, B.Ed

Stanley Thornes (Publishers) Ltd

First published in 1989 by Hutchinson Education

Reprinted in 1990 by
Stanley Thornes (Publishers) Ltd
Ellenborough House
Wellington Street
CHELTENHAM GL50 1YD
England

Reprinted 1994 (twice)
Reprinted 1995 (twice)

British Library Cataloguing in Publication Data

Leader, William G
    Fundamentals of marketing
    1. Marketing
    I. Title   II. Kyritsis, Nick
    658'8

    ISBN 0 7487 0388 8

Printed and bound in Great Britain
at The Bath Press, Avon.

Dear Student

With courses becoming more and more intensive there is a greater need for students to have *precise study information* available so that they can study more efficiently and speedily.

At the same time this enables *tutors* to devote more effort towards the understanding and analysis of the subject. Rather than give up valuable time dictating and providing notes, they can concentrate more on actively involving students in the learning process.

In this text the authors have covered all aspects of coursework providing:

- A comprehensive text on the subject
- Study and exam tips on each topic
- Self assessment tests
- Past Examination questions
- Specimen answers to selected questions
- Answers to self assessment tests

The combination of these elements will greatly improve your confidence and performance in the examinations.

Dedicated to Roberta

Acknowledgements

The authors acknowledge with thanks the advice provided by Norman Waite, Director of Diploma Studies for *The British Institute of Marketing* and The Institute for permission to reproduce past examination papers.

We also thank *The Association of Business Executives* and *The Institute of Commercial Management* for allowing the reproduction of their past examination questions.

Contents

General study and exam tips

"In many situations information is so great a part of effectiveness that without information a really clever person cannot get started. With information a much less clever person can get very far."

Dr Edward De Bono

Being successful on a course does not simply result from listening to lectures or reading a textbook. You must become actively involved in the learning process in order to acquire knowledge and skills and perform well in assessments.

There is no reason why you cannot achieve this aim. After all you are on a course of study because an examining authority believes that you have the necessary ability to complete the course successfully. If you are prepared to become actively involved and do the work required, you have every right to feel confident that you can succeed in the final examinations.

These notes are designed to make your study more efficient, to ensure that you use this manual to best advantage and to help you improve both your coursework and your examination techniques. They have been divided into four parts:

1 general study tips
2 improving the quality of your work
3 examination technique
4 studying with this text

■ 1 GENERAL STUDY TIPS

An eminent physicist once said: 'Thinking is 99 per cent perspiration and 1 per cent inspiration'. Take his advice and that of most of us who have had the benefit of a good education. Ignore the advice of those who believe you can prepare yourself for the examination in one or two weeks. Knowledge and skills of any value are not easily learned. For most of us it takes time to understand and permanently remember the content of a subject; instead of forgetting everything immediately the examinations are over. Therefore start working at studying right at the very start of your course and continue at a steady pace until the examinations. Do all the work expected of you by your tutor including homework and mock/mid term examinations. Homework is good practice and the mock exams simulate aspects of the final examination. Doing them as well as you can makes your tutor more willing to help you, as he or she will see that you are playing your part in the learning process.

The knowledge and skills you will gain on your course of study are precisely the kind needed by professional business people. So approach the study of each subject as if you were in real life a business man or woman, or a person following a profession such as accountancy or law. In this way the subject should come alive for you, and your motivation to learn should increase.

To help realise this objective, read a quality daily and Sunday newspaper that has a good business section. By doing this you will discover what is happening on a day-to-day basis and be in a better position to understand the topics you are studying on the course. You will also broaden and deepen your knowledge of the subject. Professional people at work usually read a quality newspaper and monthly or quarterly periodical related directly to their discipline in order to keep abreast of the latest developments. You will probably wish to do the same when you commence work, so why not start now?

Carry a pocket dictionary with you and look up words you hear or read but do not understand. None of us has a complete vocabulary but we can improve it if we really want to be able to read and study more effectively. In the case of students it is even more important because words used in lectures, textbooks or newspapers often become misused in examinations. Some words which cause problems with their meaning or spelling are:

aggregate	disseminate	heterogeneous
antithesis	distinguish	homogeneous
constituent	evaluate	panacea
discipline	facsimile	prognosis

Do you fully understand how these words may be used in the context of your subject? Use a dictionary.

As soon as you start your course, find out if you are going to be given past examination reports for your subject, examiners' reports, specimen answers to previous examination questions and a work scheme. It is probable that they will not all be available at your school, college or university or even from the examining authority. You should, however, obtain as much information about your course of study and the examinations as possible so you know exactly what amount of work lies ahead of you and the academic standard you are expected to reach. This will help in planning your personal workload for the period of your course.

If you do not understand something ask your tutor. Do not assume that you are inadequate because you did not understand something that other students seemed to appreciate. They may be having difficulties too or your lecturer may simply not have explained the point to everyone's satisfaction. If something is overlooked by the tutor, don't be afraid to bring it to his/her attention.

Personal health is something that many students dismiss with comments such as: 'what has health got to do with ability to think?' Studies on the topic have now clearly indicated that general health and mental performance are statistically related. Within four weeks of being given multi vitamin and mineral tablets students in two separate controlled studies improved upon their written performance in intelligence tests by approximately ten points. Your commonsense alone should tell you that you cannot perform at your best if you continually feel tired or have flu or a heavy cold in an examination. Eat a varied diet that includes protein foods, vegetables and fruit, and get some daily exercise even if it is only a good brisk walk home after your day's study.

Contrary to the belief of many students, the best academic work is not done at night-time. Once again research shows that students perform better in the early part of the week, in the daytime – particularly mornings – and in a place where there is natural daylight to read and write by. Therefore plan your study schedule so that it is completed in the day. This will also leave you the evenings and weekends free to relax and enjoy yourself.

■ 2 IMPROVING THE QUALITY OF YOUR WORK

The earlier in the course you bring your work to a satisfactory standard the more likely you are to exhibit a good standard of work in the examinations. Obviously, academic standards do relate to the thinking abilities of the student but they also depend on motivation, and a logical approach to one's work if effective presentation at the appropriate academic standard is to be achieved. Here are three tips that will help you develop a logical approach to the presentation of your work.

Read the question carefully

When undertaking essay or numerical work make sure you read the question very carefully. Underline the key words in the question so that your mind is concentrated on the essential aspects. For example, distinguish between the two main types of question.

DESCRIPTIVE QUESTIONS
A descriptive question is one in which you will be expected to describe or explain something and possibly distinguish it from alternative or similar items or ideas. Two examples are:

(a) *Describe* and *distinguish above-the-line advertising* from other forms of *advertising*.
(b) *Explain* with the *aid of graphs, how the price* of a product is *determined* in a highly *competitive economy*.

Some of the key words have been emphasised in italics to give you an idea of which words are at the heart of the question. Always underline or highlight the key words yourself before attempting to answer.

ANALYTICAL QUESTIONS

These include the purely analytical question, or the analytical question that requires you to evaluate a statement (indicate your level of support for an idea/ give it a value) or only to present your own ideas. Examples of these are:

(a) *Solely analytical*: Analyse the contention that there is no such thing as fixed costs.

(b) *Analytical and Evaluative*: How far do you support the idea that adult behaviour is predominantly related to one's early childhood experiences?

If you have been presented with a minicase (short story) or case study (extended story) detailing opposing opinions regarding a problem a company is faced with, you may be requested to offer your own solution. In this event your answer should analyse the value of all the opinions offered in the case as well as possibly suggesting your own.

Consider also the way a question is structured. If it is in two or more parts give equal time to each if equal marks are awarded to each part. If more marks are awarded to one part than another, allocate your time in the same proportions as the marks awarded. For example, if a Question has marks awarded: part (a) 5 marks, part (b) 15 marks (total 20 marks), you should spend a quarter (5/20) of your time answering (a) and three quarters (15/20) on (b).

Sometimes the time you should allocate to a part of a question is indicated by the implied requirements of the question, rather than by marks. For example

Q1 (a) Briefly outline 'actual' and 'ostensible' authority.

(b) Brown and Brown Ltd contracted with a married woman for the laying of new carpets. After the work had been done, the woman's husband refuted the contract and refused to pay for the carpets. Advise Brown and Brown Ltd and the woman on their legal position.

By using the words 'briefly outline' the examiner is indicating that much less time should be spent on answering part (a). The question requires more marks to be awarded to part (b) as the analytical and applied nature of this part indicates that it is more difficult to answer.

With numerical type questions, such as in accountancy and statistics, do not assume that all you have to do is arrive at the right answer. Your tutor – or an examiner – will expect you to explain what you are doing as you introduce each set of workings, graphs, illustrations or tables. After all, how is your tutor to know how you arrived at the right answer if you do not explain? Even more importantly, even if you give the wrong answer, at least you will be given some marks for those parts of your calculation which are correct. Such subjects involve a large element of communication and if you do not communicate effectively in your answer what you are doing you will lose marks.

Construct an essay plan

Always spend a few minutes constructing an essay plan before answering a question. This only requires jotting down a few notes for each paragraph which indicates the approach you will take to your answer and the points you will include. This will make sure that you construct your essay in a logical manner and that you keep to a target when writing your answer.

Follow up with your tutor

To understand fully what is required when answering questions, ask your tutor about the work you have handed in and had marked if he or she has not commented sufficiently on your script, informing you of where you were right and wrong and why.

■ 3 EXAMINATION TECHNIQUE

If you are studying at college you can start improving your examination technique in the mock/mid term examination which will help you in the coursework assessment during the second half of the course as well as in the final examination. Here are a few tips on improving your presentation.

- *Always do rough workings*. Use essay plans and/or numerical workings to plan your answer, but on a page other than the one on which you start your answer to the question. Cross through your rough working before starting to answer the question.
- Select the questions you intend to answer and *start with the one you think you will find the easiest* to answer. In this way you may gain your highest marks early in the exam which is very important in case you do not complete the examination.
- *Keep an eye on the clock* so that you allow about the same amount of time for answering each question (unless one is a more difficult, compulsory question). Noting the time in order to complete all the questions you are required to answer gives you a better chance of achieving high marks.
- Allow at least a third to half a page for illustrations or diagrams. In this way they look like illustrations rather than scribblings and you have sufficient space available if you have to return to your illustration to add more detail later in the examination. Always explain what your illustration is supposed to illustrate.
- Unless otherwise instructed, use a complete page of graph paper for presenting graphs and make sure that you provide a title for any entries you have made. Explain what your graph illustrates.
- Do not present workings for numerical subjects such as accounts and statistics without explaining what you are doing and why.

If you would like a deeper understanding of study skills and exam techniques a useful book containing a wealth of tips and examples that will help you to succeed in examinations is *How To Pass Exams* by W. G. Leader, also published by Stanley Thornes.

■ 4 STUDYING WITH THIS TEXT

Stanley Thornes' student texts have been specifically designed to act as study aids for students while on a course, as well as present the contents of a subject in a way that is both interesting and informative.

Use this text as part of your study activities, adding your own or your tutor's notes at appropriate points. Study your textbook in great detail, making notes on the chief points in each chapter so that the ideas have gone through your own head and down onto the paper in your own words – though perhaps with key quotations from the text.

Don't get bogged down in any one chapter. If you really can't follow the chapter leave it and go on to the next, returning at a later date. What seems difficult at the start of your course in September will be easier by December and child's play by March! You are going to develop as you do the course – so don't give up too early. Perseverance is everything in acquiring professional status.

Do not just read the specimen answers provided at the end of certain sections. Study their content and structure in the light of what you learned in the particular section and what you learned earlier in this section. In this way your skill in answering questions set by your tutor and/or the examination should improve.

At the end of each section there are examples of past examination questions. Where the answer is to be in essay form jot down beside the question the major points that you think should have been highlighted when answering. Then check back with the appropriate text of the particular section to see if your answer would have been correct. If you are still uncertain, discuss the problem with your tutor.

Talking with the tutor and fellow students is essential for developing the ability to analyse problems.

Always complete the self assessment part of each chapter as they are designed to reinforce what you have learned and improve your recall of the topics. Check your answers with those provided in the manual. As repetition of a process improves one's memory, it is very useful to re-test yourself every few weeks or let someone else read the questions to you and tell you if you got them right.

If the subject covered by the particular manual involves value judgements do not assume that what is mentioned in the manual is the only correct version. Your tutor may have other opinions which are just as valid. What matters is that you have sufficient knowledge of the subject to illustrate a firm understanding of the topic in the examinations.

One of the best ways to study is to buy a lever arch file and make dividing pages from brown paper for each subject or chapter. File your notes, and your essays and any newspaper cuttings, articles, etc. that are relevant in the appropriate topic position. You will then have an easy-to-revise and lively set of notes. If you find it a bit bulky to carry, use a ring binder instead and then at the end of every week or two weeks transfer the notes you have made to the lever arch file, keeping it at home for safety.

Now that you have read these Study and Exam Tips you should feel confident to continue with your studies and succeed in the examinations. It just remains for ourselves and Stanley Thornes to wish you every success on your course.

1 Marketing

The Consumer is King

■ INTRODUCTION

Marketing is a business activity which is little understood by the general public and yet it is an essential part of most organisations intent on expanding within democratic countries that have a highly sophisticated economy. In fact, in such countries a majority of the very senior positions in industry are now taken up by candidates who have worked in an area of marketing such as selling, promotions, marketing research or distribution. This is an indication of the importance organisations place on having an efficient team of marketing men and women, who are not only knowledgeable in marketing, or an area of marketing, but who are also creative, original and highly motivated – personal attributes that are essential to being a successful marketer in what is a rapidly expanding, creative and challenging area of business.

So, what is marketing? Well that is a question we hope to answer for you in this first chapter by explaining the term marketing and providing you with an overview of marketing in action.

However, to obtain a comprehensive and broad overview of marketing we feel that it is necessary to look at four aspects of the subject, namely:

1 The historical development of marketing
2 The marketing function within organisations
3 The marketing concept and definition
4 The role of marketing within society

For this reason Chapter 1 has been divided into four parts each dealing with one of the above topics.

Subsequent chapters will concentrate on the detailed work involved in marketing such as pricing, product planning, promotions and distribution so that whether you are a student, already working in a marketing department or simply wish to know more about marketing this manual will provide you with a firm appreciation of the subject.

■ 1 HISTORICAL DEVELOPMENT

The germination of the marketing concept as we know it today can be seen in the writings of Adam Smith, the 'father' of economics, at the start of the British Industrial Revolution. In his book *Wealth of Nations* he states that 'Consumption is the sole end and purpose of production'.

This still applies for marketing people today when they claim that:

The Consumer has Sovereignty or
The Consumer is King

In other words, marketers are claiming that a company should first discover **what potential customers wish to purchase** and how much they are willing to pay for a particular product or service. The company should then determine if the desired product can be produced and sold by the company **at the price customers will pay** *and* **at a profit to the company.** It is in essence a simple concept. After all it seems nonsense to produce something that you cannot sell at a profit, and yet many companies have done just that, with the result that they became bankrupt.

The reasons why many companies have made profits was not through pleasing the majority of potential customers but through circumstances that may have existed at the time. This can be illustrated by looking at the period relating to the Industrial Revolution, in the nineteenth century.

The Industrial Revolution signalled the beginning of production of many products by machines – rather than by hand – and thus it became possible to supply goods to a greater number of potential customers. Most companies, however, were **production** rather than **marketing orientated**. In other words, manufacturers were more concerned with gaining a reputation for producing an excellent product, or a product that they personally thought was good (production orientated), rather than considering whether it was what the majority of people needed or could afford (marketing orientated).

These companies succeeded mainly because of the great demand that existed and the high level of supply of inexpensive raw materials available to manufacturers. Bear in mind that many people had previously not had the opportunity to buy many goods because, being handmade, they were very expensive. Thus, the major competition mainly existed between customers for the goods and not between manufacturers.

Up to the beginning of the twentieth century the following changes in production took place: changes that were to cause several companies to consider a marketing approach in the sale and distribution of their products.

1 As early manufacturers rapidly expanded, new entrepreneurs entered into the same areas of production as they saw the profitable opportunities.

2 Competition started moving from customers to the manufacturers, and so manufacturers found themselves competing with each other in terms of prices and volume of sales. The level of supply and demand, as a consequence, came closer together.

3 The supply of many raw materials and power for the production of goods started reaching levels of scarcity which gave them a greater value and therefore made profit margins tighter. This caused manufacturers to consider cheaper forms of production even if it meant a change in the materials that constituted a product.

4 Technology improved the means of communication, transport and production, thereby reducing production and transport costs and enabling manufacturers to sell over greater geographical areas.

5 Manufacturers began looking at their products in terms of the consumer's understanding of quality and style instead of the intrinsic value of the product and their (the manufacturers') own idea of quality and style.

Nevertheless, even with all these developing changes, most industries had only reached the point of **sales orientation** by the turn of this century. With sales orientation, obtaining immediate sales by intensive personal selling and promotions was the most important aim, particularly as sales people played such a significant role in a company's efforts. This was also due in part to there being a lack of mass media advertising services and, for that matter, public literacy. The belief was that sales could be maintained by investing more on selling the product rather than re-evaluating the product in the light of changes in the buying patterns of a market. There seems little sense in trying harder and harder to sell gas lamps when electricity is taking over or valve radios when transistorised ones are much lighter and more reliable. Therefore, sales orientation was not taking account of the broader social and trading environment that was affecting customers.

In the early part of this century Henry Ford, the founder of the Ford Motor Company, wittily stated that customers could purchase his new, mass produced 'Model T' car, first produced in 1908, '. . . in any colour they wish provided it is black'. Thus many writers on marketing have credited him with inadvertently announcing the start of modern marketing attitudes in business. He was, in effect, claiming that he would adjust his product and price whenever possible to meet the needs of potential customers. This, of course, he was only willing to do provided it meant that he could sell more cars at a profit. It is *this willingness of an organisation to reconcile the needs of customers with those of the organisation* that is essential in the understanding of the term **market orientation.**

Unlike production and sales orientation, market orientation starts by analysing what potential customers – who constitute a market – require and at what price, and then attempts to systematically direct the efforts of the organisation towards meeting the requirements of customers. That assumes of course that the organisation's needs and those of the market can be reconciled. Sufficient numbers of potential customers forming the market will not purchase if the price isn't right, and the organisation will not produce, distribute and sell if it does not obtain a satisfactory profit.

It was also at the turn of the century that the activity of marketing was being studied seriously as a systemised function in commercial companies. The addition of the marketing activity within companies has gathered momentum ever since, and today it is an essential aspect of most medium and large sized commercial organisations.

The expansion of marketing in many modernised western countries was also given new impetus by the Second World War and the resulting rapid growth of technical innovation. The war effort caused many manufacturers in Europe and America to produce exceptional amounts of their product. It was hoped that these high levels of production and sales would continue after the war. However, mass production requires mass markets for purchasing which in turn require the knowledge and skills of marketing personnel to identify, anticipate and stimulate demand to high levels and maintain that demand. The war effort had also stimulated rapid technical innovation and/or development which has continued ever since in the fields of transport, communication (e.g. television, telephones and telexes) and production (e.g. automation, robots, computers), all these being helpful to effective marketing. Thus, the usual 'push' and 'pull' characteristics of trading were amplified: industry wanting to 'push' demand to sell more and consumers demanding new and/or better products and services. This caused a 'pulling up' of demand and acceleration of changes to products and services.

The position today

We can see this today if we consider a few of the thousands of changes to trading and ways of life that have taken place in the industrialised countries in the last twenty to thirty years: the use of televisions and videos for domestic use, training, industrial and security purposes; microwave ovens and deep freezers in homes to make the storage of food and convenience of cooking easier; the use of advanced plastics by industrial and domestic users for storage units, fittings in aeroplanes and cars, window frames, gutterings, etc., making rusting and constant repairs almost a thing of the past; the growth of supermarkets and hypermarkets with carparks attached enabling shopping to be done once a week or less; computers acting as word processors for typing instead of the traditional typewriter. A credit card explosion has also enabled people to have more instant credit to pay for food, insurance, holidays, secondhand cars – in fact most purchases they may make. This of course increases demand as there is more credit available for purchasing.

Fast food service restaurants have invaded our high streets specialising in hamburgers, pizzas, jacket potatoes, fried chicken to name just a few. Many of the fast food restaurants, and for that matter shops, are now franchised establishments. In other words, individual owners (franchisees) operate the establishment but under a name that is known nationally, so the shop owners benefit from the mass advertising and marketing knowledge of the national franchisor. These franchised shops not only include food retailers but instant print services, clothes shops, photo processing and shoe repairs.

The general public too are being encouraged to buy shares in large companies and buy and sell items themselves. For example, it is possible to operate a mail order service from home or put on house parties (party planners) to sell items such as baby clothes, jewellery, plastic food containers, toys, towelling and many other specialised items. In the last decade 'boot fairs' have also grown in popularity where the general public may sell from the boot of their car any new or secondhand objects they have.

Family purchasing

And how have all these changes to trading affected the way of life of the individual or family? Well in the first place women are spending less time in the kitchen as machines take over some of the more mundane chores. People are preparing and/or buying more international foods and dishes as a result of spending holidays abroad and visiting restaurants offering an international menu. The same applies to alcoholic drinks, with the drinking of wine and lager growing rapidly. More people are watching television and hiring video films from shops, causing a fall-off in cinema attendances. People are living increasingly on credit as banks and building societies give more personal loans and encourage the use of credit cards. Household shopping is tending to be done by men and women together, instead of by the woman alone. People are travelling abroad much more for their holidays due to lower transport costs. As a result, hotels and holiday complexes are being built specifically to meet the needs of the holidaying market. Many old age pensioners, too, are being encouraged by hotels to live abroad during the winter months, when hotel prices are very low, in an effort to cover operating costs until the summer holiday season commences again.

However, one of the most significant changes in a family's expenditure is the way the individual family members now purchase goods and services. The modern family is tending to purchase fewer items as a group in which the mother and father were the sole influencers and deciders over what is purchased. The individual members of families today are more likely to purchase products and services for their personal use. Part of this movement has been caused by the increased spending power of young people, part by an increase in the amount and variety of products and services available for sale and part through parents taking a much more liberal approach towards their children's purchase of items.

If we could look into the home of a family of five today we may not see them all preparing to go to the cinema or sitting watching television together. It is more likely that one will be preparing to go to the cinema with a friend, another with a set of headphones stomping around the room to the latest pop music, two watching a video on the television and the fifth quietly reading a book with a glass of wine in his/her hand. The members of the family are, therefore, exhibiting much more of their individual character within the family unit.

In turn, movement towards personal purchases has caused the family unit to become more sophisticated purchasers discussing with each other the products and services available and their usefulness for the price paid. This has been reflected in the way companies promote their products. Increasingly they have to consider the individuals within the family and not just the mother and/or father.

Of course this may not yet apply in every country but do not assume that it will not. One of the ways marketers look for new product ideas and predict future movements in purchasing tastes within their country is by looking at other countries who have a similar social structure to their own but whose economic development is currently more advanced. From analysing what people are currently purchasing in such countries the marketer has some idea of the way purchasing tastes and habits will move in his or her own country.

The future will probably see the increased use of television for ordering goods and controlling one's own bank account. Stores and shops will be increasingly linked to credit houses by computer to check immediately if a customer has sufficient credit to buy the item(s) he or she has in mind. The variety of personal computers will grow and their cost become so low that most households will be able to purchase one for a number of uses. It will be possible to dictate complete books to a computer eliminating the need to learn to type.

By now you may be wondering why we have dwelt so long on a few of the most recent developments in society which the efforts of marketing have so strongly influenced. The reason is really quite simple. We touched at the beginning of this chapter on the idea that marketing starts by trying to discover what potential customers want and so you should study marketing more from the point of a potential customer rather than a student or producer. If you attempt to study marketing as if it has unchanging rules and regulations that you simply have to remember then you will never be good at marketing. You must study marketing as a living, changing subject. This requires, therefore, that you retain an open mind; be able to relate theory to real life situations; and think positively in order to convince others that you personally have the best marketing idea.

■ 2 THE MARKETING FUNCTION

We have already discovered that a company does not have to be large and have a full marketing department to have a marketing approach.

However, it is useful to examine the structure of marketing departments in large organisations to evaluate the functions of sections that make up the department, such as sales and marketing research.

The structure of a marketing department and the responsibilities of the marketing director or manager will differ from company to company but Fig. 1.1 illustrates what may be classified as a typical structure. In the real life situation there would of course be differences in the structure of departments according to what the managing director and board of directors consider the aim of the organisation should be. For example, an international organisation may

Fig. 1.1 *Marketing department*

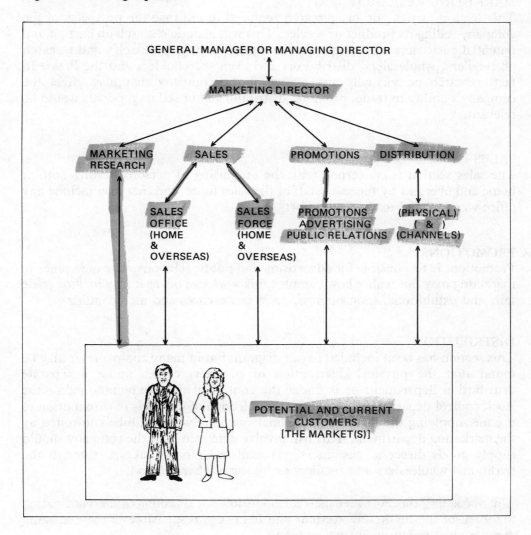

GENERAL MANAGER OR MANAGING DIRECTOR

MARKETING DIRECTOR

MARKETING RESEARCH   SALES   PROMOTIONS   DISTRIBUTION

SALES OFFICE (HOME & OVERSEAS)   SALES FORCE (HOME & OVERSEAS)   PROMOTIONS ADVERTISING PUBLIC RELATIONS   (PHYSICAL) (&) (CHANNELS)

POTENTIAL AND CURRENT CUSTOMERS [THE MARKET(S)]

have marketing departments in every one of its overseas subsidiaries (i.e. area), with the marketing director and a skeleton staff operating from head office directing and checking on the efforts of the overseas marketing departments.

The double pointed arrows in the diagram indicate how every part of the marketing function is communicating with its market(s) and relaying important direct and indirect information received about the market up to the marketing director and possibly on to the managing director.

We will consider the work done by each section of the marketing department in more detail later in this manual. At this point though we can briefly describe the function of each section to obtain an overview of its work.

MARKETING RESEARCH (MR)

This section carries out any research required to improve the prospects of the company selling its product or service. This will include research on current and potential customers who constitute the market (market research), and research on retailers, wholesalers, distributors and even shareholders and the Press. In fact, research on virtually any aspect of the company that may affect the company's ability to trade, promote, distribute and/or sell its products would be relevant.

SALES

The sales section is concerned with the organising of personal selling both at home and overseas by the sales staff of the sales force, and that may include any office work related to the sales effort.

PROMOTIONS

Promotions is responsible for advertising and public relations. The newcomer to marketing may not realise how complex this work can be, as it may include trade fairs and exhibitions, sponsorships, press conferences and merchandising.

DISTRIBUTION

This section has been included in our diagram but in many companies it may be found that the physical distribution of products comes under a separate distribution department or is under the control of the production and/or the stock control department. However, the selection of channels of distribution to use for supplying the product to the final customer would still be controlled by the marketing department. This will involve determining if the company should supply goods direct to customers, via mail order organisations, through the traditional wholesalers and retailers or by some other method.

The **marketing director**/manager is responsible for directing and co-ordinating the work of the marketing sections and is in turn responsible to the managing director/chief executive of the company.

In adding detail to the work of the marketing department, you may like to note that collectively its sections would probably be responsible for most or all of the following functions.

Selling	Selection, methods and	Public relations (PR)
Transportation	channels of distribution	Marketing planning
Branding	Financing of sales and	Product (good, item) or
Pricing	credit	service design and
Marketing research	Advertising	development
Labelling	Packaging	After sales service
Production scheduling		

Organisation of the marketing function

ORGANISING BY FUNCTION

In Fig. 1.1 we illustrated the marketing department organised according to the specialised functions of each section, i.e. promotions, marketing research, sales and distribution.

The advantages of organising on a function basis is that

1 Increased specialisation in each function may be obtained and used as a source of expertise.
2 As the marketing director is in direct control he or she can, through his or her authority, ensure that departments work efficiently together.

Disadvantages exist however, where:

1 The company deals in a great variety of unrelated products making it difficult for the marketing director to keep abreast of the characteristics and changes to individual products.
2 It can sometimes be difficult to accurately identify faults where products do not sell as well as expected as each department may be claiming that it was partly the fault of other departments.

Understandably therefore, organising by function may be the best method where a company sells one or few related products to the same markets.

PRODUCT ORGANISATION

Where there are a number of unrelated products being sold by a company some of the problems associated with organising by function may be overcome by organising by product (or groups of products). In this case individual product managers (PMs) are responsible for marketing a particular product or group of products.

They may use the services of the other specialised sections as and when they consider it appropriate to fulfil their marketing aims. Alternatively, if the company does not have a particular specialised section, such as promotions or marketing research, the product manager may use the services of an outside advertising and/or marketing research agency.

A typical structure of a marketing department organised by product is illustrated in Fig. 1.2.

This method also has the added advantage of making one person predominantly responsible for successes and failures of products under his/her supervision, thus improving motivation and placing the product manager in the role of entrepreneur.

However, there are disadvantages which include:

1 It is difficult to obtain people with the abilities of a successful entrepreneur.
2 PMs may have insufficient knowledge of the work of other functions to be able to have an adequate overview of the correct marketing methods that should be used.

Fig. 1.2

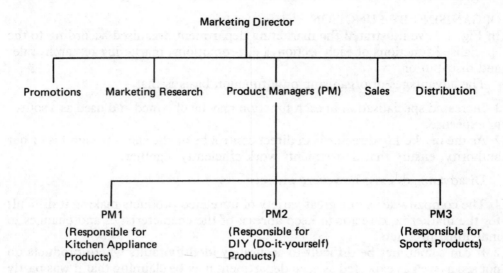

3 The PM will invariably lack the authority to direct the efforts of other functions towards fulfilling the activities considered necessary for successful marketing of the products.
4 PMs may spend more time liaising with other functions rather than with work directly associated with achieving increased sales.
5 The PM may see success in terms of the product (product orientation) rather than the needs of the market and thus overlook marketing opportunities.

Sometimes product managers are called *brand managers*, 'brand' being the name of an individual product (see Chapter 4).

ORGANISATION BY MARKET
A third method of organising is by particular markets that need a company's product or products. Marketing managers (MMs) will be responsible for marketing to the particular markets (current and potential customers) that require a significantly different marketing approach.

For example, a steel producing company may have a structure similar to that shown in Fig. 1.3.

The advantages of this structure are that:

1 It keeps the organisation marketing orientated.
2 MMs become very familiar with the market's needs.
3 Opportunities in the market become easier to identify, even if this means changes to products or the development of new products.
4 MMs once again act as entrepreneurs.

However, this method of organisation suffers from the same disadvantages as indicated in 1 to 4 of product organisation above.

Fig. 1.3

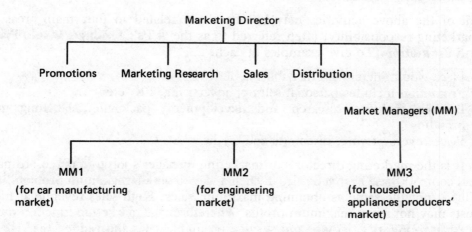

COMBINATION/COMBINED STRUCTURE

Large companies are often forced to combine one or more of the above methods of organisation, in order to accommodate highly diversified operations. A company, for instance, may operate in many different markets worldwide, involving a number of related or unrelated products. To illustrate the point, the company may have to use a structure similar to that shown in Fig. 1.4.

All methods of organising have their merits according to the size of the company, its volume of sales and the variety of products it sells. The advantages and disadvantages identified in relation to each structure can serve as guidelines to the appropriateness of structures to different situations.

Fig. 1.4

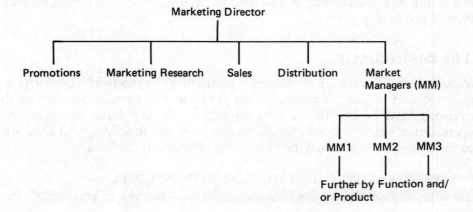

The marketing mix

All of the above activities may be effectively related to four main areas of marketing responsibility, often referred to as the '4 Ps': **Product, Place, Price** and **Promotion**. To give examples of each:

1 Place would include all distribution activities.
2 Promotion includes personal selling, advertising, PR, etc.
3 Product includes research and development, packaging, labelling and branding.
4 Price covers pricing, discounts and credit.

It is the marketing director's or marketing manager's job to mix (co-ordinate and control) these four activities in such a way to obtain maximum profitability. This is not the same as obtaining maximum sales. High sales revenue at high costs may not mean maximum profits. Therefore, the marketing function must attempt to **identify, isolate** and **service** profitable sales and **reduce the risk of losses**.

The 4 Ps also fundamentally determine the way potential customers will view the company, its service(s) and/or its product(s). When anyone is buying a product they are affected and influenced by the usefulness of the *product* to themselves, the *price* of the product, how well it has been *promoted* with particular regard to information supplied and the availability and/or rapid delivery of the product, i.e. to the *place* of purchase. Therefore, the 4 Ps represent the mix of ingredients that constitute the *marketing cake* to be presented to potential customers. For this reason the way the 4 Ps are arranged to facilitate sales has become known as the **marketing mix**.

To understand the marketing mix more clearly, think for a moment about how you would *price* and *promote* fur coats, the variety of fur coats you would offer (*product*) and where you would consider they should be sold (the *place*). Then compare the mix you have arranged for the 4 Ps with regard to fur coats with the arrangement of the 4 Ps that you would adopt for the sale of another product, say, ice cream. This simple exercise should illustrate how different the marketing mix is according to the trading circumstances (environment) and the type of product or service.

The environment

Mixing the 4 Ps to ensure the effective marketing of a product(s) however, is not quite so easy a task. The marketing function has to take account of those environmental factors that may indirectly or directly have an effect on the organisation's ability to sell. Organisations, just like individuals, operate within an environment which may be loosely divided into three levels.

INTERNAL ENVIRONMENT (MICRO-ENVIRONMENT)
All companies have an internal environment just like a household. People

sometimes agree and sometimes disagree in everyday life. The same applies to personnel and departments in a company. In the majority of cases this friction leads to the generation of new ideas, the motivation of staff and progress of the organisation. Occasionally it is destructive to an integrated approach, a point we will examine shortly.

MESO-ENVIRONMENT

This refers to the industry in which a company operates and the industry's market(s) and can be separated into three environments.

Task environment

- Suppliers to the company of raw materials or product parts for assembly
- Distributors of a company's product or service such as wholesalers and retailers
- A company's customers and the general market – their attitudes towards the product and company

Competitive environment

- The company's and competitors' share of the market (market share)
- The image of competitors
- Competitors' customers, suppliers and distribution network
- Competitors' products/services offered to the market

Public environment

- Financial publics, i.e. the people who constitute a group willing to supply finance or who can affect the current financial position of the company, such as shareholders
- The media – its coverage, availability, attitude to the industry or company
- Citizen groups, i.e. consumer and environmental groups
- The general public, i.e. potential customers

MACRO-ENVIRONMENT (NATIONAL ENVIRONMENT)

- Government directives or intervention
- Legal constraints
- Interest rates
- Inflation, deflation and unemployment
- Availability and level of credit in the economy
- Technological change and development
- Social changes
- Political stability, philosophy and policies
- Income levels within the community
- General patterns of consumer purchasing

Micro-environment, task and competitive environments will have a constant and generally more rapid effect on the company's ability to produce and market its product or service. Public environment and macro-environment will probably affect the company more intermittently. As the company is part of the environment it will, in turn, affect its environments to a greater or lesser extent.

The marketing manager must be aware of the effect of the various elements that compose these environments, particularly if measures are needed to counter unfavourable intentional or unintentional moves against the trading stability of the company. Likewise the likely effect of the company's activities on these environments must be considered if they are not to be antagonised.

Much of the way a company attempts to enhance its image with the publics who constitute each environment is by **public relations (PR)**. The service the PR section offers to the company is considered in the section on promotions.

A company will be constantly receiving feedback about all aspects of its environments from all of its operating sections, such as the sales force, marketing research, as well as directly from customers, the local and national media and organisations in the channels of distribution.

An integrated marketing approach

We have considered the need for a market orientated approach if a company is to succeed in a strongly competitive environment. This approach implies that all personnel and departments within an organisation should make the identification and satisfaction of customer needs their overriding priority. However, this is often not the case. Individuals within an organisation may be more concerned with whom they know and please within the company rather than with what they know about the product or service and how to be effective in meeting the needs of the customers. Again departments may be more concerned with what they perceive to be the purpose of the business rather than with determining how they can play their part in the organisation's overall attempt to satisfy the needs of current or/and potential customers.

Table 1.1 indicates how the marketing department and other departments may have opposing operating desires.

It would be naive to assume that the marketing department is right and the rest are wrong. This is not the case at all. Each department has a distinct function to perform and sensible objectives for its operation. What must be achieved is a balance between the opposing views with the idea of working

Table 1.1

Other departments	Other departments' desires	Desires of the marketing department
Research and development	A lot of time for developing innovations and new designs. Limited range of products and models.	Fast development of innovations to gain and keep market lead. Many products and models to spread risk of failure.

Purchasing (raw materials and/or parts for assembly)	Prefers to purchase standard parts. Likes economical purchase quantities. Fixed purchasing intervals.	Prefers non-standard parts so product has unique aspects. Rapid purchasing of parts so customers are not kept waiting for spare parts.
Production	Long production runs with plenty of warning of production needs (lead time). Standard orders. Easy assembly. Exacting quality control not preferred.	Short production runs, changing constantly to other products in the range to ensure regular supplies. Make size of production run equate to demand to ensure cost effectiveness. More complex assembly to ensure product and pack is pleasing to the eye. Good quality control to reduce after sale maintenance, returns and complaints.
Stock control	Few product lines. Fast movement of stock. Economic stock levels.	Prefer high stock levels with many product lines and models to ensure constant supplies to all segments of the market.
Finance	Strict controls on spending. Inflexible budgets. Pricing individual items to cover total costs.	Prefers individual justification for spending. Wants flexible budgets to meet changing conditions. May like to price some items to cover variable costs and prefers pricing that also develops future marketing opportunities and control.
Accounts	Prefers regular prices with straightforward transactions. Would like full financial details of customers. Low and severe credit terms and inflexible collection procedures.	Prefers to be able to employ as needed special prices and discounts as a strategic weapon against competitors and to develop sales. Leans towards minimum credit restrictions and liberal collection methods.

together to please current and potential customers in order to obtain and maintain sales. If all departments and personnel are working towards this end and the 4 Ps (product, place, price, promotion) are mixed in an effort to satisfy customers, then the company is said to have an **integrated marketing approach**. In other words all departments would be:

1 Focusing on identifying, anticipating and continually satisfying customer needs.
2 Working closely together, considering each other's role in the overall effort of producing a saleable product or service.
3 Aiming for profitability through a mutually acceptable exchange.

Fig. 1.5 illustrates the flow of an integrated marketing approach using a typical marketing orientated company.

Fig. 1.5 *Promotional messages and movement of product towards customers*

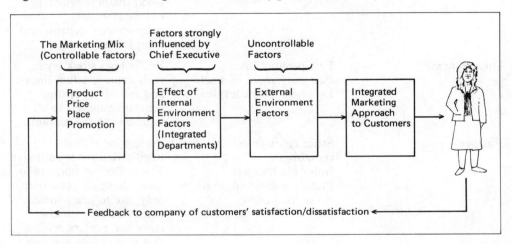

Feedback from the customers to the company may be verbal, non verbal or written. For instance, feedback may take the form of verbal complaints to salespersons, written or verbal complaints by customers to the company, answers to market research questionnaires, or simply, refusal to buy.

Customers may also complain or make constructive suggestions to individual departments within a company regarding delivery, incorrect invoicing, etc. This has the effect of making departments aware of customer needs and can help towards developing an integrated marketing approach and the reduction of friction within the organisation as departments and individuals appreciate the pressures on one another in trying to satisfy customers.

However, a reduction in internal friction and the development of an integrated approach can only be effectively achieved by a company's personnel and/or departments *systematically* and *regularly* considering the value of the company's products and services to customers.

This can be achieved by heads of departments meeting regularly to discuss the company's products in relation to market needs and then each head conveying the message to his/her own staff via departmental meetings. Many companies make this a more formal arrangement by forming a **value analysis team**, which is considered again in Chapter 4. Further means are the sending of non confidential reports of the marketing department to all heads of departments; regular meetings of the directors to consider policies and actions and group training of staff in new procedures related to newly introduced products or services. All these help to create a team spirit, as do in-house journals which inform all staff about problems, successes and expectations, particularly in relation to companies that have many branches.

Banks are now introducing closed circuit television in their branches connected to their central training department so that new customer service practices can be communicated immediately to all their staff throughout the country. Some companies use suggestion boxes for staff to recommend change to the product or production process, or encourage recommendations from customers through competitions, usually in the media or on the product pack.

Meetings with distributors, wholesalers and retailers to obtain their opinions and involve them in accomplishing the aims of the company can also be effective. If organisations in the channels of distribution can be united in achieving the company's goals, then a **totally integrated marketing approach** can be achieved. This aim is often encouraged by a company's advertising and sales personnel visits to the trade to ensure that the trade fully understands what the company is trying to provide for the final customer in the form of products and services.

Positive marketing

We have considered the importance of understanding the environment in which a company exists, in forming an integrated marketing approach and in ensuring the correct marketing mix to influence customers to purchase.

All of these activities rely on a company and its marketing department developing and maintaining a positive and progressive approach to the marketing of its products or services.

A company may do one of the following:

1 Remain passive and inflexible which will ultimately result in its extinction.
2 Change in keeping with changes by competitors and/or with the purchasing tastes of customers.
3 Initiate change and turn changes in the environment to its advantage.

Number 1 is not too difficult to accomplish but it is points 2 and 3 that market orientated companies would like to achieve. This may involve introducing new products or services, takeovers, mergers, diversification, gaining control of outlets or, if the company is a major outlet, such as a chain store, gaining control of one of their suppliers' organisations.

It is the duty of the marketing department to help in identifying profitable business and reduce risk of failure, regardless of whether this requires cutbacks, expansion of sales, mergers, takeovers or diversification into new products or services, because it is essential that *the business stays in business*.

■ 3 MARKETING – CONCEPT AND DEFINITION

If we visualised for a moment an *open air market* we would see the general public viewing the goods for sale at the stalls and traders who own the stalls attempting to sell the goods. In addition, manufacturers' vans may be delivering goods to the stalls for sale by the traders; mobile snack bars may be serving tea and coffee, and staff of the organisers of the market may be ensuring that everywhere is kept safe and tidy.

We might not see all the ancillary services that would be needed in order for these activities to take place. Services like buses to take some of the public to the market, insurance policies that traders may need, and repair services for stalls and vehicles. The reason that the services are needed is because the public and traders want the trading activities of the market to continue.

Seen nationally or internationally this is what is taking place every day. The world is like one gigantic market within which all of us are both helping to produce products and services and are also buying products and services. Indeed the trading (exchanging) is essential for societies to survive and prosper.

Marketing is interesting because it is concerned with the study of this **arena of potential exchanges**. Why do people buy certain products or services in preference to others? What effect does a company's sales effort have on potential customers? In what ways do changes to a company's product or service influence current and potential customers who form a part of the total market? These are just a few of the questions marketing attempts to answer.

Of course exchanges don't always have to be between a commercial company and its customers. It may be that the exchange is 'goods for goods' between two companies, two countries or just two people. Exchanges may even apply between a political party and potential voters such as when the political party promises to take certain action when it is in government in return for the vote of potential voters. Indeed, marketing activities are needed by many non profit making organisations such as charities, unions, clubs, institutes, societies and even celebrities, to name but a few. Communist governments too, are now using marketing activities to improve their economies within an overall communist framework. All these organisations or individuals have one thing in common: they wish to communicate with a market with a view to providing a product or service in return for a money payment, or other goods or services.

As an extreme example, to illustrate the point, a few years ago a government employed marketing services to find out why old age pensioners were not claiming from the government the money to which they were entitled. A marketing company, retained by the government, discovered that some pensioners saw the payments as charity and therefore didn't take the money; others didn't know of the offer, and the rest found the government's claim forms just too difficult to understand and fill in. By employing correct communications, the marketing company, on behalf of the government, resolved the problem. The pensioners were convinced that they were entitled to these payments because of the taxes they had paid during their working years. In addition, the claim forms were simplified and overall satisfaction was achieved. Exchange, therefore, still applied.

This idea, of exchange, is important not only for the understanding of markets but also in understanding the concept of marketing. If we do not appreciate the concept of marketing or, put another way, the **marketing concept**, it is difficult to grasp the overall purpose and approach to marketing.

Marketing concept

Philip Kotler expressed the marketing concept in the following way.

> The **marketing concept** *is a* **customer orientation** *backed by* **integrated marketing** *aimed at* **customer satisfaction** *as the key to satisfying organisational goals.*

Kotler proposes therefore that there are *three essential conditions* to the philosophy or concept of marketing, namely:

1 customer orientation
2 integrated marketing
3 customer satisfaction

①By using the words '**customer orientation**' he was proposing that an organisation should look towards the needs of current and potential customers in determining what the company should be producing and at what price. You may argue that this approach doesn't account for inventions where neither a company nor the public could possibly know if there is a demand for the invention – such as television – until it becomes available to potential customers. Here, however, we must assume that there is an implied need for televisions by the public as they were purchased when they became available. It is part of the work of marketing personnel to **anticipate** and **identify** the needs of potential customers for new or proposed products.

We must also assume that the word 'customer' as used in the concept includes **current and potential customers** as it is only through attempting to satisfy the needs of both that an organisation expands. In practice, however, an organisation can only hope to please a limited number of potential customers in the market as its competitors will also be satisfying the needs of customers with their own variation of the same product. For instance, in the total market for tinned beans there are many suppliers, such as Heinz and Crosse & Blackwell, each satisfying different tastes.

②We have already considered the concept of '**integrated marketing**' so you should now appreciate Kotler's reason for including it in his concept of marketing. To recall: it was pointed out that, if an organisation has an integrated marketing approach there is constant encouragement of all departments to work together and fulfil their role in pleasing the customer.

This may not fully apply to single operator concerns where there may not be a 'thought out' integrated approach to marketing. Nevertheless, the sole proprietor of a business which is successful probably has an integrated marketing approach in the way trading is conducted. Indeed, if the company were to grow and take on numerous employees, departments and branches, the proprietor would then have to think about how to instil in all the employees his or her desire and ability to please the customer; in other words, how to integrate their marketing effort.

③'**Customer satisfaction**' no longer assumes that the customer is always right. It merely indicates that we should start from the idea that the customer is right and always attempt to produce and supply goods or services that customers want at the price acceptable to the customers and the producer.

We must also assume that the word 'organisation' as used in Kotler's concept covers individuals such as presidents, prime ministers, pop stars and other celebrities, commercial companies, governments and non profit making organisations.

One implication of using the word 'organisation', however, is that marketing is for the good of the organisation paying for the service and does not help society as a whole. This we could not infer from what Ohio State University in 1965 considered marketing to be, namely,

Marketing may be considered as **the process in a society** *by which the demand structure for economic goods and services is anticipated or enlarged and satisfied through the conception, promotion, exchange and physical distribution of goods and services.*

Here we understand that marketing and its rewards are not solely the province of business activity but are also an understandable and acceptable national and international economic and social process. Ohio University may have some support here from communist countries which believe they are using marketing for predetermined social goals of their society.

Keeping Ohio's approach in mind, justifiable additions to Kotler's concept may be the words **continually** and within a **society**. The concept may now read:

The marketing concept is a customer orientation backed by integrated marketing aimed at **continually** *ensuring customer satisfaction as the key to satisfying the goals of an organisation within a* **society**.

The word 'continually' was added to emphasise that marketing is not a one-off operation but a continuing daily process. 'Society' is meant to include national or international societies and indicates that organisations *must* take into account current and anticipated *social* and *legal requirements* of society when satisfying customers.

Marketing definition

The marketing concept outlined the overall philosophy of marketing but it didn't define what people involved in marketing are attempting to do. Kotler defines the actual activity of **marketing** as follows:

> *Marketing is the set of human activities directed at facilitating and consummating exchanges.*

A weakness in this definition seems to be that it may be possible to imagine political negotiations as 'marketing' when independent negotiators bring opposing sides around a table and attempt to persuade them to exchange pieces of land with each other in settlement of a dispute. Nevertheless, he does acknowledge the exchange idea and doesn't lead us to assume that marketing is solely concerned with consummating exchange on behalf of organisations.

The American Marketing Association (AMA), on the other hand, defines marketing as:

> *The performance of business activities that direct the flow of goods and services from producer to consumer or user.*

A major weakness of the AMA's definition is that it ignores customer satisfaction or reconciliation which indicate that marketing is a two way process. The two way communication process arises because an organisation continually informs the customer of what it has to sell and at what price and likewise customers respond by buying or not buying and indicating their attitude to the company by complaints or praise, etc.

The British Institute of Marketing's (BIM) definition appears only to concern commercial enterprises and clearly indicates that the definition should include the management function, when it states:

> *Marketing is the management process responsible for identifying, anticipating and satisfying customer requirements profitably.*

Kotler prefers to include management only in his definition of marketing management and states:

> **Marketing management** is the analysis, planning implementation, and control of programmes designed to bring about desired exchanges with target audiences for the purpose of personal or mutual gain. It relies heavily on the adaptation and co-ordination of product, price, promotion, and place for achieving effective response.

By now you may be somewhat confused by this discussion of marketing concepts and definitions, but don't despair. Whichever concept or definition you choose to agree with, in part or total, is not as important as analysing and considering the value of each. If you are a student, examiners are more concerned with your ability to show that you have an understanding of the overall philosophy of marketing and the marketing approach as applied by organisations than with your ability to recall half a dozen definitions or concepts. Most examining bodies quite rightly take the view that marketing within society has a major role to play and one that has ethical considerations attached. It is essential, therefore, that anyone practising the discipline has at least some idea as to its purpose in relation to business, the individual and society.

■ 4 MARKETING AND SOCIETY

If you ultimately take up a career in marketing there is little doubt that you will one day find yourself discussing the role of marketing with people who believe that marketing has an adverse affect on society. Many questions may be asked and accusations made; but the more usual ones are detailed here (1–5) so that we may then assess their value from the point of view of a marketer.

1 Marketing manipulates and exploits people

Many companies have manipulated and exploited people long before the marketing function emerged. This probably occurs to a greater degree when companies do not exactly produce what people want; then, the company is more likely to try harder to convince potential customers to buy by unscrupulous sales techniques.

Increased use of advertising through the media – which are tools of marketing – has meant that there are more clear claims publicized about the usefulness of a product to which the salesforce and company must adhere if the company is not to be sued. This must be better than leaving every individual salesperson to determine his or her own message in order to make a sale.

Since more companies are using marketing methods to communicate their messages to the public, we, the public, are more aware of the alternatives available. We have, therefore, more choice and we are less likely to be influenced by only one company. For instance, when a car is technically out of date its future is invariably doomed, no matter how much a company tries to convince people to buy, because the public is aware of technical advances or price incentives of the company's competitor(s).

2 The marketing function is an added cost to the product

Research has shown that effective marketing can actually reduce costs. By first determining the number of people who want to purchase a product at a certain price level, companies can plan their efforts to accommodate that demand. In doing so they eliminate as much waste as possible, become cost effective and thus make larger profits (or compete more effectively against competitors).

It is better for a company to do this than to produce what it hopes will be the demand and then find that there are massive surpluses of unsold items. Just think of the mountains of stored food in the modern world because countries subsidise the production of items or food (often for political ends) instead of directly encouraging producers to produce only as much as the market demands. All of us, innocent of these actions or not, have to pay for this needless storage via government taxes or increased prices.

It is the effective use and distribution of scarce resources that is the basis of **economics**. If we accept that consumers should, in a democratic society, have the right to determine what they will buy, then marketing is an effective means of ensuring that resources used by the world relate to the demand of governments and individuals. For the benefit of us all, we must avoid the waste of the world's resources and production surpluses. Marketing can help to fulfil this aim by determining the extent of demand to ensure that supply matches demand and doesn't exceed it.

In the strictest sense, if marketing is considered to be an added cost of production then accounts, personnel, stock control, distribution, research and development must also be considered in this way.

3 Marketing encourages the production of products that people don't need

This depends on how you define the words 'need' and 'want'. If 'need' is intended to mean that which is essential to life, then most of what we have is not needed. On the other hand if people are to be allowed to choose what they will buy in relation to the standard of living in their society then in that sense they 'need' it. 'Want' would not suffice as it does not imply a driving force inside people that causes them to buy. Likewise, 'want' is often more loosely used to indicate something we would like but which is often outside our current purchasing power.

If we consider some of the products that have appeared in this century it will cause us to think very carefully about the words 'needs' and 'wants' in relation to ourselves personally and society as a whole. Do you think for instance, products and services such as buses, lorries, motor cars, aeroplanes, computers, robots, hovercraft, televisions, radios, videos, electric lighting and power and the use of telephones to name but a few are 'needed' or simply 'wanted' in modern society? Do you think they improve the standard of living by aiding industrial production as well as personal quality of life? Food for thought.

Of course, we are all able to mention products we do not consider remotely essential, but we would probably finish up arguing over the choice. Arguments that have existed long before marketing departments were established. These may be products such as fur coats, gold and diamond items, luxury furniture, first class travel and, for that matter, overseas holidays. Also, what is not considered 'needed' by society at one particular time may be needed at another. Consider, for instance, home insulation, double glazing and 'compact homes' to reduce the cost of energy both nationally and domestically.

It has been shown, in industrialised countries, that over the last eighty years, personal incomes haven't risen to enable individuals to afford those originally costly items that are now found in every household. Good design, technical advancement and mass marketing have resulted in the fall in cost and, therefore, prices in relation to incomes have come down to suit the pocket of the ordinary person in the street.

For instance, cars were originally very expensive being mainly hand-made and purchased by the wealthy. Now, however, car bodies are pressed out, seat covers are predominantly vinyl, not leather, and cars are much smaller, with the result that most adults in the community can now afford a new or second-hand car.

4 Marketing is only interested in short term gains

The easy answer to this is to consider the initial investment in aeroplanes, oil rigs, ships and the development of inventions. These all require long term investment in the hope that there will be a future market at a satisfactory price. Nevertheless, marketing departments have to advise their companies on such investments. They realise that if a company is to remain in business, evaluating short, medium and long term prospects and balancing the three to ensure continued profitability is a necessity. The long term investment in computers and cars in the West, undertaken mainly by commercial companies, has meant that the West is currently far ahead of the communist bloc countries in the technical development of these products.

5 Marketing causes inflation and unemployment

Both of these claims are bogus. Unacceptable levels of inflation and unemployment have occurred at regular periods for at least a century. Their cause has often been too much spending power in an economy, rising costs of production, underproduction, overstimulation of the economy, world trade cycles or war.

Invariably this condition requires action by the particular government to reduce or increase spending power in the economy, increase or decrease investment, initiate an incomes and wages policy or possibly make changes in the value of the currency.

Marketing personnel do not want unemployment or inflation as both will ultimately limit people's real spending power. Marketing is more concerned with only producing what is required and with encouraging transactions in an economy. For this to take place regularly money should be kept circulating and working and not left to stockpile without any purpose.

General ethical considerations

It would be wrong to assume that marketing doesn't have an ethical basis. All areas of life, including individuals, are subject to moral considerations. How many people for instance, have sold their secondhand car without telling the buyer all that was wrong? How many political parties have made promises to the public in order to get into office, promises that they were not quite sure they could fulfil when in office?

The best guarantee we can have of desirable trading practices probably exists where everyone in society has a sense of fair play and governments take on the responsibility of protecting our environment through antipollution, consumer, and fair trading acts, directing the economy efficiently and ensuring the just distribution of wealth so that we can all enjoy the fruits of our contribution towards a more productive society.

Voluntary consumer protection groups have helped accelerate the pace of change towards better controls to prevent exploitation, develop a better ecological environment and improve the safety of products. The efforts of these groups, of which there are many in most industrialised countries, are often collectively referred to as **consumerism**. Their efforts however, are no longer solely directed at large, private enterprises. Increasingly it is professional bodies, state owned or controlled companies or the state itself which are becoming targets of their efforts.

It is, of course, the government that should take care of our well-being, but often it is too concerned with the current political situation or is too cumbersome to be able always to identify and take action quickly enough where problems concerning trade arise. Therefore, we are probably always going to need these groups to act as the healthy conscience of us all, to protect us from unscrupulous people in positions of power or simply for putting forward alternative points of view.

We have mentioned in this section the problems communist countries have had in the development, production and distribution of their goods. This is changing rapidly as many communist countries are now beginning to adopt marketing methods. The intention is for these developments to be directly overviewed by the state and the benefits that accrue to be in line with the overall philosophy of the community. This is a bold move as it is difficult to return to an austere production-orientated economy once a public has become used to purchasing what it considers it needs. With Western governments imposing more exacting controls over public and private enterprises and Eastern governments allowing more freedom of production, the methods of trading of the East and West are coming closer together.

One certainty is that marketing personnel will increasingly consider the needs of society when considering the needs of the organisation and its customers.

SUMMARY

Having overviewed the need for marketing and the role of the marketing activity we may now encapsulate much of what has been covered in the essence of the **marketing policy**.

The **marketing policy** within a market orientated company is to:

1 Identify the potential customers at **whom** the marketing effort should be directed.
2 Determine **what** products or services the company should be providing.
3 Define **how** the marketing activities should be organised and the activities that should be undertaken to ensure that potential customers are encouraged to purchase and that products are efficiently distributed to customers.

The marketing policy therefore, may be considered as the **What?**, **Who?** and **How?** of marketing. The first two points listed above will involve the formal and informal continuous gathering and interpretation of information about the market and its needs which we will consider in Chapter 3. The third point will involve the efficient mixing and directing of the 4 Ps which we will start to consider in the next chapter as we look at the markets, products and services with which marketing is concerned.

Throughout this chapter we have spoken of the role and purpose of marketing in general terms but in the next chapter we will begin to analyze more closely the major markets, products and services, as well as assess the value to marketers of segmenting markets

■ STUDY AND EXAM TIPS

1 If you anticipate that you will have to answer questions on the marketing concept ensure that you have remembered at least two concepts and definitions so that you can draw comparisons.

2 When answering questions on marketing, wherever appropriate, use examples of which you personally are aware as they add credence to your answer and make the examiner aware of your broader interest in the subject. With this aim in mind it helps to keep your eye on what is happening in your local shops and supermarkets.

3 If you are still having difficulty understanding concepts and definitions, try to remember that a concept gives a *general idea* of a subject, whereas, a definition *provides a clear description* of the subject.

4 Unless you are very confident – or unable to answer an alternative question – avoid questions which tend to be more abstract, like the marketing concept or definition as it is easy to become confused over concepts, definitions and the role of marketing. Instead, try answering those questions which are more factual (such as the marketing function or the historical development of marketing).

■ SELF ASSESSMENT QUESTIONS

Answer the following questions and then refer to the answers given at the end of this manual to determine the marks you achieved. Award one mark for each complete question you answer correctly. If you read the chapter efficiently you should obtain ten or more marks. Re-read those parts of the chapter which relate to the questions you failed to answer correctly.

Time allowed for answering all questions 7 minutes.

1 Complete the following sentences
  (a) The consumer is _KING_____
  (b) The consumer has _SOVERIENTY_____

2 Name three types of business orientation.
  (a) _____Product_____
  (b) _____Sales_____
  (c) _____Market_____

3 Marketing is always concerned with private companies and profit.

  | ☐ TRUE   ☑ FALSE (tick appropriate box) |

4 Is marketing a one way or a two way communication function.

  | ☐ ONE   ☑ TWO (tick appropriate box) |

5 It is solely profit orientated organisations that use marketing activities.

  | ☐ TRUE   ☑ FALSE (tick appropriate box) |

6 During the industrial revolution many manufacturers of non essential consumer goods were successful because:
(a) They produced items of standard quality

(b) They used cheap labour
(c) There was a position of demand in excess of supply
Which statement is the more correct?

☐ (a)   ☐ (b)   ☑ (c) (tick appropriate box)

7 What do the 4 Ps stand for?
(a) _Promotion_
(b) _Price_
(c) _Product_
(d) _Position/Place_

8 Name the three types of environment in which a commercial company operates.
(a) _Meso_
(b) _Macro_
(c) _Micro_

9 Which of the following do you consider to be the most fundamental to effective marketing?
(a) to have a good quality product
(b) to commence by identifying and analysing the needs of the market
(c) to ensure that the organisation has all the necessary marketing functions
(d) to have a production unit

☐ (a)   ☑ (b)   ☐ (c)   ☐ (d) (tick appropriate box)

10 To be totally effective a marketing director should be in charge of four areas within the company. Three of these are the sales, promotions and marketing research departments. Which of the following is the possible fourth?
(a) Advertising
(b) Sales Office
(c) Distribution
(d) Production
(e) Market Research

☑ (a)   ☐ (b)   ☐ (c)   ☐ (d)   ☐ (e) (tick appropriate box)

11 The way the 4 Ps are blended is referred to as the
Marketing Mix

12 Complete the following:
   When the 4 Ps are effectively mixed, and all departments of a company are working in harmony towards satisfying customer needs and the channels of distribution understand and are supporting the efforts of the company, then it may be considered that the marketing effort is fully _ _ _ _ _ _ _ _ _ _ _ _ _ _ _ _ _

13 State one of the definitions of marketing as used in Chapter 1.

14 State one of the concepts of marketing as used in Chapter 1.

_____
_____
_____

15 One way of organising the marketing department is by function. Name two more.

(a) _____

(b) _____

■ EXAMINATION QUESTIONS

The British Institute of Marketing

1 Marketing is increasingly being used by non profit organisations such as colleges, libraries and political parties. Discuss the relevance of the marketing concept to the non profit organisation and suggest why such organisations are making more use of the techniques of marketing.

2 Outline and discuss those factors which you believe have given rise to the need for companies to be marketing orientated.

The Association of Business Executives

3 In principle, all functions of a business should co-operate harmoniously in the pursuit of common objectives. In practice, deep rivalries and misunderstandings are common. Outline some of the major reasons for conflict between a marketing department and the production department of a firm. How might friction be reduced?

4 'Consumption is the great end and object of industry.' In the context of marketing and the marketing concept, discuss the relevance of this statement.

The Institute of Commercial Management

5 How would you distinguish between the following:
The production orientated company,
the sales orientated company,
and, the marketing orientated company?
Include in your answer the reasons for the need for a company to be marketing orientated in today's business environment.

6 In a marketing orientated company what range of activities might take place in the marketing department? When implementing the marketing concept what problems might arise?

IMPORTANT! IMPORTANT!

Do not continue to read any further without firstly reading *General study and exam tips* (see pages xi–xvii)

2 Markets, products and services

People buy what products and services can do for them.

In the previous chapter we gained an overview of the various aspects of the marketing philosophy and we established the major benefits of such an approach to a company and to the consumer.

It is necessary now to put some detail on that overview by considering the markets, products and services that are at the very heart of marketing activities.

The aim of the three parts of this chapter is, therefore, to consider the following:

1 The meaning of the term 'market' and to gain an understanding of the major markets that exist.
2 The characteristics of the products and services that are available and their classification.
3 How major markets may be analysed and divided into smaller segments to improve marketing opportunities.

Once we fully understand these basics of marketing we can more effectively analyse the application of marketing activities such as promotions, pricing and distribution in later chapters.

■ 1 MARKETS

Having considered the economist definition of a market in Chapter 1 as 'an arena of potential exchanges', it is now necessary to consider the definition of a market used by marketers. Marketers do not tend to include sellers when they define a market although in a way they should, for when a company enters a market they invariably encounter competition (sellers) as well as buyers, and often a completely new trading environment. Instead marketers adopt a very concentrated and positive approach by relating their definition solely to the buyers in a market with the definition:

the market is all individuals and organisations who are actual or potential customers for a product or service

In terms of the main body of work of marketers this proves a useful definition, though, when it is used, it is essential that it is used precisely. If for example, you asked a person actively marketing wine, 'What is the market for wine?', it is doubtful if you would receive an instant reply. Instead he or she would ask you questions to discover exactly which wine market you are referring to: questions like 'Do you mean the world or home market for wine?' or 'Are you speaking of our particular type of wine?'. Therefore, when marketing people mention a market they are careful to define the market they are speaking of in clearly defined terms such as 'What is the market for dry red wine in the southern states of America if we sell it at around $25 per 70 cl bottle?'.

It is only by being this precise about a market that they can begin to consider if it is worth marketing their product and it is only when a possible market is identified for the company's wine (the **target market**) that the feasibility of selling the wine in the area can be assessed.

Sometimes, however, we cannot always clearly determine if a market exists. This may have to rest on the experience of the marketer rather than on absolute knowledge. There is an old story that illustrates this point. Two salesmen from different shoe manufacturers went to a country to see if there was a potential market for shoes. Having arrived in the country and found that no one wore shoes one salesman wrote back to his company requesting to return claiming there was no market for shoes as no one wore them. The other salesmen wrote to his company, 'Wonderful news! This country has great potential. No one here wears shoes.' Therefore, the way that we assess situations obviously depends to a great degree on our knowledge, experience and personal attitude.

Of course the company of the second salesman would then ask him to make some sales of shoes so that they can, at least, confirm that people will buy. The story does however, illustrate the need for a realistic but positive approach to marketing if marketing opportunities are not to be overlooked.

Major types of markets

Having analysed the term market let us now consider for a moment the market in terms of who may buy a particular product, for example milk.

There is the general public who will buy milk in bottles or small cartons in order to drink it, use it to whiten their tea or coffee or even use it as a basic food for themselves or their children. They are purchasing to obtain personal satisfaction through **consuming** the product.

Other people, like restaurant owners may buy milk in larger containers in order to use it in the process of making a different product like tea, coffee or a milkshake. A manufacturer of desserts may buy milk in bulk (very large quantities, not packed) to produce desserts which may be for sale in restaurants or through shops or supermarkets. Another group of people, like shopowners, may buy a substantial number of bottles or cartons of milk in order to resell them to the general public. In these instances the purchasing motive relates to **using** the milk towards making a profit rather than consuming the product itself for one's own personal satisfaction.

Finally another group of people, e.g. a charity organisation, may buy many pints of milk in order to give them free of charge to people in need, such as the sick, homeless, orphans or the very poor. The motive for the purchase in this example is quite different from the reasons behind the other purchase situations described. They could, in fact, be considered to have a social motive for purchasing the milk but once again they are purchasing and **using** the milk for providing a social service rather than personally consuming it.

From these simple examples we can see that the **same product can be purchased by many different people or organisations for different reasons**. If you have understood the examples used above, then you already have an insight into the two **major markets** which marketers need to consider. These are

1 Consumer markets
2 User markets

and they can be broadly distinguished by the **types of people** (or **organisations**) buying a product, and the **motive** behind the purchase.

Consumer and user markets

Consumer markets may be defined as individuals or groups of individuals making the *final purchase* of products or services to *consume* them for *personal satisfaction*.

User markets may be defined as organisations or individuals purchasing products or services in order to *use* them as part of providing further products or services in the effort to fulfil a *profit* or *non profit making goal*.

You may understand these definitions a little more clearly if you firstly follow the process by which a product is produced, distributed and finally purchased. As a simplistic example we will use motor cars as our product and in Fig. 2.1 trace the production and final sale of cars and then analyse the markets that may be involved.

INDUSTRIAL OR PRODUCER MARKETS
As the name suggests this market is concerned with the production of goods and services and may be defined as:

> *a market consisting of individuals and organisations purchasing products and services for use in the production of further goods and service for sale, lease or rental at a profit*

Fig. 2.1 *An outline of the process for producing, distributing and selling cars*

INDUSTRIAL MARKETS

A. Companies extracting the basic raw materials
   for the production of cars.

   Iron ore for making steel,
   Rubber for making tyres,
   Crude oil,
   Sand for glass, etc, etc,

B. Producers of parts for car manufacture,
   and ancillary service and suppliers ie, construction
   services and office suppliers.
   Parts include: radiators, wheels, gearboxes,
   electrics, windows etc, etc,

C. Car manufacturers.
   Produces more parts such as the engine
   and body and assembles all parts to
   make the finished car.

INDUSTRIAL MARKETS

D. Resellers

RESELLER MARKET

   National and regional distributors,
   agents, wholesalers and retailers sell the
   finished cars to companies and individuals
   in other user markets and consumers in the
   consumer market.

iv. **Metamarkets,**
   Government
   Councils
   Charities
   Unions etc,

iii. Consumers, (**Consumer Market**)

   Consumers purchasing for personal satisfaction.

USER MARKETS

It would include extractors, processors, agricultural producers, the construction industry, manufacturing organisations, the transport industries and service industries to name but a few of the major industries.

RESELLER MARKET
The reseller market may be defined as:

the market whose purpose it is to acquire goods and services in order to sell, lease or rent them to others at a profit

Its main functions are the distribution and resale of finished products and services. Included would be national distributors, wholesalers, retailers, agents and auctioneers – in fact, almost any individual or organisation who acts as an intermediary (person in the middle) between those who produce goods and services and those who want to purchase them. The most well known segment of this market is **retailers**, i.e. shops, supermarkets, department stores and other organisations selling direct to the final purchaser in this chain of distribution, the consumer.

There are, however, many other intermediaries not so well known, such as the exclusive agents of rock stars who control the singing services of the star, agents of producers in the industrial market selling to others in the industrial markets and auctioneers of industrial or consumer products.

THE METAMARKET
'Meta' means 'related to or extension of the main body' and that is what the metamarkets are: that group of producers and/or suppliers of goods and services who cannot easily be classified in the other main markets, such as charities, government services, clubs, political parties, institutes and associations, unions, etc. Unlike organisations in other markets the organisations within the metamarket do not always aim to make a profit surplus to their operating costs. A social or political cause is more likely to be central to their aims.

Depending on the organisation, part of their operation may be directly involved in industrial market operations, and another part in the reseller market. Part of an organisation may make a profit while the whole organisation itself does not:

- A charity may own profitable retail shops which sell items to the public to obtain money for the production of goods and services to be given to the beneficiaries of the charity.
- A government may own all health services to provide a non-fee paying health service, but may also provide a few medical services for those who want the service – such as overseas visitors – and are willing to pay.

CONSUMER MARKETS

The consumer market is concerned with purchasing goods and services for final consumption; hence the word **consumer**. The market consists of men, women and children constituting potential or actual final purchasers who purchase for personal satisfaction. We have already defined this market but we will be considering its characteristics and purpose further in this section because of its importance in marketing.

The point is, therefore, to use the classification of markets mainly as a guide to what individuals and organisations are doing, why they are buying and who they are serving. Markets and marketing are organic parts of life's activities that are constantly developing and changing and the subject should be treated this way rather than as a subject that has inflexible laws and definitions – otherwise you may not recognise developments and changes if and when they do occur.

SERVICES

Services such as transport and insurance may be allocated to market areas in much the same way as producers depending on the market they are intended for, an aspect we now consider.

The purchaser and the product or service

Figure 2.1 is a simplistic illustration of the production and distribution of a car. This was to clearly identify and explain the various markets. In the real life situation however, the manufacturer may be producing some of the cars for use by his or her own staff and may be selling them to staff members. Distributors would also be selling to other companies or individuals wishing to purchase a car to carry out their work and not just to the consumer market. Indeed many products other than cars are sold to both user and consumer markets – products such as milk, Sellotape, vacuum cleaners and services like window cleaning and building to name but a few. Therefore, to be clear as to whether a product or service is being purchased by a member of the user or consumer market determine the answers to the following questions as implied in the earlier definitions of the two markets.

1 Does the purchase represent the **final purchase** in the chain of distribution?
2 Will the product be **consumed**? Consumed means to be used up so that it is no longer new or in its original finished state. Therefore, a car is consumed over years through being worn out as a result of use. A tin of beans is consumed when the beans have been eaten.
3 Is the product being purchased solely for **personal satisfaction**? If we eat a box of chocolates we derive personal satisfaction but if we give it away as a present we have still purchased for a personal reason/satisfaction and the person who receives and consumes the actual chocolates hopefully derives personal satisfaction.

If the answer to **1, 2** and **3** is **yes** then it is a product or service being purchased by a member of a consumer market. If not then it is a product being purchased by a member of the user market.

A car may be purchased by a doctor for personal and professional use. Therefore, the further test – within **3** above – to determine the prime reason for the purchase is to assess if the person (doctor in this case) would have purchased the very same car if he or she could only purchase it for personal use.

The marketer needs to understand major markets and the purchasing needs and behaviour of buyers in the markets in order to devise a marketing mix that will influence the *particular* market. This naturally leads us on to consider the features and needs of user and consumer markets in relation to the planning of the marketing mix.

Comparing the features of user and consumer markets

Marketing management concentrates on developing a marketing mix designed to satisfy the needs and wants of a particular market: a mix which will ultimately lead to satisfactory levels of profit for the company. Product, price, promotion and place – the elements of the marketing mix – will be affected by the expectations and actual needs of the markets.

In Table 2.1, therefore, we summarise more closely the features and differences of user and consumer markets and more importantly identify the **implications** of the features in the design of a marketing mix appropriate for influencing the market.

Table 2.1 Features of the markets

Consumer markets	User markets
(a) **Tend to have relatively large number of purchasers**	(a) **Tend to have relatively small number of purchasers**
Thousands or even millions of consumers may be interested in a particular product or service and consequently marketers will rely heavily on the media, like national and local newspapers, commercial television and radio or posters to promote products or services to these large audiences.	Although the number of manufacturers – or resellers – forming a particular market may run into hundreds or a few thousands, this total is small in relation to the hundreds of thousands or millions of consumers seeking the products being offered by manufacturers.
	The relatively small number of purchasers to be reached may, therefore, enable direct personal sales visits by sales personnel and be a major means of promoting sales. Buyers may also be contacted by phone and sent direct mail literature. Advertising may be possible through sales journals which are purchased only by people in a certain position or profession.

(b) Low value purchases dominate

Consumers tend to buy small quantities of particular products and even in the case of a very expensive product the actual financial outlay will be small in relation to the outlay witnessed in user markets. Consider for instance, a speciality product like a car. Individual consumers may have to spend a considerable amount of their income in order to purchase a car, but a car agent will have to spend a much larger amount of money in order to stock a variety of cars from which consumers can select.

(c) Emotive buying behaviour is widely evident

Consumers purchase products or services to satisfy personal needs often in a way which is not considered consistent or rational.

Actual advertisements often reflect emotive buying behaviour by projecting feelings, sensations and 'social acceptance' themes concerning their product, e.g. how the product will make you more attractive or encourage friendships or provide you with a particular sensation, as with cigarettes and the taste of chocolate, ice cream, etc.

(d) Equal purchasing power among consumers is often assumed

Consumers may buy varying quantities of a particular product but, due to the numbers purchasing, it is unlikely that any particular individual will dominate a market through his or her personal purchases. Therefore, each individual has similar purchasing power to the other individuals who constitute the market.

(b) High value purchases are widely evident

User market purchasers tend to buy large quantities of component parts, raw materials or finished goods necessary for the effective performance of their operations. A supermarket, for instance, may have to buy 1000 pints of milk per day, in order to satisfy the daily demand of its customers. A shipping company may buy a ship for millions of pounds.

Individual user market customers, therefore, are usually given more consideration by companies selling directly to them.

(c) Rational buying behaviour is widely evident

The nature of the operations of user market companies and the high value of purchases force buyers in user markets to be more rational in their evaluation and selection of products and services they purchase. Consumers can easily afford to be irrational over the purchase of a bar of chocolate but a supermarket purchasing to resell may have to commit its finances to hundreds of bars, so a rational and proper evaluation of all the alternatives will be necessary.

Promotional themes aimed at user markets, therefore, will attempt to promote efficiency of a product, its professional image and most importantly the assistance it can provide in fulfilling the profit or non profit goals of the organisation. (See also the section dealing with decision making units, pages 39–41)

(d) Unequal purchasing power must be assumed

In user markets there is often a handful of companies who dominate a particular market.

As a result they are considered as prime customers from which market information and large sales may be obtained. Consider for instance a large organisation involved in retailing and compare its power within

Consumer markets	User markets

The power of consumer markets tends to be considerable in total rather than by individual purchasers or small groups. Therefore, complaints of individuals tend to be viewed in numbers and as an underlying indication that the company's product or service is beginning to meet problems.

the market with the operations of a small corner shop with limited resources, expertise and market coverage. In fact with user markets the term '80:20 ratio' is sometimes used (often referred to as Pareto's Law). This is to indicate that it is often the case that 20 per cent of companies in a user market may dominate 80 per cent of the market both in their purchases and sales. Do not take the figures presented too literally: 20 per cent simply implies a small number while 80 per cent implies the majority.

In user markets the very value of individual purchases would cause a supplier to try to resolve a customer's problems immediately.

(e) Relatively unevenly dispersed

We have already mentioned the similarity or uniformity of individuals in their purchasing power within a consumer market, but it is also important to note that consumer markets also tend to be evenly dispersed throughout the market place, although concentrations of consumers will exist in towns and conurbations.

Therefore, a complex distribution network that penetrates deeply into the market is usually needed to ensure the product or service is available for purchase throughout the market. This means that producers of the finished product often have to rely on the reseller market to ensure that their product is sold to the market and much of the promotional effort will be directed at pleasing and encouraging retail outlets, in particular.

(e) Tendency towards an even dispersion

The user market and in particular industrial markets may be concentrated in geographical areas such as steel manufacturing, iron ore extractors and mining pits, often based where raw materials are plentiful.

Supermarkets and departmental stores – though well dispersed throughout a country – also tend to be near large towns. Therefore, producers of the finished product can often sell and deliver direct to such customers in large quantities. A less complex distribution network than for a consumer market is therefore often possible.

Comparing the decision making unit in user and consumer markets

In marketing jargon, the people responsible for determining if a purchase will take place are referred to as the **decision making unit (DMU)** and the profile of the DMU, its needs and the number of people constituting the DMU will usually be different according to the market.

Generally speaking, the higher the value of a purchase the greater will be the number of people involved in making the purchase. Thus, user markets will usually have more people involved in the decision making process.

Imagine for example, that you are trying to sell an expensive machine to a company for use in producing plastic containers. The **buyer** for the company may be responsible for tracing suppliers of plastic carton producing machines and processing the final purchase. However, the person who will **use** the machine, if it is purchased, may be an unskilled worker in the factory. The person who may have the most **influence** over the purchase may be the production director. Finally, the ultimate **decider** may be the managing director who signs the cheque for the purchase.

Thus, the decision to purchase may involve four (or more) people: a **buyer**, **user**, **influencer** and **decider** collectively referred to as the *decision making unit*. Alternatively, just one or two people could be responsible for carrying out all these roles. For example, when purchasing paper clips for a small office, the secretary may represent the buyer, user and influencer with the manager of the office simply signing the invoice (the decider). If the four functions are separable then the people involved may have different needs. The buyer, for instance, may have wanted to purchase the cheapest machine possible; the worker may have wanted the easiest machine to operate; the production director may have wanted the machine that produces the most cartons within a given level of quality control; and the managing director may have wanted the machine that would maximise profits.

The marketing director, with the help of the marketing research and sales team, will try to determine what each person in the DMU needs when trying to increase sales. He or she will be particularly interested in highlighting **benefits** relevant to the person who will **influence** the sale, but these will be balanced by also covering those relevant to other people who form a part of the DMU.

When selling to consumers, it is often the case that one person represents all or most aspects of the DMU. A mother may be the decider, influencer and buyer of clothes for her young child even though it is her child who will have to wear them (the user). The child may prefer the most expensive and highly colourful clothes, but the mother's concept of what her child should wear may be different and she may not have sufficient money for the most expensive items. Thus, the child's clothing needs, as perceived individually by mother and child, may be different and the marketing director again must be aware of the needs of each and try to find a way of pleasing both to obtain a purchase.

On the other hand, if the family of which the woman is a part had been buying a house for all the family to live in it is quite possible that everyone in the family would have been involved in arriving at a purchasing decision. Making a sale to a consumer market may also, therefore, involve not just 'deciders' but 'purchasers' (people who actually buy the product), 'influencers' (people having the strongest effect on somebody else's decision making) and 'users' (individuals who actually use the product for personal satisfaction and thus consume it).

The marketer must attempt to identify and distinguish between the various DMUs, whether he is selling to the user or consumer market, determine their particular needs and reconcile those needs if sales are to be made.

The importance and size of the user and consumer markets

Students of marketing often tend to concentrate their attention on consumer markets in the erroneous belief that they are the most important and in money terms, of the most value.

The consumer market does not in fact have as much monetary value as the user market. If you return for a moment to Fig. 2.1 you will note that many transactions have taken place before the sale of the car to the final purchaser. Thus, money has changed hands many times.

Consider for a moment that you purchase a radio for £100. Before you purchased the radio four transactions may have taken place as follows: the extractor sold the iron ore necessary for making the radio to the processor for £20, who in turn produced the steel for the manufacturer for £40, who assembled the radio and sold it to the importer for £60, who sold it to a retailer for £80, who finally sold it to you for £100 (the consumer market). You paid £100 but before this £20 + £40 + £60 + £80 = £200 was exchanged within the user market. Therefore, in terms of monetary importance the user market is more important than the consumer market. The great importance of the individual consumer markets lies in their significance as final purchaser because all work undertaken before consumers purchase does so in the belief that a consumer will purchase. Thus, if their needs are not considered first then the whole production and distribution effort may prove worthless.

Indeed even extracting and processing companies study changes in the consumer markets to determine what they should be doing in the future. If a steel producing company sees that car sales are declining it knows that demand for its steel will also start to decline, and the company will, therefore, seek additional customers to car manufacturers to minimise the risk of a decline in sales.

Being aware of the features of consumer and user markets will help a marketing manager:

- identify possible markets for the company's products and services *and*
- plan the marketing effort in keeping with the needs of the individual market.

However, to be fully conversant with the needs of markets and/or individuals we must also be aware of what products and services they purchase and the benefits they expect from purchasing, which constitutes the content of the next section.

■ 2 PRODUCTS AND SERVICES

Introduction to products, services and benefits

When we refer to **products** we imply something tangible, a physical entity. But purchasers may obtain different benefits from the same product. When we buy cosmetics for instance, we may be seeking 'youth', 'beauty', 'hope', 'social acceptance', while when we buy a car we may be looking for 'speed', 'comfort', 'status', and, of course, 'a means of transport'. These likely benefits represent the many aspects of a product's concept and they are used in the establishment of a specific personality for a product that can readily be identified by people who feel they need the benefits it has to offer.

The benefits that customers derive may be imaginary or intangible, such as the belief that drinking alcohol makes us more socially acceptable, but they will, nevertheless, be associated in the mind of the customers with the product, which *is* tangible. Advertising campaigns associated with the particular product will attempt to emphasise those benefits common to many potential purchasers in order to achieve maximum sales.

Consumers select products which match their own personal expectations and evaluate the performance of a product in terms of benefits enjoyed. Most of us own a wrist watch but we may expect different benefits from the same product. Some seek to impress their friends, relatives and business associates and may invest a lot of money on a reputable make that may be made in gold. Others with specific hobbies, like tennis or squash, may prefer a watch which is shock proof, while a third group of consumers may settle for a simple inexpensive watch designed to offer outstanding time reliability. All are purchasing an item that is essentially for telling the time, but each are seeking different additional benefits for which they are willing to pay.

Industrial customers may not be purchasing for personal reasons but they too are often deriving different benefits from the same product. One customer may want a water pump to empty a well, another to pump water around machinery that can overheat and yet another to spray water for irrigation – the same product providing different benefits to different groups of customers. In fact purchasers are not really buying a water pump. One is buying a 'well emptier', one 'a machine sprayer' and the third an 'irrigator'. If something could fulfil their needs better they would purchase it in preference to the water pump as it would be offering more benefits.

Therefore, people do not just buy products or services, they really buy **what products and services can do for them** which are collectively described as **benefits**. A horse and carriage may look attractive but the extra benefits offered by cars caused them to become virtually obsolete.

Services

Services may be offered in the form of activities or advice/opinions, but like products they too will carry a variety of benefits.

Cleaning windows for example, is a service. We do not buy a product but the 'activity' of cleaning. Our solicitor does not provide us with a product; he provides us with professional advice or opinions, his knowledge and skills remaining his own. Banking and finance, communications, transportation, education, etc. are just a few of the many types of services available. Services have many of the same characteristics as products but there are some discernible differences which we can consider.

SERVICES ARE INTANGIBLE
When we buy a pen or a paper pad we can see it, touch it, show it to our friends and select the colour, shape and size we prefer. Tuition as a service, on the other hand, lacks a physical entity and a direct assessment of its full value is much more difficult to undertake. You may assess the building, the classroom, the teaching aids used, the appearance of the lecturers, etc., but you cannot assess the benefits of the tuition immediately – nor all the benefits that may be derived.

LACK OF CONSISTENCY
Most of the products we use are manufactured on a mass basis, usually providing millions of identical units. Services on the other hand, lack this exact level of consistency. Think of a lecturer who has taught students for a number of years and who has covered a particular topic many different times. The lectures given will not be identical because situations change drastically, i.e. subject knowledge, health, mood, personal problems, composition of class, etc.

OWNERSHIP IS NOT PASSED ON
When you buy a product you become the legal owner of the unit in question which you can resell in its exact form at a later date. With services this is rarely possible. If you attend lectures and obtain knowledge you cannot pass on that exact knowledge to another person.

SERVICES ARE PERISHABLE
Consider your last holiday or social outing. You may have photographs to remind you of it, or souvenirs to show to your friends, or a nice gift to give to somebody, but generally the holiday or outing after the occasion is simply memory: good, bad or average.

The intangibility of services can be overcome in part, through some physical proof of the service. When you complete a course of study you obtain a diploma or certificate to prove that you successfully passed certain examinations, but you do not remember in detail all lectures you attended nor all the topics you were taught. If you employ the services of a carpenter to build a shed you have the shed to constantly remind you of the service that you witnessed.

HEAVY PERSONAL INVOLVEMENT
As already indicated benefits from services are not immediately apparent and our initial evaluation of alternative, similar services available is difficult to assess.

Marketing of most services, therefore, relies on the 'personal touch' so that mutual trust between the purchaser and the service supplier can be established, for most services involve personal interaction between the purchaser and supplier of the service.

Characteristics of industrial/producer and consumer products

Before considering consumer and industrial products separately let us firstly consider from where all products are derived and the production processes they undergo before they can be used or consumed.

There are basically four stages of production providing raw materials, finished or semifinished items.

EXTRACTIVE INDUSTRY PROVIDING EXTRACTIVE PRODUCTS
These are the raw materials of production – the world's naturally occurring resources – and have to be extracted from land, sea or air. They include, oil (petroleum), sand, salt, coal, iron ore, copper, tin, water, natural gas, sulphur, nitrate, wood, cement, fish, oxygen, diamonds and gold, to name but a few. Some of the items such as sand and coal are ready for human use the moment they are extracted; others will need processing. Even air is ready for human use, as we use it to help propel cars, planes and most machines, although we fortunately do not need to purchase it.

PROCESSING INDUSTRY PROVIDING 'PROCESSED PRODUCTS'
This constitutes the second level of production and often heavily relates to the production of items by employing natural phenomena such as the production of glass through the heating and rapid cooling of sand with other minerals. Others would include steel, petrol, manufactured gases, usable oil and most chemicals. Once again some would be immediately ready for use whilst others would need to become a part of the manufacturer's process before they can be used.

AGRICULTURAL INDUSTRY FOR 'AGRICULTURAL OR FARM PRODUCE'
Agricultural produce is produce that results from cultivating the soil, producing crops and the raising of livestock, and to some degree the preparation of this produce for sale. It will include eggs, meat, fruit, vegetables, milk and in some cases wood and fish (from fish farming). Many of these products are ready for consumption upon production, but a few may become part of a production process, such as the production of cakes, yoghurts, or wooden furniture.

MANUFACTURING INDUSTRY FOR 'MANUFACTURED PRODUCTS'
These are products which have undergone refinement and assembly, by hand or machinery, before they are provided to consumers as a finished product. They are material items that have been invented and fabricated by mankind and are generally the ones that consumers in particular are most exposed to. Included in an inexhaustible list would be cars, tables, chairs, knives, forks, clothing, heating equipment, aeroplanes, ships, machinery, household fittings and office items.

As you may have gathered, some raw materials naturally occur and can be extracted while at the same time they may be processed or cultivated. For example, fresh water may be safely consumed in some parts of the world, but in other areas it may need processing before it is fit for human consumption. Forests naturally occur providing wood, but unless new trees are planted and cultivated, provision for the future will not be met. Some raw materials, therefore, are exhaustible at the rate they are used, while others such as water, air and the sun appear inexhaustible within our concept of time.

As far as the marketer is concerned there are two common factors in this production process: people and their needs. The vast majority of this process occurs because of human needs and the processes of production exist only because of humans. Indeed most processed and all manufactured items do not continue to exist unless man discovers or invents a process and shows a continuing need for an item.

Consider rubber for instance. If mankind had not devised a process for reshaping and strengthening rubber to fulfil needs such as tyres for vehicles then rubber trees would not be cultivated for their rubber content. Do not assume therefore, that there is a finite list of processed, cultivated or manufactured items, because what does not exist in one era may exist in another.

Knowing what exists, however, does not really tell us much about the life span of products in the market place or the speed with which they are replaced. To assist us in this regard we can evaluate the **durability** of products and their **replacement cycle**.

Durability
This is length of time products tend to last before they have to be replaced – in other words their life span. Table 2.2 lists the durability of a variety of products.

Replacement cycle
This is the length of time that will elapse between replacement purchases. A television set may be working satisfactorily but the owner may feel that he/she would like a more up-to-date version.

Of course, many items can last a very long time if left unused but the categories do assume normal usage. After all we do not purchase soap or shampoo to leave it on a shelf for years.

Durability by itself is not a completely satisfactory criterion for division

Table 2.2

Main categories	Consumer market goods	User market goods
Durables – Survive constant use over a long period of time. Normally, 5 years or more	cars, TVs, radios, tables, chairs, kitchen utensils, houses, etc.	shelving, heavy machinery, mobile offices, etc.
Semidurables – Survive many uses. Normally 1 to 10 years	shoes, clothing, curtains, carpets, bedding, etc.	office furniture, light machinery, office equipment, etc.
Non durables – Survive one or very few uses by the purchaser. Normally used within days, weeks or months	food, tobacco, newspapers and magazines, soap, toilet paper, etc.	component parts, raw materials and items ancillary to manufacture, i.e. paper and paper clips, etc.

because it does not fully reveal the speed with which products are replaced or what they represent in terms of purchasing behaviour. Take, for instance, a pair of shoes and carpeting. They are both semidurable products but the nature of the products and the cost of purchase involved will lead to different patterns of purchasing behaviour among consumers. It is therefore important to seek a more detailed or informative classification of consumer products which we can obtain through the use of the replacement cycle as an added means of classification.

Three types of consumer goods can be identified in the replacement cycle.

1 CONVENIENCE GOODS
These are products which are often bought on impulse and represent relatively minor purchases in consumers' lives. They are products bought frequently, they are relatively inexpensive and they tend to involve minimum mental effort by consumers in their evaluation and selection. Typical examples of convenience goods are everyday family food, boxes of matches, bars of chocolate, newspapers, sweets (candy), crisps, chewing gum, etc.

2 SHOPPING GOODS
Shopping Goods are bought on the strength of their quality, price and suitability. They are invariably more costly than convenience goods, they have a longer useful life and consumers are willing to make an extra effort to locate them, evaluate them, try them and, if convinced, buy them. They are products which can be related directly to a consumer's personality and expectations in terms of appearance, style, shape, colour, etc. Examples of shopping goods include items of clothing, shoes, books, bedding, decorative items for the house, etc.

3 SPECIALITY GOODS

They represent major purchases in consumers' lives and are purchased infrequently, i.e. over years. They may be characterised by their complexity, high cost and long useful life. Evaluation and selection of speciality goods is extremely complex and consumers must collect a large variety of relevant information before they are in a position to select the product which will suit them best. Examples of speciality goods include motor cars, television sets, video recorders, etc.

Another feature of some products is the high level of *post-purchase anxiety* which consumers may face after the purchase. Such anxiety may relate to doubts or worries about the product's performance, quality, durability, value for money, reactions by other people towards the purchase, etc. Manufacturers of speciality goods must try to reduce or remove post-purchase anxiety. They may attempt to achieve this through guarantees, money back offers, free trial periods and through advertisements designed to emphasise the quality and performance of the product.

In the case of durables and semidurables their speed of replacement will also depend on the quality of the product, fashion and the development of additional benefits to customers. A high quality carpet may last 30 years or more but it may be replaced after 10 years because the owner may see a carpet which he/she considers more useful or/and attractive. Therefore, durability and replacement categories are a general guide to patterns of purchasing behaviour and not an absolute.

Consumer market services

Generally speaking, services can be classified according to the area of operations they relate to and they often **supplement** the use and purchase of products by consumers. A car for instance may need a repair, so the services of a car mechanic may be required to ensure continued use of the car; a new dress will eventually require dry cleaning services. The marketing implications of products and services are discussed in detail in Chapter 4, but in order to further appreciate the variety and importance of services in consumer markets we may consider a few of the many services available through glancing at the following classifications.

FACILITIES AND POSSIBLE SERVICES PROVIDED

- *Agencies*: theatrical, employment, holiday and travel, estate
- *Insurance*: brokers and consultants
- *Housing*: conveyancing, renting, repairs
- *Household*: gas, electricity, telephone
- *Personal*: legal, banking, doctors, undertakers
- *Transport*: bus services, car repairs, car parking, driving schools

- *Recreation*: clubs, theatres, cinemas, sport centres
- *Religion*: baptism, burials, counselling, social services
- *Clothing*: repairs, cleaning, laundering, storage
- *General*: hairdressers, beauticians, window cleaners, baby sitters

Now that we have an appreciation of the complexity and variety of consumer products and services we have a basis from which to analyse user market products and services more closely.

User market products and services

As indicated earlier in this chapter, products or services involved in consumer or user markets may be the same. It is important, therefore, to identify the major user market purchases, which we can do by placing them into five general categories as follows.

MAJOR EQUIPMENT
This category comprises products that are necessary for the initial creation of a manufacturing or service unit or its physical expansion. They include buildings, machinery, office furniture, display units, delivery vans, etc. Generally speaking they represent the capital assets of a business. Products in this category may be specialised or custom built in order to satisfy the particular requirements of the individual user. From the accounting point of view, they represent a company's fixed assets.

OPERATING SUPPLIES
In general operating supplies are services but they do include products. These are used in the manufacturing or reselling process but they are not part of the final product or service provided by the companies using them. Major equipment, for instance, may need operating supplies like electricity, petrol, oil, gas, etc. for their operation, and the organisation may also need transport, cleaning, external accountancy services and labour. These supplies will be part of the total cost associated with the operations of the company, but are not part of what is actually sold by companies.

COMPONENT PARTS
Consider a car of your choice and try to visualise the hundreds, if not thousands, of parts which have to be combined in order to create a product like a car. These products represent the **component parts** of a product and they can be defined as *finished goods used in the creation of another finished good*. Many component parts may also be sold individually. A car owner, for instance, may wish to buy a tyre, car battery or spark plugs.

RAW MATERIALS
These are products supplied by agriculture, extractive or fishing industries that

may be used in the creation of a processed or manufactured good. Raw beans, for instance, will be needed by manufacturers of canned baked beans, while tobacco will represent the basic raw material for cigarettes and cigars. Caution is necessary at this stage because the description of raw materials could be confused with the description of component parts as both types of products may form part of another good. The distinguishing feature of the two types of products is that component parts have already undergone some form of manufacture, while raw materials are used in the form they are found in. A car battery, for instance, must be manufactured before it is used as part of a car, while raw carrots can be used in their natural form for producing a carton of mixed salad.

PROCESSED MATERIALS/PRODUCTS

We have mentioned finished processed products such as glass and petrol, but it is often the case that processed products are used for the creation of certain finished goods and, though they are part of the finished product, they may not always occur in their original form. Next time you purchase a can of fizzy soft drink, refer to the ingredients of the product which are listed on the can. You will find that the ingredients are often unpronounceable chemicals which have been combined for the creation of the drink. These ingredients are the **processed materials** and although consumers do not always understand them, they actually use the product without much hesitation.

User market organisations

User markets consist of profit as well as non profit making organisations. Most organisations in the user market can be classified according to the principal types of activity in which they are engaged with the following general categories representing the main activities.

- *Banking and finance:* includes all nationally and privately owned banks
- *Insurance*: encompasses stock companies, mutual associations, fraternal insurers, state funds, and other insurers of less importance
- *Communications*: an extremely wide spread 'industry' that includes the postal service, telephone and telegraph services, radio and television broadcasters, and publishers of newspapers and books
- *Public utilities*: the suppliers of electricity, natural gas, and water
- *Road building and maintenance*: a major industry that markets its services almost exclusively to federal and state governments
- *Transportation*: includes railroad, truck, bus companies, pipeline operators, airlines and shipping lines
- *Agriculture*: includes farmers, livestock producers, lumber companies, and fisheries
- *Drilling and mining*: includes drillers for fuels, gas and water, mining organisations for minerals and oils
- *Construction*: includes residential, commercial and industrial builders

- *Manufacturing*: includes a wide variety of manufacturers
- *Reseller*: includes brokers, wholesalers, agents and retailers
- *Services*: includes those who render both personal and business services, such as automobile mechanics and appliance repairers, owners of amusement parks and other recreational facilities, motels, hotels and restaurants

In addition, the *user market* may include non profit making organisations such as trade associations, labour unions, charities and hospitals which supply social and community services. There would also be professional people such as architects, physicians, lawyers and accountants who are also industrial users when they buy products and services needed in the provision of their work.

It is important to appreciate fully the variety of goods and services available or the ones that are purchased by user markets in order to answer adequately questions in marketing where the answer requires the use of examples.

This knowledge of products and services will now help you in understanding market segmentation.

■ 3 MARKET SEGMENTATION

It is often impossible to develop *one* product or *one* service which will be equally appealing or satisfying to all consumers within a large national market. This is due to the fact that consumers may buy different goods or services according to their sex, age group, income, occupation or even geographic location. It should, therefore, be evident that marketing organisations must attempt to develop or adapt products or services to satisfy specific **groups of consumers**. This need brings forward the concept of **market segmentation** which refers to the notion that the total market for a product, such as clothing, is composed of a number of subgroups called **segments**, who have different needs. Once these subgroups are identified, and their needs are understood, a company may be able to develop a marketing mix appropriate for servicing a subgroup it considers a potential and, of course, profitable market. Market segmentation can therefore, be defined as:

> *the process of dividing a market into the homogeneous segments that collectively constitute the market that is being segmented*

each of which may be a minor market. For example, children's books are a segment of the total market for books.

In order to understand the process of segmenting, we can refer to a large market comprising consumers with differing characteristics and expectations. The UK coffee drinking market for instance, consists of men and women, scattered throughout the country, many of whom have different expectations of a cup of coffee, and is composed of individuals who use different quantities of coffee on a daily or weekly basis. As already indicated, one product cannot satisfy everybody and individual companies cannot provide a product that will meet the needs of all members of the market. A specific but large enough group of people showing similar characteristics and expectations may therefore be selected as a **target market** that the company is able to supply and from which the company can make a profit. A series of criteria are needed which will enable the marketing manager to **divide** the market into small groups or segments. This process may involve a number of **segmentation methods** which use different means of division.

Segmentation methods

There are four major methods used for segmenting a total market into its main parts which are:

1 demographic
2 geographic
3 buyer behaviour
4 psychographic

1 DEMOGRAPHIC SEGMENTATION

This method of segmentation uses people's characteristics such as sex, age, income, race, social class, religion, occupation, size of family, political voting preference and level of education as a means of dividing a large market into smaller segments. The family characteristics or life cycle of the family may also be used, i.e. young single, adult single, unmarried with child, married no children, young married with children, etc.

Governments generally tend to divide people according to their income, but marketers do not consider this adequate enough for their purposes. It is difficult to determine the way in which a person may act solely as a result of the income that they earn or the wealth that they possess: one person earning a higher weekly income may watch soap opera on TV, while another on a lower income may watch opera at Covent Garden.

Therefore a popular demographic method of classifying people used by marketers is by linking their occupation with their income in order to gain an understanding of the way certain groups of people may or will behave. This grouping is a **socio-economic** classification or grading.

This knowledge of social habits linked to income is of particular importance to marketing managers as it enables them to target such marketing activities as public relations, advertising and selling more directly at people they wish to influence. This may involve advertising in the quality newspapers or/and teachers' magazines to reach teachers, while advertising in the popular daily newspapers to communicate with the manual worker on the shop floor.

Socio-economic groups are divided into six classifications: A, B, C1, C2, D and E. A and B represent the upper classes and upper middle classes, C1 and C2 the middle and lower middle classes, D and E the working classes and those people obtaining transfer incomes from the government, such as pensioners, the disabled and the unemployed. A more detailed classification is given in Table 2.3, but bear in mind that these are guidelines to the division of society and must not be rigidly interpreted.

Table 2.3

Social grade	Status	Occupation
A	Upper class	Higher managerial, administrative or professional
B	Middle class	Middle managerial, administrative or professional
C1	Lower middle class	Supervisory or clerical, junior managerial
C2	Skilled working class	Skilled manual workers
D	Working class	Semi and unskilled manual workers
E	Those at lowest level of subsistence	Pensioners, casual or lowest paid workers, unemployed

Although the socio-economic groupings have been identified under six classifications it is more common to use just four classifications, namely, AB, C1, C2, DE. This is because, useful as the classifications are, there are still many grey areas. For example, there can be a situation where one professional person such as a lawyer or surgeon is earning ten times more than another in the same profession.

Socio-economic grades are reviewed every few years, as is the general way in which members of each group tend to behave. Most advertising agencies will make sure that they have access to this information so that they can advise companies using their services on the best ways to promote to certain segments of the market.

2 GEOGRAPHIC SEGMENTATION
This is the method that uses geographic locations such as countries, counties, cities, suburbs, rural areas, etc. as a means of division. Climate may also be used where there are distinct differences in climate within a market such as the USA as climate also affects what people purchase. Drinking, eating and clothing habits are just three of the many purchases that would be affected by climatic conditions.

3 BUYER BEHAVIOUR
The way people behave during and after purchasing is continuing in importance due to the rapid integration of social class attitudes. This has been caused to a

great extent by programmes or/and articles of the popular media that are now seen worldwide, causing most people to constantly re-evaluate the way they behave. For instance, a number of people from every social class may now drive the same make of car and wear the same kind of clothes, possibly from the same national chain of clothing stores. Therefore, class is gradually becoming less important than buyer behaviour and many companies are aiming their promotions at the total market in the knowledge that people at every level of society may be interested in what they sell.

Some indicators within the area of buyer behaviour that are measurable are:

- Usage: the amount that different people buy and use.
- The end use to which the product is put, i.e. one person may use a car for family pleasure while another buyer uses the same car predominantly for business purposes.
- Loyalty to the brand: some buyers remain persistently loyal to a brand while others are easily affected by the advertising of competitor products.
- Inquisitiveness: many purchasers are constantly evaluating new products while others do not appear to be aware of changes to what is being offered.

In Chapter 3 you will read how observation by researchers and consumer panels are sound methods of measuring the way individuals or groups behave. In fact, one eminent examination body has 'Behavioural Aspects of Marketing' as a separate subject.

4 PSYCHOGRAPHIC OR PERSONALITY SEGMENTATION
A growing awareness of the need for more explanatory criteria has led to the greater use of psychological variables. This method has been advanced through improvements in psychological measurement. The variables involved range from general personality traits to specific product field requirements.

The market is segmented by using such personality variables as autonomy, compulsiveness, gregariousness, conservation and ambition. This form of segmentation arose as a result of discovering that buyers' needs may often be differentiated along life-style or personality lines. Thus, there are buyers who are fast livers seeking up-to-date or/and latest trend purchases; status seekers who tend to buy goods that will indicate a high status; and buyers who seek ordinary, unfrilled goods that do their job.

Several years ago in the USA Ford owners were at the time described as 'independent, impulsive, masculine, alert to change and self confident', while Chevrolet owners were described as 'conservative, thrifty, prestige conscious, less masculine and seeking to avoid extremes'.

The reasons why the above four methods are still popular means of segmentation are because they can be understood, they can be measured, they can be reached with promotions and distribution and they often represent substantial market segments and are, therefore, frequently profitable to service.

However, other methods of segmentation are now beginning to gain favour, in particular **benefit segmentation**.

BENEFIT SEGMENTATION
In this form of segmentation buyers are subdivided in relation to various forms of benefits that the buyer may be seeking from the particular product. In the case of clothing, there are customers who tend to seek different benefits such as warmth, style, status or low price. Research may then determine the most sought after benefits, and the company will emphasise the major benefits when promoting.

In one study Russell J. Haley characterised purchasers of toothpaste as: those seeking 'decay prevention' as worriers; 'bright teeth' seekers as sociables; those seeking a particular taste as sensories; and 'low price seekers' as independents. Depending on the particular concerns of the market at the time, a toothpaste company will choose one or two of these benefits to highlight in its advertising campaign and possibly on the pack.

If we take psychographic segmentation we will find that we can often identify particular types of people with the benefits they seek. For example:

(a) *Status seekers*: a group which is very much concerned with the status or image the product bestows on purchasers.

(b) *Swingers*: a group which wants to move with fashion. Their brand choices reflect this tendency.

(c) *Conservatives*: a group which prefers to stick to large successful companies and popular brands, has little desire to change and may often view new versions of products with suspicion.

(d) *The rational*: a group which looks for benefits such as economy, value, durability, etc. and is willing to change to a new product if it appears to offer more benefits.

(e) *The inner directed*: a group which is especially concerned with self-concept (how they see themselves). Members consider themselves to have a sense of humour, to be independent and/or honest.

(f) *Hedonists*: a group which is affected primarily by sensory benefits such as a pleasant aroma, taste and looks of a product.

(g) *Quality seekers*: These people will check as much as possible to see that a product has quality in terms of what it can do often to the point of watching consumer programmes and reading consumer magazines whose staff have tested what they consider to be the main aspects of the product.

Figure 2.2 illustrates a few of the prime expectations/motives of the total adult market for clothes. Some or all of these segments appear among the markets of most products and services.

Fig. 2.2

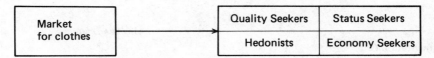

Combining methods of segmentation

Individual segmentation methods are rarely applied in isolation. The methods invariably have to be **combined** in order to obtain a large enough homogeneous segment. For instance, demographic segmentation may uncover a potential consumer market consisting of women, 35–50 years of age, in the C1/C2 socio-economic group. However, there may be tremendous differences in the geographic locations of these consumers, in the benefits they seek and in their attitudes towards the product. A combination of segments must, therefore, be sought to identify a large enough market to service. Figure 2.3 illustrates the characteristics of a potential segment of the total tea drinking market suitable as a target market.

Reasons for segmentation

(a) To improve profits through increases in sales.
(b) Once specific consumer needs in relation to market segments are known, the marketing budget and effort – whether towards the total market or segment(s) – can be allocated and targeted more precisely to reconcile these needs.
(c) To give the company stronger control of the total market or a market segment and/or to protect itself against potential or current competition.
(d) Segmentation can help the company in assessing its relative strengths and weaknesses with regard to the 4 Ps as well as opportunities and threats.

Requirements for segmentation

There are three important requirements that have to be met before segmentation becomes a possibility.

1 MEASURABILITY
Before segmentation is carried out information relating to the total market as well as individual segments must be collected. If information is not available or cannot be ascertained and **clearly measured** a criterion for division does not exist.

2 ACCESSIBILITY
Before segmentation is carried out an evaluation of the company's financial

Fig. 2.3

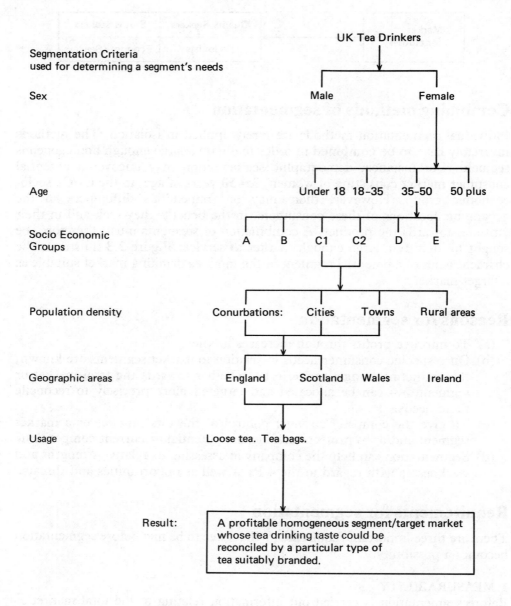

Segmentation Criteria used for determining a segment's needs	UK Tea Drinkers

Sex — Male, Female

Age — Under 18, 18–35, 35–50, 50 plus

Socio Economic Groups — A, B, C1, C2, D, E

Population density — Conurbations: Cities, Towns, Rural areas

Geographic areas — England, Scotland, Wales, Ireland

Usage — Loose tea. Tea bags.

Result: A profitable homogeneous segment/target market whose tea drinking taste could be reconciled by a particular type of tea suitably branded.

production and marketing resources is needed as well as an analysis of the distribution network available for distributing the product. The strengths of the company and the distribution facilities available will determine the **degree of access** the company has to different market segments.

3 SUBSTANTIALITY

Individual market segments must be **large enough** in terms of value as well as volume and, therefore, profitable before the cost of segmentation undertaken can be justified.

User market segmentation

To explain and illustrate the basics of segmentation we have concentrated on consumer markets, but most user markets can be and are segmented by marketing managers to maximise profits and minimise the risk of failure. They are, in fact, segmented by a classification closely related to those used for consumer markets.

(a) By individual characteristics of organisations, i.e. size of company, type of company, the markets they serve and the type of products they purchase, the make up of the DMU within companies, etc.

(b) Buying behaviour – rate and volume of purchases by companies, end use of purchased products, utility requirements, loyalty to brand, etc.

(c) Geographic – distribution of the industry, climate and location of resources such as oil, coal, etc.

Even benefit segmentation can be used and opens up useful possibilities for targeting the marketing effort at segments. For example, one company may feel that it benefits from buying a non-flammable paint because it creates a safer environment for workers in its factory; another company may only buy the same paint for the benefit of profits that result from reselling it.

Segmentation and targeting marketing activities

As already briefly mentioned, marketing activities and particularly the marketing mix will change and become more segmented the more we segment a market. For example, if a company was producing ice cream it could firstly split its total market into the user market and the consumer market. Thus the company may deliver the ice cream in bulk without labelling to such establishments as catering organisations and hotels, and also put the ice cream into small decorative packs for the consumer market (indeed, using different packs according to whether the people purchasing are adults or children). It may further divide the consumer market into other subsections such as by climate, purchasing behaviour, etc.

Probably the most common delineation of user markets is into:

• size of company
• type of company a supplier is dealing with
• type of industry the customers are in
• type of customer being supplied
• purchasing needs

To understand this further, we will consider two of the segments mentioned, taking firstly, size of companies. If we were supplying steel we may find that we can design a classification that will reflect the value of purchases of the companies who purchase from us, or indeed, by the industries to which they belong. Thus we may classify them in the following way:

- Companies capable of purchasing over 1 000 000 tonnes of steel per annum
- Companies capable of purchasing   500 000 up to 1 000 000 tonnes
- Companies capable of purchasing   250 000 up to 500 000 tonnes
- Companies capable of purchasing   100 000 up to 250 000 tonnes
- Companies capable of purchasing   50 000 up to 100 000 tonnes
- Companies capable of purchasing under   50 000 tonnes

We may then classify them according to the industry to which they belong, i.e. re-rolling, stockholding, bright drawing, engineering, motor manufacturing, construction, shipping industry, etc.

The effective marketing director will use knowledge of these characteristics to ensure that the company's total marketing efforts reconcile the particular needs of the particular type of customer. The company may formulate pricing policies and discounts which encourage large potential customers to place orders and attract small and medium sized companies to purchase larger amounts in order to benefit from the discounts offered. It may also use different trade magazines to reach the buyers in the different industries.

Likewise, a sales manager for a printing concern may train sales representatives to service customers' accounts more effectively through knowledge of each market segment's particular printing requirements. Thus, some companies purchasing printing services such as financial reports, statements, etc. (referred to in the trade as 'city printing') may be more concerned with quality, design and delivery time rather than price, whilst publishers requiring trade periodicals or books printed regularly may be very price conscious.

User markets may also be broken down by the demographic characteristics of the people who influence any purchase. For example, managing directors and other senior managers will probably fall into high socio-economic groups and, therefore, tend to read the quality newspapers, which is extremely useful information to companies advertising management consultancy, finance and investment services for several industries.

It is essential to realise therefore, that while consumer and user market characteristics are by and large separable it is still people who do the purchasing in organisations and their personal characteristics can and do often affect the purchase they make for the organisation.

Race or nationality may also be a critical factor particularly with multinational companies in consumer markets, as social and cultural habits of different races or nationalities may cause them to purchase not only different things but also in different ways. Advertisements in which the children play with unwrapped sweets may be considered acceptable in the UK but unhygienic by the Dutch advertising authorities, reflecting the general attitude of the people towards food hygiene. Certain colours such as reds and blacks used with effect in one country may have the opposite connotation to people in another country. Even at a more subtle level, it is generally recognised that some races or nations like very colourful packs whereas others prefer packs in uncluttered designs and more sombre colours.

We have dealt in brief with some of the ways in which we can segment markets, but it must be remembered that in a large market orientated company, continuous study of these markets is a regular function and not something that is just done once at the beginning of a new product launch. Purchasing habits change, markets come and go, so the marketer must be constantly assessing markets if opportunities are not to be missed.

Segmentation strategies

Expansion of business was based some years ago on the standardisation of products to serve the high volume mass markets. The tendency to standardise led to similarity of products between manufacturers and thus increased competition. Eventually the intensity of competition pressed manufacturers into developing **product differences** to give their product its own identity and uniqueness.

Now the emphasis is on **market segmentation**. Starting with current and potential customers and by distinguishing and identifying their specific characteristics and needs, companies attempt to identify segments of the market they would like as their target market(s). They have, therefore, also tended to determine a segmentation strategy that defines the approach to (a) market(s) they will adopt.

A segmentation strategy represents a commitment to particular markets or segment(s) of those markets and involves a selection between the following options:

1 Differentiated marketing
2 Concentrated marketing
3 Undifferentiated marketing

DIFFERENTIATED MARKETING
A company may decide voluntarily, or be forced through the efforts of competitors, to operate in all or most segments of a market but may have different packs for each. e.g. Coca Cola and Pepsi Cola are sold in cans and several bottle sizes direct to consumers as well as in dispensing barrels for bars and restaurants that have the appropriate dispensing units. More total sales are created but supply costs may or will be higher due in part to:

● Pack modification costs for supplying different segments
● Administrative (and promotion) cost: separate planning and marketing effort for targeting each segment

- Inventory costs: safe stocking margins to be kept for many pack sizes
- Delivery costs: due to the smaller quantities or mixed items on each lorry

For an example a company may select to operate in three different segments of a market which it feels are segments which it can service and may offer three distinct products designed to meet the needs of those segments (see Fig. 2.4). Though such segmentation will involve more effort, advantages may be a firmer control of the market through sales into the main segments as well as lower production and supply costs resulting from an increase in the amount of the basic product produced, i.e. the drink itself.

Fig. 2.4

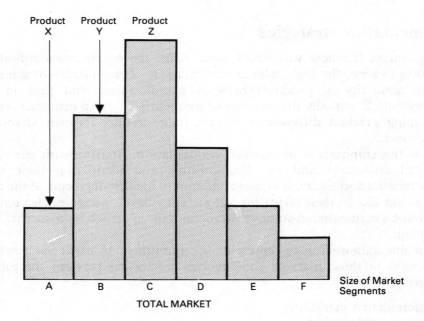

It is worth pointing out that this approach may also involve the introduction of *one* product which can appeal equally well to *more than one* segment. A specific make of car may be presented as speedy, economical, comfortable, reliable and relatively inexpensive to purchase, and as a result these features may lead to acceptance of the car by consumers in more than one segment. The tendency today, however, is to make minor modifications and additions to the basic car to create different versions such as the two door, three door and five door version; engines of different sizes; and the GTi and Turbo verions, in order to satisfy as many different segments of the market as possible – at a profit.

CONCENTRATED MARKETING
A company may decide to concentrate its resources and activities on a specific segment of the market rather than spreading its operations thinly over many

large segments. It is a popular and justifiable approach by relatively small companies which try to specialise in one area of the market rather than compete on unequal terms with larger competitors in highly competitive segments. This specialisation is often risky because small markets are more prone to unexpected changes which could prove extremely problematic to the supplier who has specialised solely in that one segment.

Figure 2.5 illustrates a company concentrating its marketing efforts on one segment which they may attempt to dominate through specialisation.

Fig. 2.5

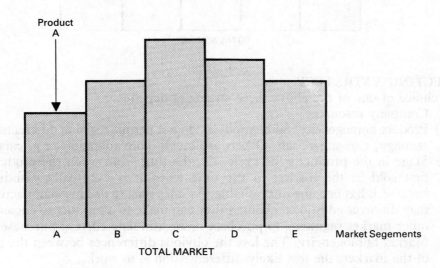

Small companies often grow by servicing a small segment of a market and when successful with this operation move on to service larger segments.

UNDIFFERENTIATED MARKETING

This strategy involves the introduction of products or services and promotional messages designed to reach a large number of consumers *in most segments* and on occasions *the total market*. It will usually involve the company in fierce competition with companies operating in a number of segments within the total market and it could prove very costly because the marketing operations will need to be geared towards total market coverage.

The companies that adopt this strategy are usually those who gain considerably from not changing the form (differentiating) or packing of their products.

A company introducing a product to the total market, without allowing for any segments or differences in expectations among segments, is illustrated by Fig. 2.6.

Fig. 2.6

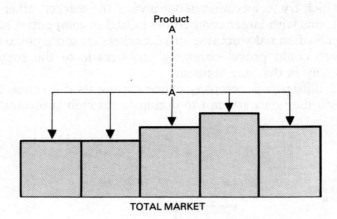

SELECTING A STRATEGY
The choice of one of the above three strategies depends on:
  (a) Company resources.
  (b) Product homogeneity. Some products do not permit a strong differentiation strategy, e.g. sugar, salt. Others are much more adaptable, e.g. cars.
  (c) Stage in the product's life cycle, i.e. the time from when the product is first sold in the market to the time when it is eventually withdrawn because it has become unprofitable. As sales start to decline manufacturers may discover additional changes they can make to a product to encourage other market segments to purchase or re-stimulate current purchasers.
  (d) Market homogeneity. The less the obvious differences between the parts of the market, the less likely differentiation is to work.
  (e) Competitive marketing strategies. Segmentation by competitors may demand a segmentation policy for the company.

The worth of segmentation, therefore, must be calculated carefully with each separate market being assessed for its short, medium and long term profit potential.

STUDY AND EXAM TIPS

1 Important. The classification of all markets into the categories *user* (industrial/ producer, reseller and metamarket) and *consumer* closely follows the American classification.
  However, some examination bodies only divide into consumer and industrial

markets taking the view that resellers, producers or providers of social services are all producing a product or service. While the preference of the authors is the former – simply because they more closely define distinguishable markets – students are advised to ask their tutor or particular examining body the classifications they adopt.

2 Make sure that you can clearly define consumer and user markets and distinguish them by their features.

3 Consider closely the underlying business and marketing logic of market segmentation, not just the methods by which a market may be segmented.

4 Do not confuse *methods of segmentation* with *segmentation strategies*.

5 The features of user and consumer markets or/and the segmenting of a market will have a direct effect on recommendations relating to the planning and targeting of the marketing mix. Become familiar with the different marketing mix strategies that may be employed due to changes in the market the company intends servicing by relating what you will learn about the 4 Ps to markets and market segments.

6 Use aids to your memory for memorising key information associated with this or other sections. For example, the words *DUC strategy* could be used to recall segmentation strategies when they are mentioned in an exam. DUC would stand for the first letter of the strategies: Differentiated, Undifferentiated and Concentrated.

■ SELF ASSESSMENT QUESTIONS

Answer the following questions without reference to the text and then refer to the answers given at the end of the manual to determine your score. Award yourself 1 mark for each complete question that you answered correctly. If you score 12 or more you are reading efficiently. Where you answered wrongly check back in the chapter to see what the answer should have been.

1 Complete the sentence.
There are two major markets which are referred to as the consumer and the _ _ _ _ _ _ _ _ market.

2 Which answer completes the following sentence? People buy what products and services can do _
(a) in a given situation.
(b) for them.
(c) in the future.
(d) to other products and services.

| ☐ (a) | ☐ (b) | ☐ (c) | ☐ (d) (tick appropriate box) |

3 Define market segmentation as in part 3 of this chapter.

_____
_____
_____

4 The user market may be subdivided into three main markets, two of which are the industrial market and metamarket. Name the other one.

_____

5 Define the consumer market as in part 1 of this chapter.

_____
_____
_____
_____

6 Define the user market as in part 1 of this chapter.

_____
_____
_____

7 There are two criteria that can be used to help classify products. One is the replacement cycle. Name the other.

_____

8 The replacement cycle classifies goods into three categories, one of which is convenience goods. Name the other two.

    (a) _____
    (b) _____

9 What does the abbreviation DMU stand for?

_____

10 The DMU may comprise four different people (or functions). One is called the buyer. Name the other three.

    (a) _____
    (b) _____
    (c) _____

11 A large consumer market may be segmented geographically. Name three other ways in which it may be segmented.

    (a) _____
    (b) _____
    (c) _____

12 One of the six alphabetic (alpha) and alphanumeric grades of socio-economic groups is C1. Name the other five.

    (a) _____
    (b) _____
    (c) _____
    (d) _____
    (e) _____

13 There are three important requirements that have to be met before segmentation becomes possible. One is measurability. Name the other two.

    (a) _____
    (b) _____

14 One segmentation strategy a company may select as part of its marketing policy is undifferentiated marketing. Name two others.

(a) _____

(b) _____

15 Which answer do you consider should complete the following sentence?

All people really buy are

(a) products and services.

(b) benefits.

(c) future promises.

☐ (a)   ☐ (b)   ☐ (c) (tick appropriate box)

■ BRINGING IT TOGETHER

People studying marketing for the first time often find it difficult to see the interrelatedness of markets, products and services and market segmentation. This is often reflected in the essays students submit on the topics.

For this reason it was felt that it would be useful to demonstrate some of the ways in which they are related in the form of a specimen question and answer. It was also felt that concluding in this way would provide students reading this manual with the opportunity to study the structure and form of presentation of one particular type of question and answer.

The question is designed to show students how to allocate their time spent answering a question in accord with the marks the examiner is prepared to award for the successful answering of parts of the question. Parts (a) and (b) in the question are definitive type questions and are awarded less marks than part (c) which is an analytical and evaluative type question (see *General study and exam tips*, pages xi–xvii).

Note when you read the essay how the work allotted to each part is in approximate accord with the marks possible for each part. The total length of the essay is in keeping with the time available for answering during most examinations, i.e. 38 minutes.

Question – 20 marks possible

(a) Define market segmentation.   4 marks

(b) Define four methods by which a market may be segmented.   6 marks

(c) Discuss the value of and limitations to segmentation.   10 marks

Answer

(a) Market segmentation is the process of dividing a market into those homogeneous segments that collectively constitute the market that is being segmented. Each segment identified as a target market should represent an homogeneous segment with characteristics that distinguish it from other segments.

(b) Markets may be segmented in one or more of the following ways:

1 *Geographic*, i.e. by climate, region, state, country, etc.

2 *Demographic*, segmenting by people's characteristics which may include socio-economic groups, race, age, sex, religion, marital status, etc.

3 *Psychographic*, by personality traits such as gregarious, dependent or independent, conservative, radical, ambitious, etc.

4 *Buying behaviour*: segmenting people by their purchasing behaviour, i.e. frequency and quantity of purchases, use to which the product will be put by different groups of people, patterns of purchasing, etc.

Other methods do exist of which segmenting by the benefits different groups of people obtain is probably the most popular.

(c) By identifying, understanding and servicing the particular needs of segments of a market a company may make more profits and/or reduce the risk of a downturn in the demand for its product. As an example, the market for a particular make of car may be segmented into industrial and reseller markets purchasing cars for use by their salesforce and executives and the consumer market purchasing for personal pleasure. Through understanding the needs of segments of these major markets the company may be able to adapt its car to appeal to various segments and direct its marketing efforts, more closely targeting them at each segment to encourage purchases.

Where new products are concerned there may be several reasons for segmentation. In some instances a company may wish to identify a segment of a market so that it can initially service one segment and then when that segment is saturated break into other segments.

A small specialised company may want to discover and supply a segment of a market that it feels it can cope with satisfactorily. It may also be that a company intends trying to identify a lucrative segment of a market to introduce its product at a high price in order to recoup development costs before supplying a less expensive version to other segments or the total market. This is an approach that some computer companies have adopted before developing units cheap enough for use in most homes.

There are of course limitations to segmentation. To segment with success the elements used for segmentation must be measurable, potential purchasers in a segment must be capable of being reached with promotions and supplies, i.e. accessible and the segment must be substantial enough in value to the company to warrant supplying. And even after all this effort it may be that supplying a substantial segment would not be sensible.

Several years ago when the desire for T shirts was at its height a T shirt company discovered that approximately half of its men's T shirts were being purchased and worn by women. Should it, therefore, promote separately to men and women and possibly produce T shirts for the female segment? Further research led the company to believe that it should continue as normal – producing for and promoting to men – as women, consciously or subconsciously, were purchasing the T shirts because they were associated with men. Nevertheless, the exercise taught the company more about its market, and the findings probably proved invaluable when purchasing patterns and tastes did change.

The degree to which a marketing manager may segment a market will depend on the existence of segments in the market and the amount of information that can be collected to clearly distinguish any segments. The lesson is that marketing managers should segment if possible but only service those segments that will ensure increased profits or will help minimise losses by preventing a decline in overall sales.

■ READING ON

We have analysed markets, indicated the value of thinking of products and services in terms of benefits and considered the ways in which markets may be segmented. What we now need are sources for providing information on which decisions regarding the analysis of a market and the mix of the 4 Ps may be taken, and that is the subject of Chapter 3. But before you read on you may be pleased to learn that if you have understood Chapters 1 and 2, it is most probable that you will readily understand the rest of the manual as it is based on a firm appreciation of the topics you have already covered.

■ EXAMINATION QUESTIONS

The Institute of Marketing

1 What are the requirements of market segmentation and targeting?
What are the benefits of effective segmentation and targeting?

2 Write notes on the following:

(a) Convenience goods.
(b) Shopping goods.
(c) Speciality goods.

The Association of Business Executives

3 To what extent should a company pursue a strategy of market segmentation?
If the market is to be segmented, upon what basis should this be done?

4 Explain what you understand by the terms:

(a) Undifferentiated Marketing.
(b) Differentiated Marketing.
(c) Concentrated Marketing.

5 The markets for industrial products are likely to have some characteristics which differentiate them quite markedly from the markets for consumer products.
Identify such characteristics and suggest how each is likely to affect the practice of marketing.

The Institute of Commercial Management

6 With a product/service of your choice discuss how you would approach the tasks of market segmentation and targeting.

3 Marketing research

Running an organisation without adequate marketing information reduces business decisions to guesswork.

Studies have shown that most businesses that fail do so because they have not obtained, analysed or acted upon market information regarding their product or service: information that is often readily available.

Running an organisation without continuous and adequate marketing information reduces business decisions to guesswork; guesswork that may adversely affect the lives of many people and the existence of an organisation. Could you imagine for instance, a car manufacturer spending tens of millions of dollars on the production of a new car without firstly analysing through research: what a market is seeking from cars in the near future; how much they are willing to pay; how many can regularly be sold if the needs of the market are met?

If you obtain a firm grasp of marketing research therefore, you will have moved a long way towards understanding where the marketing effort begins and towards becoming professional in marketing. To provide you with a firm grasp of the fundamentals of marketing research we have divided this chapter into three parts as follows.

1 Defining marketing research (MR) and providing an overview of areas that may involve MR studies
2 Outlining the sources and type of information available.
3 Taking you through the basics of conducting an MR survey.

By the end of the chapter you will find that you will be familiar with MR terminology and at the very least you will be able to understand the work involved.

■ 1 DEFINING MARKETING RESEARCH

Marketing research may be defined as:

> *The planned and systematic gathering and collation of data and the analysis of information relating to all aspects of marketing and the final consumption of goods or services*

It is common practice to divide research into two general areas, namely: **market research** and **other marketing research**. This division is shown in Table 3.1.

Table 3.1 Division of marketing research

Market research: may be defined as research involving current and potential customers who constitute a market. Major areas of interest include the study of:	Other marketing research: may be undertaken by companies to improve marketing decision making. Major areas of interest include the study of:
1 The size and location of current and potential markets. 2 Buying habits of potential and/or current customers. 3 The segments that may be part of the market. 4 Personal characteristics of the consumers. 5 Structure of the market. 6 Current and future demand and purchasing trends. 7 Attitudes of consumers towards the product or promotions. 8 Analysis of market shares. 9 Influencers and deciders in the buying decision.	1 Analysis of the strengths and weaknesses of competitors. 2 Product design and development. 3 Study of distribution (channels and physical). 4 Economic, social, legal and technological changes and trends. 5 Pattern and effectiveness of the marketing effort, such as: salesforce routing, PR expenditure etc. 6 Cost effectiveness of advertising. 7 Trade attitudes towards the company, its product and its competitors.

Market research may be further divided into **consumer market research** and **user/industrial market research**. It has also become common practice to name research in accord with the element of marketing that is being researched such as **advertising research**, **product research** and **sales research**.

■ 2 MARKETING RESEARCH INFORMATION

Data and information

Until factual (or non factual) aspects of a group of people under study are gathered and collated such facts are simply ungathered **data**. For instance, our common sense tells us that millions of people smoke a variety of cigarettes but such knowledge is meaningless for decision purposes until it is quantified. It is only when data is gathered and collated in some form understandable to people – such as tabled or graphed – that it becomes **information**.

When we collect data directly from people through research questions or observation, we refer to it as **primary (first hand) data**. When we use data already collected by others for their own purpose we refer to it as **secondary**

(second hand) data. Both primary and secondary data or information is important to marketers for taking decisions but obviously a marketer is more confident of the results of information he or she has personally been in control of collecting, analysing and collating.

Field and desk research

The collection of primary (raw) data involves *field (primary) research* which is directly undertaken by the organisation – or an agency whom the organisation pays solely for conducting its research under its authority – on an aspect of marketing or the market, involving the collection and collation of primary data.

The collection of secondary data or information involves *desk (secondary) research* which is obtaining information or data that is already in existence (secondary information or data). Information that is already in existence may have to be restructured into a new form to suit our needs, e.g. changed from a table into a graph or matrix form.

SOURCES OF SECONDARY DATA OR INFORMATION
To be cost effective the experienced marketing research manager will always start any research by checking what information is already available from sources internal or external to the organisation. It is often the case that there is a wealth of information in existence that the company just could not afford to research at first hand with its own financial resources.

Internal sources
These are sources internal to the organisation, and include the following:

(a) The *accounts department* may provide the production and delivered cost of the product; value of sales by segments of total customers; total cost of discounts given; value of creditors and debtors; cost of returns; cost of after sales service. This is a very useful source of information to a marketer when considering which customers are essential to the survival of the company or what effect a change in price and discounts may have or the additional cost of providing an after sales service to customers.

(b) Information possible from the *sales department* includes: speed of handling orders; dispersion of current customers; pattern of complaints and enquiries; total sales for each product in the range. All of this is invaluable information for understanding what is happening in the market place on a day-to-day basis.

(c) The *despatch department* can give information regarding mode and method of physical distribution; type of packing (home and export); problems associated with distribution of the product from the company. This may be extremely important when considering accepting overseas orders that have special packing and delivery requirements and when wishing to make a quick sale of a large quantity of stocks.

(d) The *production department* will have details of materials used; type of products returned and problems associated with stocking; productive capacity; order scheduling time. This is essential information to the marketing department when promising to customers – particularly in the industrial market – delivery times or alterations to the basic product.

(e) The *personnel department* is the source of information about the method of recruiting marketing staff; the cost of staffing the total marketing team and their reasons for starting with and leaving the team. This department therefore can supply information that helps the marketing manager evaluate the cost of increased staffing to try for a marketing opportunity and generally plan staffing levels in the marketing department.

There is much more information still available from other departments that may exist in the organisation, such as the *public relations* and *advertising* departments. Try to think for yourself of some other useful marketing information available from departments within an organisation and discuss it with your tutor and/or fellow students.

External sources

Internal sources of information are obviously of importance when determining what the organisation can do and when considering the likely effect on finances of changes to current operations. External sources, however, are helpful when the company is considering new areas of operation such as opening an overseas branch, entering into a new market, evaluating competition or determining future social, economical and trade trends that affect the organisation. Sources of information may include

(a) International information: available from international organisations such as the OECD, EEC Commission, IMF, World Bank, international marketing agencies, etc.

(b) National: government departments such as Customs & Excise, export intelligence and information from publications, including censuses and statistical abstracts.

(c) Domestic (and possibly worldwide): trade associations, local councils and social service, chambers of commerce, embassies, unions, universities, institutes and societies, advertising and marketing agencies, reports and publications, newspapers, periodicals and trade journals, libraries – both general and specialised.

(d) Panels: Some MR agencies are particularly important for supplying secondary information that is up to date. These are agencies that operate panels of consumers or retailers on a continuous basis, such as:

(i) *Consumer panels*: These are groups made up of a large representative sample (group) of consumers of the particular product(s) under study. The panel is established on a permanent basis so the marketing research agency controlling the panel is able to obtain marketing research on a continuous basis. Each person on the panel is asked to provide information regarding their purchases and this information is passed on to the companies subscribing to the service. This method is cheaper than continuous researching by the company itself and can usually be instigated quickly. The company does not require MR staff and because of the lower costs involved the obtaining of continual information on the purchasing behaviour by the market is possible. Subscribing companies, however, do not have control of the research or exclusivity of information.

(ii) *Retail audits*: A representative sample is organised by an independent agency but this time it is made up of retail outlets rather than consumers. The agency staff enters the panel of retail outlets and checks (audits) on behalf of its subscribers (companies) wanting the collated data the sales of subscribers' products and that of their competitors, over a given time. In this way subscribers can evaluate how well they are doing compared with their competitors, in which areas sales are increasing or declining and which retail outlets are performing better than others. Once again, however, individual subscribing companies do not have control over the research or the information obtained.

Primary data

A few sources of primary data from consumer and user markets include: consumers, retailers, wholesalers, factors, brokers, suppliers of goods and services and manufacturers, extractors, processors, voters or donators and beneficiaries in the case of charities or members of trade unions.

One method of obtaining primary data is through **field surveys** undertaken by the company. This involves the company or a marketing research agency on behalf of the company directly undertaking a planned marketing research study on interviewees/respondents. The advantage is that the company has direct control of the research and obtains information exclusive to the organisation. The disadvantage is that it is costly and involves considerable expertise.

Research may be **ad hoc** (one off), usually to obtain information at one point in time for making a particular marketing decision. This is especially useful where secrecy is important such as analysing a market for the development of a proposed new product. There are, however, times when **continuous** research is more suitable, if for example an organisation wishes to keep continually abreast of a changing market. Cost usually prohibits most companies from undertaking continuous research on their own, and this highlights the importance of 'consumer panels' and 'retail audits'.

Data obtained through marketing research may be:

(a) **Quantitative**: this is data capable of clear objective assessment, such as the number of cars that pass a particular site for a proposed petrol station in any one week.
(b) **Qualitative**: This is subjective data, such as the attempt to assess people's attitudes or motivations.

Field research carried out by a company's marketing staff is obviously very expensive and requires considerable expertise. Therefore, the tendency is for the larger companies to undertake some research of their own while still using secondary sources including consumer panels and retail audits.

Nevertheless, even the smallest of companies or sole proprieters can and should undertake research in one form or another before committing their finances to a project. Indeed it is the skill with which many entrepreneurs fulfil this function before starting a company that often determines their success: the application of business acumen to forecasting future events. As one businessman said, 'There is no such thing as a large company. Only successful small ones.'

■ 3 CONDUCTING MARKETING RESEARCH SURVEYS

When we undertake research to extract and evaluate quantitative or qualitative information, regarding a sample of people as representative of a total market, we refer to the study as a **survey**.

There are four popular methods of obtaining data from respondents to questions that form a part of marketing research surveys, namely:

1 postal questionnaires
2 telephone interviews
3 personal interviews
4 observation

The major advantages and disadvantages of each are given below. You will find it useful to note that the advantages of one method often imply the disadvantages of another. For example, deeper probing into the answers given by respondents is possible where personal interviews by interviewers are used which is not possible with postal questionnaires as there is not an interviewer present to ask questions designed to discover the reasons behind some answers.

Postal questionnaires

These involve posting questionnaires to respondents in order that they may complete them and return them to the company.

ADVANTAGES

- Postal questionnaires are economical. This makes them a popular method of collecting data from respondents.
- They are useful where there is an extreme geographical dispersion of the respondents, as the cost and time of travelling to respondents is saved and initial responses may be obtained faster.
- Bias (through interviewer attitude or approach), which may result from personal or telephone interviewing, is avoided.

- The respondent has time to consult with others who the researchers may want involved in answering the questions, such as members of the family.
- The company undertaking the research does not require a team of skilled researchers.

DISADVANTAGES

- Low response. Twenty-five per cent may be considered very good. Therefore, follow up reminder cards are usually necessary to increase the response rate.
- Questionnaires invariably must be short, if an acceptable level of response is to be achieved. This reduces the depth and quality of information which may be collected.
- Further probing of replies is not possible.
- The reason why a respondent did not or would not answer (non response) cannot be ascertained.
- We cannot always predetermine if the respondent is exactly the type that we require, i.e. typicality.

Telephone interviewing

This involves telephoning respondents so that the interviewer can ask the respondent questions and complete a questionnaire.

ADVANTAGES

- Invariably cheaper than personal interviewing.
- Can interview respondents who are widely dispersed, and re-call them if they were not immediately available.
- Conversations can be recorded so that they may be considered again in greater detail at a later date.
- The response rate is higher than for postal questionnaires: sometimes as much as 90 per cent.
- Particularly useful in industrial market research as most companies have a telephone.

DISADVANTAGES

- Owners of telephones may not be a totally representative sample. Much of the market may not own a telephone.
- It can be expensive where respondents are widely dispersed and require calling in the daytime.
- If personal characteristics, such as the exact colour of a person's hair, are important, these cannot be precisely determined (i.e. typicality).

Personal interviewing

Personal interviewing involves trained interviewers in talking to the respondents face-to-face.

ADVANTAGES

- More questions may be asked as the respondent's interest can be stimulated by the interviewer.
- The typicality of the respondent can be ascertained before continuing the interview as he/she can be seen and asked questions – by the interviewer – to determine typicality before the actual research questions are asked.
- It is possible to explain questions that would be difficult to answer employing other methods.
- The opportunity to probe into a question more deeply or to obtain details of other potential respondents from the person being interviewed can be afforded.

DISADVANTAGES

- Cost per interview is the highest of all methods.
- Sometimes it is found that inexperienced and insufficiently trained interviewers allow their own attitude to lead the respondent wrongly.
- Training of interviewers can be very expensive.
- Sometimes, as in industrial markets, only three or four interviews can be conducted in a day, thus prolonging the survey.

Observation

This involves the observer in obtaining data by noting the behaviour of people: such as the number of people who pass through a certain railway station or store within a given period.

ADVANTAGES

- It does not involve interviewing or questionnaire filling in and thus does not require highly skilled staff.
- A considerable amount of survey work may be completed in a day.
- Typicality of what is being viewed can be quickly assessed.
- A more objective, and thus measurable, approach is possible than with other methods as interviewer and respondent bias is minimised.

DISADVANTAGES

- It is a method that tends to answer questions like 'How many?', 'Where?', and 'How?' but not 'Why?'.

- It is often a characteristic of widely dispersed sampling and can, therefore, involve considerable travelling by staff.
- Verification of findings of individual interviewers (observers) may be difficult or/and expensive. In the case of personal interviewing (see above) for example the MR manager can telephone a random sample of respondents (provided they have given a telephone number) to check if they were interviewed.

Types of marketing research questions

When asking respondents questions only four types of questions may be asked whether orally or in written form. These are:

1 dichotomous questions
2 multiple choice
3 semantic differential scales
4 open ended questions

1 DICHOTOMOUS QUESTIONS
These are **close ended** two sided questions, in that the respondent can only answer 'Yes' or 'No', 'True' or 'False', etc. The respondent can choose from only two options.

Example

Q Do you smoke?   YES   NO   Please circle your answer

2 MULTIPLE CHOICE QUESTIONS
Again **close ended** but the respondent is given more possible choices than two.

Example

Q If you smoke, on average how   1. 1 to 9   Please circle your answer
many cigarettes do you smoke   2. 10 to 20
each day?   3. 21 to 30
                                                      4. 31 to 40
                                                      5. 41 or over

Thus, multiple choice questions are a compromise between the inflexibility of close ended questions and the possible vagueness of open ended questions.

3 SEMANTIC DIFFERENTIAL SCALES
Semantic differential scales go that little further than multiple choice questions as, while they limit the reply the respondent may give, they do allow freedom of response by the respondent within the governing extremes on the scale.

Example

Q Mark with a cross 'X' the point on Scale A which reflects your liking of the ice cream that you have just tasted.

Scale A

I ——————————— I
Hate it   Adore it

4 OPEN ENDED QUESTIONS

It may be justifiably reasoned that **open ended** are the better types of questions, as they allow respondents to express fully their own opinions. The main problem is the effective interpretation and collation of answers, as the replies may be vague and extensive. For this reason, respondents are often asked to limit their replies to a set number of words. Open ended questions are very useful where a company is attempting to determine if there are aspects of consumers' attitudes and/or behaviour they may not currently appreciate.

Example

Q Why do you believe you smoke?   Please write your answer here.

_____
_____
_____
_____

Essential rules when designing effective questionnaires

When designing questionnaires to be used by interviewers or sent directly by post to respondents there are generally rules which the marketing researcher must observe. Ten of these are:

1 Make the questions and questionnaire as short as possible so that respondents do not feel that answering is too much of a chore.
2 Make questions as simple as possible so that they are more easily understood.
3 Keep questions on the same topic in the same section of the questionnaire so that respondents develop a full awareness of what is being asked.
4 Ensure that questions are in a logical order. For example, start with questions that determine if the respondent is a representative subject.
5 Do not use questions that lead the respondent. For example, a question like 'Do you believe that red coats are the most attractive?' would probably be inappropriate. A more correct question would be 'Which colour for coats do you consider the most attractive?'
6 Ensure that questions are not ambiguous to prevent misunderstandings.
7 Avoid asking two questions in one sentence as the respondent will not know what question he or she is answering. Example of a sentence that contains two questions, 'Do you often fly by plane and travel by PAN AM airlines?'.

8 Choose questions appropriate to the survey method being used, i.e. postal, telephone, personal interviews.
9 Ensure that the layout and design is pleasing to the eye.
10 Leave very personal questions until the end in case the respondent chooses not to answer these particular questions.

Methods for pre-checking the questionnaire

Even when the first draft of a questionnaire has been designed considerable errors can occur if a researcher does not firstly check the questionnaire with other researchers and on respondents in the market he/she is intending surveying. Therefore, to test the questionnaire the researcher must:

1 *Make allowance for his/her own bias* by ensuring that researchers with different opinions analyse an outline questionnaire and then assist with the final construction of the questions and questionnaire design.
2 *Conduct some free-ranging interviews* with representative individuals or groups of respondents to see if the right questions are being asked before they become part of a research questionnaire and if there are any unforeseen problems, such as difficulties in obtaining typical respondents.
3 *Conduct a pilot survey* and include the method of double interviewing.
   Pilot surveys are small surveys of say 100 representative respondents to check if the draft questionnaire is ready to use in a full survey. **Double interviewing** is used in pilot surveys in which the interviewer asks the question on the questionnaire and after the response asks the respondent what he or she thought the question was trying to determine. Respondents often infer different things about the same question. In this way ambiguity regarding each question is avoided.

Sampling

Now that we know the fundamentals of designing questionnaires the next step is to select a sample of people to interview to ensure that they are representative of the total people (**universe**) we wish to research.

We are able to select a representative number of people (**the sample**) from consumer markets because they tend to be large in number and homogeneous. Most importantly they abide by two laws of statistics that must apply when selecting a representative sample from a larger group. These are:

1 **The law of inertia of large numbers** which asserts that large groups of people are less likely to change rapidly in their patterns of behaviour than small groups. This is important as a survey may take several weeks and we do not want the market from which we are taking a sample to be constantly changing in its behaviour, otherwise our findings will not be representative of current behaviour.
2 **The law of statistical regularity** which maintains that a large enough sample

of a very large group of people (or items) will be representative of the characteristics of the large group.

Determining the actual size of a sample and its accuracy in representing the universe is beyond the scope of this manual. It is necessary, however, to understand the characteristics of samples to ensure that no matter how large the sample it is representative and also to help keep costs to a minimum.

Samples may be selected in two ways, namely randomly and non-randomly.

RANDOM (PROBABILITY) SAMPLES

This is where items or persons who collectively constitute the universe are selected to be part of a sample in such a way that each one stands the same chance of being selected to be part of the sample. Therefore, a purely random sample requires that all items or persons who represent the universe are available or known so that a random sample may be selected. As a simple example, if we had a large bag of thousands of marbles of various colours that had been thoroughly mixed together it is reasonable to assume that if we extracted several handfuls of marbles they would have similar characteristics to those remaining in the bag. In the case of marketing we would usually select our random sample of people by computer.

A major problem when using random samples for MR surveys is that we may finish up with a sample that has too many people with a particular characteristic. For example, if we wanted to select a sample of men and women in the USA of various races to interview, we may finish up with 70 per cent of the sample being white women with no black people included at all. An extreme example but it does make the point.

NON-RANDOM SAMPLING

If we do not know all the items that constitute the universe then we cannot use a purely random sample and must be satisfied with a non-random sample. This does not mean that a non-random sample is less representative than a random sample, as it may take account of differences in the importance of people, organisations or items that can be selected. A non-random sample will also, invariably, be more cost effective than random samples when used for MR purposes. Non-random samples would include:

(a) *Stratified sampling*: The universe is divided into strata/segments that collectively represent the whole universe. For example, house owners may be stratified into owners of detached; semi-detached; terraced houses; etc. and their numbers estimated. A randomly selected proportion from each stratum may then be obtained for researching, thus ensuring that in our total sample we are sure of obtaining proportions in relation to the total universe.

(b) *Systematic sampling*: The first item is selected randomly, and then additional items are selected by equal intervals, i.e. house number 11 may have been selected randomly, and then each tenth in the district thereafter will be used for research.

(c) *Multi-stage sampling*: Multi-stage sampling is based on defined regions/ areas. Regions of a country may be selected randomly and thereafter areas within these regions. For example, counties or states may be selected at random: then local authorities within the counties or states selected; then streets within the local authorities' areas; then families in the streets; and finally individuals in the families.

(d) *Cluster sampling*: This is similar to multi-stage. Representative clusters of people are selected randomly instead of a staging process based on society's defined areas. For example, apartment blocks or streets may be used. Every person in the apartment block or street that has been randomly selected will then be interviewed.

(e) *Quota sampling*: This is possibly the most important method used by marketing researchers. The universe/population is stratified and interviewers are then given specific numbers (a quota) of types of people to interview, such as, 10 house owning teachers, 13 house owning managers etc. The attributes essential to typicality of respondents is more important than location or random selection. Therefore, if we were wanting to interview red headed women about a proposed new hair dye we may send interviewers to a city in Wales (a country where there are many red headed people) to cut down costs of the research and provide each interviewer with a quota of women of different ages to interview.

Because of costs and the need to ensure a representative sample non random sampling is the more popular method of sampling in MR. Bear in mind, however, that most non-random samples have an element of random selection in them, but they are not purely random samples as all items, or people, did not have the same opportunity of being selected. You may in fact find some books referring to certain non-random sampling methods as **modified random sampling**.

ADVANTAGES AND DISADVANTAGES OF THE TWO SAMPLING METHODS

Table 3.2

Random sampling	Non-random sampling
Advantages	**Advantages**
• Knowledge of the universe's characteristics is unnecessary. • Bias caused by the selector is eliminated.	• Relevant sections of the universe may be selected in the proportions they appear in the universe. • Geographical concentration can be achieved thus reducing costs. • It is usually a more practical method for MR sampling.
Disadvantages	
• Certain groups of people may be selected more than they should be i.e., bias in the final sample. • Errors can be difficult to detect. • May be costly, particularly where people in remote districts are selected.	**Disadvantages** • Detailed initial information of the universe is needed. • Errors in sample selection can easily occur.

USER MARKET SAMPLING

The above sampling methods are rarely used in researching user markets because companies constituting a market (e.g. the industrial market) are often so few in number that it is sometimes possible to interview all the companies involved, or a small proportion of companies that account for the majority of supply by the particular industry, plus a small proportion of the remaining companies. Where, however, a method of sampling is possible the method used will invariably be non random.

Marketing research decisions

By now you have probably realised that MR surveys call for a planned, systematic approach by the MR manager. Such an approach may follow this decision making pattern.

1 *Define the problem* and assess if a full survey is really necessary to make a decision, i.e. would it be cost effective?

   Some decisions are not worthy of massive market research surveys. For example, if an ice cream company is considering introducing a chocolate flavour and knows that people are already buying chocolate ice cream made by competitors is there much point to extensive research to discover if consumers will buy the one that the company proposes introducing? Why not simply introduce the chocolate flavour in one area of the market and see how well it sells?

2 *Set objectives.* Assuming MR is needed, 'What do we hope to discover and how quickly, and can we discover what we need to know before we have to take a decision?'.

3 *Which type of research will be needed?* Desk, field or both?

4 If field research is to be used, is there a list or table of the *details of the universe*? These lists are called **sampling frames**, such as mail order lists and the register of new cars. Sampling frames may provide the major characteristics of the universe and are helpful with any MR, but particularly for selection in random sampling. If a frame does not already exist the company may have to develop its own sampling frame such as appropriate clusters for cluster sampling.

5 *What survey and sampling method(s) will be used?*

6 *How and by whom will the information be gathered,* collated and analysed and a report presented to senior management?

Test markets

Sometimes where a national launch of a product will be very expensive an organisation may choose to test the acceptability of its product and the effectiveness of its proposed marketing effort (campaign) on a small representative section of the total market. Geographical areas in a country, such as certain towns and conurbations, used for test marketing are known as **test market areas** or simply, **test markets**.

The characteristics of the area chosen must closely resemble those of the nation in order that an organisation can use the area for testing the acceptability of the product to the national market. The area should:

1 be relatively isolated so that it is not strongly affected by passing or spasmodic purchasers;
2 have a distribution and retail outlet system similar to that nationally;
3 have purchasers and a purchasing pattern similar to that nationally;
4 have the necessary marketing communication services, such as TV channels, press, posters, etc. that are normally available nationally.

The organiser's test market must be maintained until repurchase levels are determined so that final regular, national sales can be estimated.

The major problems with test markets are that:

- They are expensive.
- They give competitors the opportunity to see what the organisation is going to launch nationally and thus the opportunity also to take counter action to stop the national launch of the product being successful.
- They allow competitors to spoil the test market results by interfering with the test through changing their own promotions in the area or buying the product under test so that the organiser believes that more have been sold and thus becomes involved in a costly national launch.

Nevertheless, even with these problems, their usefulness is such that large organisations still like to use them before committing themselves to the considerable expense of launching the product nationally. In the case of companies with hundreds of retail outfits through the country they are in the fortunate position of being able to test new products they have developed in one or several of their shops in a particular area. If it is found that the new item sells well then it may be introduced into the company's other shops in selected areas or nationally. However, this is using one's own shops as test shops and not *test marketing* where many other elements must exist for the test to be truly representative of national market and marketing characteristics.

Marketing research within the total marketing information process

When we think of marketing research we should consider it solely as part of the **information process** of marketing. The marketing director or manager may personally receive information useful to the marketing effort from sources other than the MR department – from directors of other activities within the company, from personal visits to customers, from daily newspaper and trade magazine articles, from TV and radio programmes, from talking with members of the salesforce, from suppliers, from watching competitors' efforts and from literature often supplied by government departments responsible for promoting industry.

Marketing research, therefore, both desk and field, represents just one source of marketing information but it is a major one as the information that is required is usually essential to the effective operation of the company and the manner in which it is collected employs many of the planned and systematic research techniques associated with research in the social sciences.

Marketers should grasp every opportunity to undertake any desk or field research, to become used to the discipline of research and the idea of positively searching for information required for decision making rather than negatively leaving decisions to chance.

■ CONCLUSION

Sometimes newcomers to the subject of marketing erroneously assume that marketing only applies to big businesses. This is not the case at all. We are constantly witnessing the emergence of small unknown companies on to national and international markets. Their growth in size cannot be accomplished without sales and continuously increasing sales are rarely accomplished without the proprietor constantly analysing what the market needs.

Consider for example, a woman wishing to start her own restaurant. What sort of information could she obtain through her own efforts before making the decision to open the restaurant? It should include information regarding the market, the product and for that matter many other aspects of such a business.

The following are just a few sources of information that may be worth considering before the decision to start the restaurant is taken.

FRANCHISING
If a franchise is being considered contacting a franchise association for impartial advice on the advantages and disadvantages of the venture would be useful.

THE STREET
To check how many people pass by the proposed location of the restaurant at various times of the day and week. Why are they in the locality? What sort of food they tend to buy at restaurants? What sort of restaurant they would like to have in the area? Approximately how much would they expect to spend when eating out? When do they eat out – at lunchtime, evenings, weekends, etc?

LOCAL COUNCIL OFFICES
To determine the localities in which people of different socio-economic groups live so that any promotional effort can be directed at the right people. To check on planning permission in case it is intended to establish a restaurant where one does not currently exist. For by-laws on hygiene and safety.

YELLOW PAGES AND LIBRARIES

To locate companies, wedding photographers, institutions, churches, clubs, all of whom may require meals for large numbers of people on special or festive occasions.

LOCAL RESTAURANTS

To check how similar they are to the one being considered, their level and type of customer and their proximity to the proposed restaurant. If the woman has no experience of working in restaurants it would be useful to work in one for a little time to obtain an idea of such operations at first hand.

In addition, the following would prove useful, if not essential:

- *Trade fairs and exhibitions*: such as the Hotel and Catering Exhibition to see and compare the equipment and services that are available to restaurants.
- *Books*: on starting up a business or/and restaurant to ensure some understanding of business procedures and to avoid pitfalls.
- *The bank manager*: to offer advice on financing and planning the venture, to provide the name of accountants familiar with accounting for small businesses.
- *A small advertising company*: to determine the local media (radio, newspaper, cinema) available for promoting the restaurant or any other suitable method of promoting.
- *Relatives and friends*: to test and perfect the proposed dishes/recipes that will form part of the menu. (This is known as product development, which we will consider in Chapter 4.)

As already mentioned, these are just a few areas of research that would need to be considered. The fact is that the majority of first time business ventures fail and in the majority of cases do so because insufficient research and planning was undertaken by the would-be entrepreneur. Therefore, as you read the rest of this manual do bear in mind that marketing and marketing research applies to businesses of any kind and size.

■ STUDY AND EXAM TIPS

1 Because of the detail of the subject, examiners tend to ask specific questions on one or two aspects of marketing research. Therefore, read the question carefully, identify the aspects to be discussed and concentrate your answer *only* on those aspects.

2 Always allow for the fact that researchers will rarely find perfect solutions to any problem, so where applicable present your thoughts along the lines of minimising subjective decisions and 'risk reduction'. It is senior management (board of directors) who will take the final decision, having taken into account the research findings and other organisational factors, such as alternative investment opportunities, finances available and expertise required.

3 Be willing to identify and discuss both advantages and limitations of techniques used in research programmes. One limiting factor is cost. Remember, there is no point in incurring the high expense of field research if desk research could provide sufficient answers for a management decision.

4 Research findings represent the major information input to many marketing decisions, so always keep in mind the marketing use or uses to which the findings may be put when deciding on an appropriate research method.

5 Don't forget that anyone with adequate MR knowledge starting up in business can and should still do desk or possibly some limited field research on his or her own before investing their hard earned money so do not limit your answers only to large companies unless specifically asked to do so.

■ SELF ASSESSMENT QUESTIONS

Answer the following questions without reference to the text and then refer to the answers given at the end of the manual to determine your score. Award yourself 1 mark for each complete question that you answered correctly. If you scored 8 or more you are reading efficiently. Where you answered wrongly check back in the chapter to see what the answer should have been.

1 Pilot surveys may involve double interviewing.

☐ YES   ☐ NO (tick appropriate box)

2 Market research is solely concerned with the analysis of the market itself?

☐ YES   ☐ NO (tick appropriate box)

3 There are two types of research. One is field research and the other is
‒‒

4 Primary data is obtained through what type of research?
‒‒

5 Data or information may be quantitative or ‒‒‒‒‒‒‒‒‒‒‒‒‒‒‒‒‒‒‒‒‒‒‒

6 Name three types of non-random methods of sampling.
(a) ‒‒
(b) ‒‒
(c) ‒‒

7 Name the four types of questions that may be used in marketing research questionnaires.

(a) _____

(b) _____

(c) _____

(d) _____

8 There are four ways by which marketing research surveys obtain data or information. One is by personal interviewing; name the other three.

(a) _____

(b) _____

(c) _____

9 If a sampling method is used in researching industrial markets what method would invariably be used?

_____

10 Research can be continuous or _____

■ EXAMINATION QUESTIONS

The Institute of Marketing

1 Using examples, discuss some of the main sources of secondary market research data and the uses of such data in marketing decision making.

2 Discuss the value and limitations of marketing research.

The Association of Business Executives

3 Marketing research assignments often generate data from samples of the population being investigated. In this context discuss the relative advantage and disadvantages of:

(a) Random sampling techniques.

(b) Non-random sampling techniques.

4 When carrying out a marketing research survey data can be collected by means of

(a) Personal interviews.

(b) Mail questionnaires.

(c) Telephone interviews.

Enumerate the advantages and disadvantages of each method.

4 Product policy

The best promotions in the world cannot sustain a poorly conceived product or service.

Most of us at one time or another have purchased a product that we felt we could improve, making it more useful to more people. Broadly speaking, this is what **product policy** in companies is all about: The determining of:

(**a**) what a company should produce
(**b**) when new or altered products should be launched
(**c**) in what quantities they should be produced and supplied

To examine these three aspects of product policy we have divided this chapter into three parts.

1 What companies supply, why a company needs to change its supplies, how changes may be made and what should be evaluated when changes are considered.
2 The procedure in developing and launching new or altered products.
3 The role of brand names, packs and packaging.

Without a continuing product policy a company will not be sure that it is meeting the needs of new or changing markets. If a company ceases to supply products that are profitable then the company starts to decline. Therefore, the short, medium and long term growth of a company is affected by its continuing product policy decisions with regard to current products sold by the company as well as new ones it intends launching. As most product managers would probably contend: the best promotions in the world cannot continually sustain a poorly conceived product or service.

■ 1 SUPPLIES, CHANGES AND EVALUATION OF PROPOSED CHANGES

What companies offer/supply to purchasers

Let us just remind ourselves again that what a company really offers to customers is **benefits as perceived by the customer**. Once we have determined what benefits customers need, we can then reflect these benefits in the product(s) or service(s) we supply or intend supplying.

In the case of a company producing cars it must analyse all the benefits customers derive from a car and then determine which benefits the company will reflect in the car(s) it produces and markets.

The major factor that will determine if the company will provide individual benefits for customers is **profitability**. If sufficient people are willing to pay a price for the benefit that will enable the company to make extra profit, and if the company is able to produce the benefits required, then it is most probable that they will be supplied.

To explain by a simple example, let us suppose that only two of all the people who purchase cars wanted a sunroof in their car. It is doubtful if the producer of the average priced car would provide this additional benefit. If on the other hand research showed that one million potential customers wanted the benefit of a sunroof and were willing to pay for this extra benefit, then the car producer would probably be prepared to make this slight change to around one million of the cars it produces. You can see this type of accommodation by looking at the variations to a basic car offered by popular car companies such as Ford, General Motors, Volkswagen, etc.

Therefore, to return to the initial point, bear in mind that all companies really have to sell is **benefits** which companies attempt to provide through the features of the product(s) or service(s) they have to offer.

Product mix or service mix

The word *mix* is regularly used in marketing to refer to **all the products or services offered by a company**.

If we look at Table 4.1 with a college as an example we will find the service mix in the form of courses offered to potential students by the college. The college is offering three courses – indicated by the title and level of qualification –

Table 4.1

	Courses offered		Levels offered
1	Marketing Course	1a	Certificate
		1b	Diploma
2	General business course	2a	Foundation Certificate
		2b	Higher Certificate
		2c	Diploma
		2d	Advanced Diploma
3	Communications, advertising and marketing course	3a	Foundation Course
		3b	Certificate
		3c	Diploma

to accommodate the needs of potential students from different segments of the market at which the college aims its courses or services.

Using this simple example of educational services offered by a college we can introduce the following dimensions of a service and product mix.

SERVICE WIDTH/RANGE
This refers to the number of individual services offered. In our case, courses 1, 2 and 3 represent individual educational services. The successful receipt of the service is confirmed in the form of a qualification, i.e. certificate or diploma.

Product width/range
Where a company produces many totally different products it is said to have a multi-product range. If it only supplies versions of one product it is said to deal in one line.

SERVICE DEPTH/VERSION
This refers to the variations within each service (or product) which in our case are courses 1a, 1b or 2a, 2b, 2c, 2d or 3a, 3b, 3c.

Product depth/version
Taking cars once more as an example, the one basic car may be changed slightly to produce an L, XL, GTi, Turbo, Prestige version, etc.

SERVICE/PRODUCT CONSISTENCY
Consistency refers to the relationship between the provision of courses (or products) offered and their end use. Many academic courses are similar. The same lecturing skills, therefore, may be used; the same physical facilities; the same course tutor could be in charge of all the courses; and where subjects are very similar expertise may be transferred from one course to another without any loss of standards/quality of service.

However, on completion of their course, students will use their knowledge gained and qualification for working in different areas of business: course 1, marketing; course 2, general areas of business; course 3, advertising or public relations.

There is also consistency as applied to constant levels of standards which is much more difficult to achieve with services.

In the case of most products modern methods of quality control can ensure that a product we buy today will be the same if we buy one again tomorrow, e.g. each tin of beans of the same name, such as Heinz, will taste the same as the previous one.

Therefore, consistency of standards is more possible with products than services except where products are perishable or the quality fluctuates through the forces of nature, i.e. apples may taste better or worse next year.

PACKAGE DEALS
Sometimes more than one service are sold together. When this occurs it is

referred to as a **package deal** such as package holidays in which the flight, hotel, airport-to-hotel transportation, meals and car hire may be sold as one price. The purchaser cannot tell how much each element of the holiday costs and may not be interested as they may not wish to arrange the different elements for themselves. From the holiday company's point of view package holidays generate more customers and may conceal how much they are making in profits.

A product and service may also be linked in this way, e.g. a car may be purchased with two years' garage servicing; or a one year guarantee of parts and labour with two years' garage servicing; or a one year guarantee of parts and labour and one year's road side rescue service all included in the price.

Again two products may be linked as a package deal, e.g. 'buy our washing machine before such a date and you will also receive a toaster'. Of course you are not told how much the washing machine would be without the toaster.

When a package deal represents for suppliers and customers the normal and most needed presentation, such as with package holidays offered by travel agents, then *the package* (package deal) should be considered the product or service.

Selling an experience/feeling

Sometimes what we believe we are supplying in the form of a product or service is not what the customer is receiving. Customers may be receiving personal experience and unless we can identify the main experiences that customers receive we cannot clearly evaluate what we should promote and supply.

For instance, Madame Tussauds, the London wax works (museum) which exhibits wax replicas of famous people for customers to see, recently revaluated the service they were providing. The result was that they realised that most visitors went to the museum to be close to the personalities that they personally hated or admired, rather than to see all the exhibits, and each visitor experienced different feelings when standing by the figures that attracted them. It may be hate, love, admiration or respect but it was personal to each visitor and the visitor was paying to experience those feelings. This caused the management to reconsider its promotions and pricing and it introduced a camera and film hire service with much success so that visitors could capture their moments with the famous on film.

It is a similar situation with charities. When we donate we usually do not receive the service ourselves but we do experience personal satisfaction no matter what our motive for donating. Sometimes people will buy products not for their integral worth but because they provide a feeling of status or contentment. This once again reinforces the idea that we should always consider what benefits people are seeking not what we are determined to supply.

Why make changes?

There are four main reasons why companies modify existing products, introduce new versions or new products or withdraw existing lines. These are:

1 Due to **changes caused by the market**, e.g. people may develop a taste for sweeter products so a company's product may have to be sweetened more to retain customers. Coca Cola is much sweeter now than when it was first introduced. Changes in cinema attendances have caused many large cinemas to be made into two or three smaller cinemas each offering a different film to encourage attendance.

2 **Changes caused through competitors** improving their products in relation to the needs of markets.

3 **Changes due to cost**, e.g. need to change from metal to plastic as steel is increasing in price. If price rises demand by the market may fall.

4 Changes to current products or the introduction of new products **because a company believes it will increase sales and profits.** Conversely a company may withdraw products because they are becoming unprofitable or to release resources of the company for concentrating on more profitable lines. When companies reduce the amount of products or versions of a product they produce the process is referred to as *rationalising* of the product line or range.

What changes to the product mix may be made?

Most of the changes to the product mix made by companies will fall into the following areas:

1 Addition of **new products/services unrelated to current ones** to break into a new market or spread the risk of a downturn in the demand, for one or more of the company's products, across a more extensive multi-product range.

2 **Extension of related products**, e.g. a coat manufacturer introducing a completely new coat style or suits.

3 **Differentiation of current product**, i.e. slight additions in order that the differentiated version will appeal to people in other segments of the market. For example a standard video recorder may be differentiated by the additional offerings of remote control, freeze framing, eight hour play facility, etc.

4 **Modifications to current product**: usually to reduce costs, improve style or reliability. Many products have to be modified because design faults have emerged over the time they have been sold in the market. Many cars have had their side chrome trims replaced by black plastic which – in many cases – looks just as good and is cheaper to produce.

5 Planned, fictitious or **perceived changes** possible because of the attitudes of most of us when we consider a purchase. For example, a paint manufacturer producing 5 litre tins of paint may label thousands without a brand name, thousands with a strong brand name and image and thousands again for a chain of Do-It-Yourself stores under their company brand name. Purchasers will pay substantially different prices according to which tin they purchase – although the paint inside is exactly the same – because they firmly believe that the paints are different.

It is debatable if this should come under changes to the product as only the label changes. It depends if you consider the brand as synonymous with the product. Obviously customers believe there is a difference and for that reason it has been arbitrarily introduced at this point.

Factors to analyse and evaluate in changes to the product mix

As explained the product mix of most companies may be expanded or rationalised, but before any changes to the mix are made a company will need to evaluate the outcome of any proposed changes before they are made.

Offering a multi product or service range to a market presents a company with the opportunity to spread the risk of failure of one or two products across a range of products, the opportunity to service many different market segments and to take advantage of demand trends in a variety of individual products as and when they occur.

At the same time however, providing an extensive range of products usually involves additional costs as less of each product will probably be produced and many sections and divisions may be needed to handle the production and supply of the various products. Competitors only supplying versions of one product may also prove more efficient in supplying potential purchasers and thus obtain comparatively more profit and control over a major segment of the market.

Marketing management should, therefore, evaluate the total range of products or services it will offer and the value of additional products by using a series of internal and external checks which would evaluate the following.

- Sales trends: in total, by product/service line, by product/service version and the sales trends expected from the launch of new products.
- Profit trends for individual products/services and expected profit.
- Profit trends for any proposed new product.
- The value of individual products as a means of generating purchases of other products in the range.
- Production capacity and its allocation to individual products.
- Type of resources which will be freed (or may be dispensed with) if a product or service is withdrawn.
- Opportunities to introduce products or services into other segments of the home or an overseas market.
- General market and economic trends which could affect the future of individual products or services.
- Market shares achieved and maintained by own products.
- Competitors' activities and achievements and trading trends.
- Need to retain levels of production to ensure that costs are minimised and total costs of the company are covered.
- The possibility of contracting out the production and/or distribution of one or more of the company's less profitable products/services.
- Would rationalising the range of products (reducing the range) reduce costs as

the company may then concentrate its activities on fewer lines or should it extend its range of like products so that the salesforce can carry new products to their current customers and distribution costs are shared?

● The effects on sections, divisions and/or branches of the company of the dropping or addition of new products or product versions.

The checks identified represent the main areas of concern but individual companies will introduce additional checks that they consider relevant to their particular business.

Any evaluation carried out will help marketing management to decide on: new (or altered) product or service launches, product or service withdrawal, intensity of marketing programmes for specific product or service lines, sales targets and the allocation of human, financial and physical resources.

■ 2 NEW PRODUCT DEVELOPMENT

There are four major processes or areas to consider in the development and launching of a new product or the modification of an existing one. These are:

1 the new product development process
2 the adoption process
3 the product life cycle (PLC)
4 pack, packaging and branding

The first three of these we will consider in this part with the last evaluated separately in part 3.

New product development process

The development process defines a series of activities that should be undertaken in the development of a new product to the point where it becomes commercially viable, i.e. ready for launching (introducing) onto the market. This process is illustrated in Figure 4.1.

IDEAS GENERATION STAGE
This is the beginning of the process where a company collects information and ideas in the hope that one of the ideas will ultimately become a new or adapted product or service for the company to introduce to a market.

Ideas are sought internally as well as externally to the company and at this stage no idea is rejected. Groups are formed and encouraged to forward ideas. Ideas for development may be sought from sales staff, scientists, inventors, company management, company staff (via suggestion boxes), members of the trade, members of the general public, from analysis of competitor activities or from analysis of various markets (via market research) to identify possible product or service needs.

Fig. 4.1 *Development of new products*

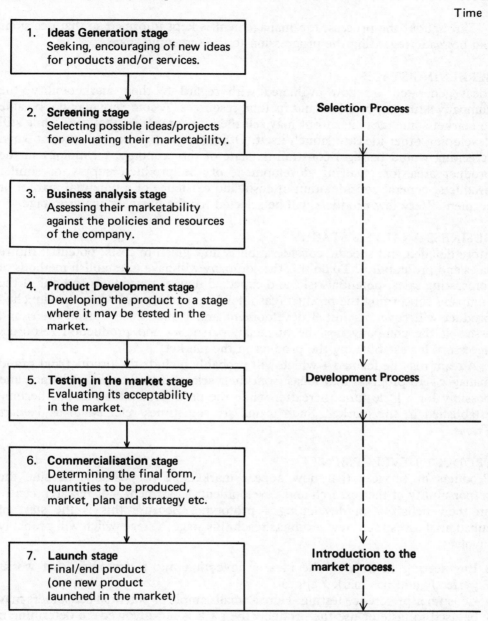

As an example marketing research may have determined from an analysis of the wine market that there is a need by a segment of the market for a wine of a particular sweetness in an instant dispensing pack. Teams comprising a senior member of each of the main departments in a company may meet regularly to evaluate the company's products and new ideas to modify and improve products in relation to the needs of customers. These are often known as Value Analysis teams.

Throughout the process, top management is kept informed so that decisions can be made regarding the progression to the screening stage.

SCREENING STAGE

Ideas generated are now evaluated with regard to their marketability, the company's future objectives and its total resources. A company may not be able to market some ideas itself but may sell them to companies that can, while still developing other ideas to launch itself. Other factors to take into account when screening would be legal constraints, state of the economy, technology in the product area for ensuring development of the product, supply of similar products, general consideration of costs and existence of a potential market or segment. Very few products will be selected for the business analysis stage.

BUSINESS ANALYSIS STAGE

More detailed and specific consideration is now given to costs, potential future sales and profitability. To do this the company will have to establish methods of forecasting sales, potential risks and expected flow of revenue in and out of the company concerning the product (cash flow) up to the point when the launched product will cover its initial development and launch costs (break even) and assess if the company has the financial, personnel and production resources necessary for establishing the product in the market.

A team may be formed – which will probably include the product and brand manager – to progress new ideas from their selection to the market launch and possibly for a little time thereafter while the product is attempting to become established in the market. Such teams are sometimes referred to as *Venture Teams*.

PRODUCT DEVELOPMENT

Products or services that now appear marketable propositions become the responsibility of the research and development department – or research centre on their behalf – in developing a prototype. Because this is the start of substantial investment few products reach this stage, a stage which will probably involve:

- Engineering to develop the idea or invention into a prototype that works perfectly and has market appeal.
- Consumer preference testing: Here a small sample of potential consumers may be used to taste or use the product (the pack is not involved) to determine if the prototype developed does really meet the needs of potential purchasers, or if it should be adjusted in some way.
- Packaging and branding: The pack is developed and may be tested on potential consumers to check its protective ability, its economy in use, its convenience and contribution towards the promotion of the product. The

name or a series of possible names may also be assessed during this stage and the overall personality of the product examined through the eyes of the consumers or potential users.

TESTING IN THE MARKET

At this stage the chosen product is tested in the market to determine its acceptability by the market before the final launch. In the ideal business situation a company would like to be able to implement a mini launch of the product in a particular region, i.e. a Test Market (see Chapter 3).

If test marketing is used it should be designed to identify specific factors which are most likely to make a product a success in the market place. This is a complex operation and companies may need to use the facilities and expertise of specialist research organisations in this field. A major operator, A.C. Nielsen (a multinational research organisation), analysed several grocery products which had been test marketed at different times within a period of 14 years. The most frequent causes of failure were found to be:

- Faulty products or packaging.
- Poor value for money offered by the product.
- Lack of adequate advertising or promotional support during the test marketing period.
- Lack of trade acceptance.

Nielsen pointed out that products which meet their marketing targets during test marketing seldom fail to achieve success when launched nationally and they broadly recommended the following advice for achieving a successful test:

- Decide on the primary purposes of the test (trade acceptance, consumer acceptance, test package, assess name, etc.).
- Be realistic in the evaluation of the findings and do not allow subjective judgement or personal feelings to interfere with rational decision making.
- If possible carry out tests in different areas in order to compare results. One test in one area for a short period of time may not be enough.
- Retain or employ professional services to advise on the appropriate procedure.
- Study competitors' sales and market shares closely.
- Examine retailer co-operation and support.
- Study repeat sales following initial purchase. Many people may buy out of curiosity but it is important to know whether they buy again.
- Try to identify all the factors which influence the sales of the product.
- Use appropriate research techniques in collecting the necessary information during the test.
- Avoid change of plans once the test is launched. It may lead to bias, confusion, etc.
- Take into account all the changes which are witnessed during the test, especially in relation to competitors' counter measures.
- Seek co-ordination of the promotion mix.

Do not launch on to the national market until re-purchase levels in the test market have been firmly established so that regular national sales levels can be properly evaluated and an appropriate marketing mix determined.

Of course small to medium sized companies with limited resources or companies that have to maintain secrecy regarding new launches may not have the opportunity to undertake a test market, but they may use one or more of the following methods of evaluating the acceptability of a product to a market.

(a) Test shops/restaurants/bars, etc. (see Chapter 3)
(b) Consumer/user preference testing (see *product development* above)
(c) Test trials

The only solution for a very small company or a sole proprietor enterprise may be (b) involving first the product only and then its packaging. Where the product is so expensive that the company could not afford a test or that testing must be done in secrecy (c) may be essential. For example, prototypes of new cars may be tested on the company's test track where secrecy may be maintained so that competitors are unaware – or should be – of the new car's specifications until it is launched on the market. Methods (b) and (c) are often used by companies supplying to the industrial market where a typical test area does not exist and where there may only be a handful of companies purchasing.

It is essential to realise, however, that (a), (b) and (c) are not the same as a test market as they do not use a representative sample of the total market that can closely evaluate purchases that will take place in the national market.

COMMERCIALISATION STAGE
It is now necessary to consider all the commercial aspects of the introduction of the product to the intended market in the amounts proposed. Thus, the marketing mix must be determined by considering the answers to questions such as: What form will the final promotions take? What is the role of the sales personnel and have they been properly briefed? What should be the final pricing and discount policy? Will the company try for a segment of the market, a national market or market internationally? Which distributors should we use? When do we launch? What should the advertising theme be? Are we happy with the brand name and the package?

The adoption process

Before a company actually launches a product it must consider the product's life cycle and the mental stages that consumers go through before they actually adopt (purchase) a new product in order to determine a marketing plan. These mental stages collectively represent the **adoption process**, the sequence of which tends to be:

awareness — interest — evaluation — trial — adoption

AWARENESS

Before a product is adopted, consumers need to become aware of its existence, its attributes, possible applications, etc. Advertising, personal selling and public relations are the main contributors to awareness building (see Chapter 8).

INTEREST

The product must be of interest to individual consumers if it is to gain a foothold in the market. Interest will result from the intrinsic or perceived worth of a product, the benefits individual purchasers will derive from the product and existing social and moral values and beliefs. Very few consumers accept ideas or products that contradict their current values or beliefs. If the product is still perceived as interesting, the interested purchaser will seek additional information through advertising, sales literature, word of mouth, distributors, etc.

EVALUATION

Once the potential consumer has obtained, or been given, additional information he or she can compare the information they have received with their own needs. Use of the product by famous members of society may cause adoption by certain individuals – hence the use of famous people in advertisements. Favourable publicity generated by a public relations department can also facilitate evaluation. Generally speaking, any source of information that can reduce negative reactions should be used.

TRIAL

In the case of inexpensive products, sales promotion methods may be used in order to induce trial. Personal selling activities can be used to show the product in action, for explaining benefits and technology or for offering additional information. Organisations in the channels of distribution may be used to encourage consumers to try the product at the point of sale without a purchase actually taking place. This may be by in-store tastings of a new butter, cheese, etc. or attaching a small sample of the new product to another product that is already selling, e.g. a small bar of a new soap attached to a shampoo bottle. Even an expensive product may be evaluated by personal trial (trial for instance at the point of sale on an individual basis, e.g. 'Try a BMW – 24 hour Test Drive'.) Evaluation and trial often of course represent one joint mental stage in the adoption process of potential customers.

ADOPTION (THE PURCHASE)

This stage is related to the actual purchase and re-purchase of the product. The majority of manufacturers will seek to establish a long term relationship with their market and will monitor the needs of the target market after adoption. Special offers, reminder adverts, product improvements, etc. may be used to revive or maintain interest, continue evaluation and achieve loyalty. After sales support can protect established relationships by removing post-purchase anxiety about reliability. Consumers may be given warranties which qualify them for free repairs, replacement units and on occasions a full refund if they are not satisfied with the overall quality and performance of the product.

Adopter categories

The rate and ease of adoption will also be directly determined by individual consumer characteristics. Some people readily accept change, while others are more traditional and are slower to react to change. There is a need, therefore, to understand and identify the various types of purchasers, in particular consumers, and five different types of major groupings tend to exist, which are:

1 INNOVATORS
These purchasers represent the smallest percentage of the chosen target market that will adopt a new product. They may treat a new product as a status symbol; be fascinated by a technological development; have a deep personal or business need for the product; like to be different; see themselves as opinion leaders; or, in the case of expensive prestigious products, simply have sufficient income to purchase. They will buy because they simply want to buy and may be part of any social class provided they have the finances to purchase. They may or may not, however, set a trend, depending on their influence on the total market.

2 EARLY ADOPTERS
This is the next type of person to adopt the product and they are the adopters who will indicate whether most new products will be successful. They normally represent the actual **opinion leaders** or **trend setters** that members of the public may follow. If we consider a new fashion you will find that it will often only become acceptable to the general public if some celebrities, such as a well known sports person or film star, actually adopt it. These celebrities may have a large consumer following and the resulting imitation of the item worn by the celebrities may create a large market for the product in question.

Bear in mind however, that there are different trend setters in different markets. High socio-economic groups may be influenced by successful people in positions of authority, while low socio-economic groups may be influenced by TV or pop celebrities.

3 EARLY MAJORITY
This group and the late majority group represent the majority of adopters. The early majority may respond to opinion leaders and accept innovations fairly quickly but purchase the product mainly for its usefulness and, therefore, are long term repeat purchasers. Marketing managers try to identify the needs and wants of this large group and product alterations or introduce variations in order to satisfy this group's expectations and needs.

4 LATE MAJORITY

These purchasers tend to react to changes slowly, waiting for the product to prove itself and for the prices to come down before they adopt. They do not follow recommendations made by opinion leaders and they rely much more on their own personal assessment of the product. Again they may be long term continuing purchasers. Allowances for their tastes and needs may also be made through the product mix offered.

5 LAGGARDS

Laggards represent the last group of people to respond to a new product. They tend to value tradition and they dislike changes to something well established and accepted. They will only adopt once the product has established a track record.

When considering the adopter categories identified you may also find it useful to consider your own reactions, as a consumer, with regard to specific products you come across for the first time. You may be an innovator when it comes to clothes, a member of the early majority when you buy records, part of the late majority when you adopt brands of food, or even a laggard when you select a motor car.

The lesson to remember here is that consumer responses will be affected by personal factors (age, sex, income, etc.), social factors (occupation, family, etc.), cultural factors (religion, nationality, life styles, etc.) and psychological factors (personality, perceptions, motivations, etc.). All these factors will have an influence on the evaluation of different types of products and will affect the speed of adoption of new products.

Product life cycle

Products, just like people, have a life cycle. They are born (introduced into a market), grow, mature and finally decline and die (are withdrawn from the market).

The product life cycle (PLC) identifies and explains the stages that a product may go through from the moment it is launched on to the market to the moment it is withdrawn. Understanding the pattern and movement of the PLC can help identify important marketing environmental factors that managers need to be aware of before they decide upon the most effective marketing effort.

There are five stages that products may go through during their PLC. These stages are illustrated in Fig. 4.2.

INTRODUCTION STAGE

At this stage the product is newly launched into the market. Competition tends to be very limited or non existent. Growth is usually rapid and profits are non existent because of research and development and initial marketing costs.

Fig. 4.2 *Stages of the product life cycle of a typical product*

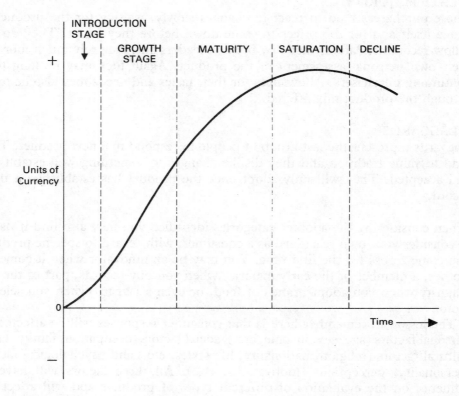

However, the company may have the benefit of high pricing or significant market penetration if the product is uniquely different.

Advertising and sales promotions are extensively used in order to build awareness, encourage evaluation and trial and initial adoption.

GROWTH STAGE

During this stage mass market acceptance will take place through early adopters. Growth will be rapid, profits should emerge and all initial costs may be covered during this stage, i.e. the *break-even point*. However, competitors may also appear, and the marketing manager may have to consider adjustments to the marketing strategy or/and early preparation of an improved version for introduction into the market.

The emphasis during this stage is on market penetration and promotional campaigns will be used in order to stress the relative merits of the product. Intensifying competition may lead to price reductions. An expansion of the distribution network will be sought in order to facilitate market penetration in the light of increasing pressure from new or current competitors.

The movement of the profit line in relation to the PLC is illustrated in Fig. 4.3.

Fig. 4.3

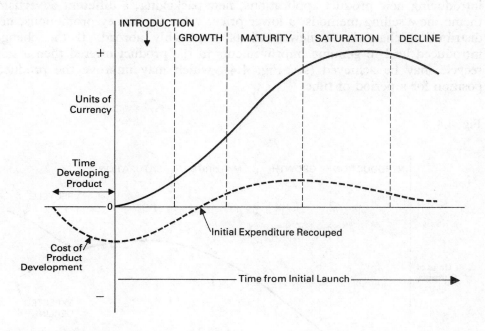

MATURITY STAGE

This stage represents the most competitive stage in the life of a product but one in which profits are flowing in steadily. Early and late majority begin to adopt the product and competitors introduce counter measures designed to attract consumers away from the product. Advertising and promotional campaigns concentrate on reminding consumers; rewarding loyal use of products; offering incentives for repeat purchases; and attracting new users to the product.

Sales are still rising but the speed of ascendency is declining.

Increased demand and resulting economies of scale allow for further price reductions and an even more intensive distribution network is sought. Subtle differences between competing products become very significant to consumers, who now have more knowledge of the variety available in the market, and poor or uncompetitive products are squeezed out of the main market.

SATURATION STAGE

There are now many competitors in the market, profits per unit have further declined and there is no growth in sales. It is time to consider new markets, changes in price, promotions, introduction of new product versions or new products.

DECLINE STAGE

This stage is associated with an initially slow but accelerating decline in sales and profits. The manufacturer may have to accept the gradual decline and ultimate withdrawal of the product from the market or may try to revitalise it by introducing new product applications, new packaging, a different advertising theme, new selling methods, a lower price, value for money promotions, new distribution channels or new markets – possibly abroad. If the changes introduced lead to genuine improvements in the product offered then a sales recycle may be achieved (see Fig. 4.4), which may improve the product's position for a period of time.

Fig. 4.4

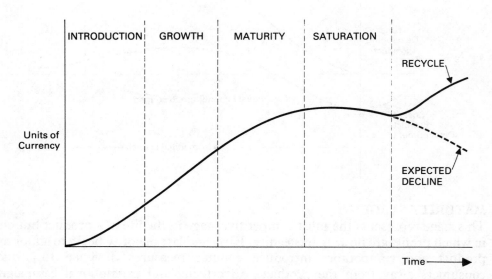

Failure to convince consumers that genuine improvements have been introduced may have the affect of accelerating the rate of decline by creating distrust and suspicion among existing/remaining users.

Before contemplating withdrawal however, professional marketers will examine all alternative courses of action available to them, as explained in the Suggested Answer at the end of this chapter.

Evaluation of the PLC

Knowledge and understanding of the PLC can help in appreciating that:

- Products, like humans, are not immortal. Therefore, marketing managers should never relax and assume that products will last forever.
- Products need to be supported by all the other elements of the marketing mix if they are to survive pressures from competitors.
- Decision making criteria used in the market place change all the time. Products must respond to these changes and they must continually prove their value and benefits to the market.

- Continuous assessment of internal and external factors will help lead to an effective marketing plan that brings results.
- All marketing functions – selling research, advertising, distribution, etc. – have to be adjusted during the phases of a product's life cycle to constantly ensure that they are accurately targeted.

In other words, a PLC for a product or service encourages marketing managers to constantly assess the progressing stages and to review their marketing plans. Knowledge of PLCs, however, does not provide concrete solutions to problems nor does it claim to deliver a definite pattern for planning purposes. Like any other theory, the PLC theory suffers from a series of limitations which can be summarised as follows:

(a) The characteristics of each stage and the recommended responses do not relate to any particular market or product. They represent a general summary of the stages which may not be readily applicable to all products. PLCs for various products will differ. In the case of fashion goods for example it would be difficult to distinguish between the separation of the maturity and saturation stages as the product is so short lived (see Fig. 4.5). Indeed, some authors always prefer to see the PLC with four stages in which the maturity and saturation stages are combined.

Fig. 4.5

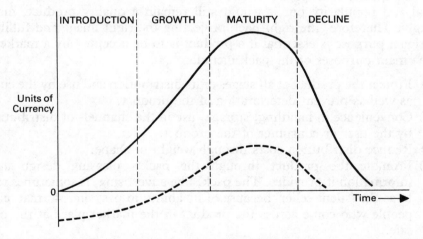

(b) The duration of each stage cannot be determined in advance, which can make planning very difficult.
(c) It is often difficult to determine the stage the product is in within the PLC. Sudden decline in sales, which may just be a temporary decline, may lead to the wrong belief that the product has entered its decline stage and plans for withdrawal may be implemented.
(d) Competitors' reactions are rarely known in advance so accurate allowances for them are difficult to make.

(e) The PLC theory/concept is more applicable to specific brands than to product groups. A particular brand of cigarettes, for instance, may lose its popularity and may be withdrawn from the market, while cigarettes (as a product class) show a healthy and continuous growth in the market. The problem here is that marketing managers may tend to use product classes as indicators of the likely popularity of individual brands.

The distinct advantage of being able to comprehend the PLC before the launch and as it unfolds is that it enables the marketing manager to plan for each stage, appreciate what may take place during each stage and have sufficient time for considering alternative marketing strategies.

■ 3 PACK, PACKAGING AND BRANDING

Pack

The **pack** in which the product is contained often becomes synonymous in the minds of customers with the product itself, which emphasises its importance in helping to make sales. It is essential to realise, however, that the pack is not the product. Paint may come packed in a tin or spray can but it is still paint. If the pack of a quality champagne was in a plastic container it would lose a lot of its appeal and popularity but it would still remain a quality product, marketed wrongly. Therefore, the right pack projecting the right image and fulfilling its functional purpose is essential if a product is to be accepted by a market.

The main purposes of the pack include:

(a) Protect the product at all stages of its distribution and use by the customer as well as prevent deterioration of the product.
(b) Convenience in handling, storage, use in the channels of distribution and by the user or consumer of the product.
(c) Reduce distribution costs through weight or shape.
(d) Promote the product through the pack's pleasing design and the information it provides. The pack, like advertising, is sometimes referred to as the 'silent seller' because of its ability to pass on information to the people who come across the product in the market place at the point of sale.
(e) Distinguish the product from others. This may be in the forcefulness of design or its intrinsic usefulness, as with car paint in spray cans. The modern trend towards self-service has made product differentiation at the point of sale vital. The eye-catching ability of the pack often facilitates product location in the store and, it is hoped, will encourage product selection.
(f) Establish product group identity, e.g. Kellogg's, Heinz and Campbells range of products.

Packaging

The **packaging** contains the pack and provides the means by which a collection of packed products may be transported, safely, economically and conveniently. The package may be made of cardboard, wooden or plastic boxes or crates holding just one product with its pack or thousands depending on the size of product and the marketing intentions of the company.

The packaging has now become a means of promoting the name of the product as well as a means by which many consumers or users may purchase in larger amounts. Oxo cubes, for example, may be more effectively displayed by a package containing several cubes, due to the small size of the individual cubes.

Summarising the pack and package

Each product or range of products has a definite identity which can be enhanced or destroyed by the pack or/and packaging in which it is contained. It is the basic aim of a company to ensure that the product's identity and company's identity are projected in part through the pack and package.

Branding

Branding is an important part in the projection of the right image of the product. A brand is

> *a name, symbol or sign that is given to products in order to help them establish their own identity, facilitate recognition by consumers and communicate what the product can deliver*

The brand invariably appears on the pack irrespective of the design of the pack and quite often the brand is associated with the producing company to create a corporate identity, rather than just the product. Shell, Heinz, Ford, Mercedes, Rolls Royce, ICI are just a few that fall into this category.

Giving the right commercial name to a product is like breathing life into it. The name must give the product credibility, it must be relatively easy to pronounce, easy to remember and it must not infringe other companies' brand name/trademark. Consider for example the 'Avon' and 'Chanel' company names – they are easily identified within the range of cosmetics.

The increasing internationalism of many products in the market has resulted in a growing need for manufacturers to devise product names that are acceptable in domestic and overseas markets. Names to be used internationally need to be checked against all major languages in order to ensure that they do not stand for anything provocative, offensive or rude. The implied nationality of the product, which results from the name given, could have a direct effect on the way consumers perceive and respond to it. For this reason, countries with a poor reputation for quality will attempt to create an international name or one that implies a country that has a good reputation for the product, such as Japan; whereas Japanese companies who enjoy a good reputation, particularly for electronic equipment, will use their own name internationally.

Companies generally employ one or more of the following three branding policies.

1 COMPANY BRAND NAME

The product offered is given the company's or corporation's name so that the favourable image of the company – particularly technological and quality attributes – are communicated to potential customers making market acceptance much easier. The purchasing public view the new product in terms of the reputation of the company: Sony, Hitachi, Hoover, etc. This branding policy cannot be used when a company moves into unrelated product areas where transfer of reputation is not automatic. After all, how readily would you purchase a Sony soft drink or a Hoover car as a result of the company's good name in other areas of production?

Private (own) brand names often given by supermarket chains to the products they sell, such as Marks and Spencer and Sainsbury, would also come within this category.

2 FAMILY BRAND NAME

Companies that offer a variety of product lines that are aimed at different target markets often use this naming policy. They will attempt to build a good image in terms of product groups. The family name chosen will rarely be related to the company name. Often manufacturers with a poor company name have enjoyed success in the market when this method was employed. An example in Britain was British Leyland with its family brand names Jaguar, Rover and Range Rover.

3 INDIVIDUAL BRAND NAME

This branding policy is extensively used by companies introducing unrelated products to markets and by companies that do not have a strong company image. If the venture is considered to be risky, long established companies that are not a household name, such as Proctor and Gamble, may not be willing to risk the company's reputation by putting their name up front and will only strongly relate brand names to the company when full market acceptance has taken place.

In certain cases a name is directly related to a specific market and transfer is not possible, e.g. a brand name suitable for one country may not be suitable for another.

Remember, however, that the symbol/logo used may be just as important and meaningful as the name.

■ STUDY AND EXAM TIPS

1 By their nature product development theories lend themselves to presentation by diagrams, so use diagrams wherever they help explain.

2 Bear in mind that new, small or medium sized businesses can benefit from an understanding of the principles of product policies so don't simply refer to large companies unless specifically requested.

3 Do not forget that the theories associated with the development of new products **do not** provide absolute answers, only useful guides.

4 Increase your awareness of companies' products, packs, packaging and brands by making it a point to study adverts whenever they appear and closely examine products when you are in a store. This will enable you to use examples in the examinations that are your own.

■ SELF ASSESSMENT QUESTIONS

Answer the following questions without reference to the text and then refer to the answers given at the end of the manual to determine your score. Award yourself 1 mark for each complete question that you answer correctly. If you scored 7 or more you are reading efficiently. Where you answered wrongly check back in the chapter to see what the answer should have been.

1 Which one of the following (a to g) is not a stage of the new product development process?

(a) Ideas generation stage.
(b) Screening stage.
(c) Business analysis stage.
(d) Product/service development stage.
(e) Distribution channel stage.
(f) Testing in the market stage.
(g) Commercialisation stage.

☐ (a)   ☐ (b)   ☐ (c)   ☐ (d)   ☐(e)   ☐(f)   ☐(g)   (tick appropriate box)

2 Complete the sentence:
A test market should not be stopped and the product launched nationally until
re _ _ _ _ _ _ _ levels have been established.

3 One of the five mental stages consumers may go through to arrive at a decision
to adopt (purchase) a product is awareness. Name the other four.

(a) _____
(b) _____
(c) _____
(d) _____

4 One of the five adopter categories is laggards. Name the other four.

(a) _____
(b) _____
(c) _____
(d) _____

5 In most cases the product life cycle comprises five stages, one of which is the
introduction stage. Name the other four.

(a) _____
(b) _____
(c) _____
(d) _____

6 Complete the sentence:
When products or services are mixed in such a way that consumers are not certain of
the price of each product or service that comprises the whole offering the mix
offered is referred to as a _ _ _ _ _ _ _ deal.

7 One purpose of a pack is to protect the product. Name another three.

(a) _____
(b) _____
(c) _____

8 Define a brand as in this chapter.

_____
_____

9 One of the three branding policies is attaching a company brand name to a
product. Name the other two.

(a) _____
(b) _____

10 Complete the sentence:
The point at which the profits from the sales of a product cover the total costs is
referred to as _ _ _ _ _ _ _ point.

■ EXAMINATION QUESTIONS

The Institute of Marketing

1 What factors should a company take into account in determining its product
mix?

2 Discuss the value and limitations of the product life cycle concept.

The Association of Business Executives

3 'There is nothing the manager can do once a product reaches the decline stage of the product life cycle.'
Comment on this statement, explaining why you either agree or disagree with it.

[*Note*: A suggested answer to this question follows and you are advised to read it carefully.]

4 Discuss the stages likely to be involved in processing an 'idea' for a new product to a position of full scale marketing.

The Institute of Commercial Management

5 Write brief notes on:

(a) Product life cycle.
(b) Packaging.
(c) Multi-product operations.

6 Before a company introduces a new product or brand onto the market what considerations should be made from a marketing standpoint?

■ SUGGESTED ANSWER TO QUESTION 3

Obviously the most worrying time for most companies who have established products in a market is the time when the sales of their product start to decline. For this reason examining bodies understandably set questions on this stage of the PLC, so it seems appropriate to close this chapter by concentrating on this topic by answering question 3 of the Past Examination Questions.

Answer

The decline stage of the PLC represents the stage in the product's life cycle when sales begin to decline, and consumers switch to more advanced, fashionable or less expensive products introduced to the market by competition or hopefully by one's own company. Competitors with comparable products at comparable prices may begin to withdraw from the market and overall profitability of the product as an investment proposition in the particular market declines.

Fig. 4.6

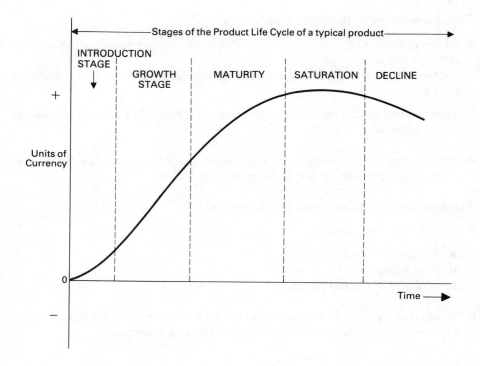

Many managers believe that the decline stage indicates the end of the product's useful life with the result that some withdrawal of the product from the market by companies may be witnessed in the hope of minimising losses.

Such actions may often be premature for in many cases the decline may be halted or another PLC for the product stimulated into action (see Fig. 4.4).

The position of the decline stage in the PLC is illustrated in Fig. 4.6.

Actions, however, to minimise, halt or redress the decline should only be taken after careful evaluation of the current situation and the options available. An evaluation may include consideration and investigation of the following:

(a) The amount of stock of the product currently held by the company and in the channels of distribution that may need to be sold before a new product version is introduced.

(b) Could special promotions, i.e. two for the price of one, coupons, price reductions etc. prevent or reverse the decline?

(c) What are the expected reactions and expectations of members of the trade handling the product to the fall off of sales?

(d) Can the product be revitalised through feature changes such as new shape, new colour, new applications or new texture?

(e) What are the overall plans in terms of the company's resources and individual products?

(f) Are there any opportunities evident in other segments of the market or in markets overseas?

The findings of such investigations allows a marketing manager to look at the problem from many different angles and possibly take action that may avoid withdrawal of the product from the market.

A few of the outcomes of such an analysis could be:

1 Introduction of the product to overseas market/s to maintain demand and profitability.

2 Introduction of consumer incentives designed to help the company off-load remaining outdated stocks at the company or in the channels of distribution – such as at an annual or end of season sale.

3 Introduction of new features to the product which could revitalise product sales and profitability for a period of time.

4 Make a cheaper or more expensive version of the product to appeal to another segment of the market.

5 Utilisation of the product as a *loss leader* for new products recently launched; stocks of the declining product are sold at a loss and the new product is helped through the early stages of the PLC.

6 Contracting out – at a commission – the rights to supply the product to a smaller company that would still find the provision of smaller quantities profitable.

7 Phased product withdrawal for the redirection of resources, preservation of company image, protection of consumer interests, control of losses, etc.

Successful responses to a declining product may not always be possible but at least evaluation of alternative actions may prove more profitable than an instant withdrawal from the market; particularly if a profitable alternative is not readily available. It is reasonable to assume that the ultimate decline and withdrawal of a manufactured product is inevitable but so often there are still considerable profits and marketing advantages to be obtained before that stage is reached.

5 Pricing

The price a company can ask for its product is a marker that indicates how efficient a company has to be to obtain customers.

Jim and Fred were constant rivals. Each owned a small supermarket facing one another. One day Jim wrote on his shop window, 'Eggs reduced to £1 for 10'. Seeing this and realising his own possible loss in trade, Fred wrote on his window, 'Eggs 80p for 10'. Thereupon, Jim erased his notice and wrote, 'Eggs 70p for 10'. In response, Fred wrote on his window, 'Eggs 60p for 10'.

Just at this moment Fred's bank manager was passing and seeing Fred's action and knowing Fred's financial situation said, 'Fred, you can't even buy eggs at 60p for 10. If you keep this up you'll go out of business.' 'Oh, no, I won't!' said Fred, with a whimsical smile, 'I don't sell eggs!'

The above story, though fictitious, does illustrate a little of the psychology behind pricing and how fascinating pricing can be. Pricing is a critical aspect of marketing because the price set for a product or service involves and affects every aspect of the organisation. It is a marker that indicates how efficient and cost effective every section has to be if profits are to be made from the price and the volume of goods the company hopes to sell.

In order to obtain a clear understanding of this area of marketing this chapter has been divided into eight distinct parts each dealing with a separate aspect of the topic.

1 defining pricing and price
2 the objectives of pricing
3 major influences on pricing
4 pricing policies
5 credit
6 discounts
7 additional pricing terminology
8 determining a price structure

■ 1 DEFINING PRICING AND PRICE

Pricing is

> *the process of determining the price that an organisation should ask from purchasers for the product or service it supplies*

The **price** is

> *the monetary value attached to the product or service at a particular point in time*

A company may be able to make a reasonable profit by asking £1 for its product but if the market is willing to pay more the company will, in most cases, ask for more. Conversely, if a company discovers that a market is not willing to pay a price for a product that will cover its cost of production and supply it will not attempt to produce the product. Incredible as it may seem some people starting in business for the first time have produced goods that they later found they could not sell in any significant quantities. Thus, determining how much a market(s) is willing to pay for a product and how many people may purchase it is fundamental to the start of a pricing process.

Price is used by purchasers as an indicator of a product's or service's quality. Consider the number of times you have rejected or refused something because the price did not represent, in your opinion, a true reflection of a product's quality. Perhaps the price was set too high and you considered the product unreasonably expensive, or the price seemed far too low for a given level of quality which the seller was promising you. You may have been right to refuse such an item, but you may have lost a real bargain simply because the price was not 'convincing' or did not feel right.

Would you buy, for instance, a 22 carat solid gold watch for, say, £20? If you had the watch tested or evaluated by an expert and found it really was made of 22 carat gold, then you would be more than happy to pay such a price for a quality item. How would you react, though, if a genuine evaluation is not possible and an instant decision is required? Would you part with your money in the hope of a bargain or would you prefer to follow the sort of logic of most people and reject it? You may or may not purchase the watch but the fact is that in the minds of most potential purchasers the price asked would create **doubt**, **worry**, **dilemma** and/or even **suspicion**.

If a price is wrongly set, therefore, potential customers may consider it to be unrealistic or unbelievable in relation to the particular product or service. Pricing must take into account people's perception of value and the price asked must closely reflect the perceptions of good value for money held by the target market irrespective of how irrational their judgement may appear.

■ 2 PRICING OBJECTIVES

Prices may be changed several times by an organisation over time across a whole range of its products in order to achieve its long term objectives. Thus a company may be involved in setting a price for a new product and/or changing the prices of its current products.

The **prime objectives** of pricing by commercial organisations will be:

1 To maximise profits in the short, medium or long term – in other words ensure profitability.
2 To minimise the risk of undue losses that may occur if a product does not obtain the sales expected.

The first indicates the positive and optimistic aspect of pricing and the second highlights the cautionary and conservative side of the process, but both are valid depending on the situation.

There will also be other major objectives that may be essential for obtaining the prime objectives:

- To enter and control a segment of the market or the total market.
- To act in counter strategy against the pricing or promotional actions of competitors.
- To assist in the product becoming a leading brand.

Many other objectives may of course be associated with pricing. They could relate to reputation building, selling off excess stocks, moving the product through the channels of distribution, facilitating the sale of other products of the company or a tactic to minimise short term losses that may result from actions of competitors, such as the launch of a new and competitive product on the market.

Consistency, therefore, between prices set and marketing objectives will help a company in achieving and maintaining a satisfactory trading position.

Having considered the objectives of profit making concerns it is also necessary to note that non profit making organisations such as local councils, states, governments, clubs, unions and charities will also have an objective in the prices they set. These may relate for example, to the provision of a social service, like the provision of heavily subsidised meals for old aged pensioners or vitamins for children. Of course the full costs involved will invariably have to be derived from other sources such as rate payers, tax payers or donators to charities who may want to know, or feel, that their contribution towards the provision of all these services is being used sensibly.

■ 3 MAJOR INFLUENCES ON PRICING

As pricing is vital to the success of most products or services every effort should be made to identify and evaluate the major internal and external influences which may affect a product's current price or the price a company may ask for a new product. Table 5.1 summarises the major influences on setting or maintaining a price.

Table 5.1 Major influences on pricing

Internal factors	External factors
1 Marketing objectives	6 Consumer perceptions and expectations
2 The other 3 Ps (product, promotion, place) of the marketing mix	7 Demand
3 Costs	8 Company reputation
4 Attitude of senior management towards pricing	9 Seasonal factors
5 Resources	10 Competitors' activities
	11 Legal constraints
	12 The economy
	13 Level and distribution of incomes

Internal factors

1 MARKETING OBJECTIVES

The right price combined with the right mix of the other 3 Ps in the marketing mix may allow a company to pursue its marketing objectives. The pricing policy and the price set, therefore, will depend on the prime and major objectives the company intends to follow. Therefore, the overall marketing objectives set must be attainable.

Likewise, however, marketing objectives can only be reached if the price is right, so the setting of objectives must take into consideration the prices that may be asked and the total profits that would result from the various prices possible and the volume of sales that may be achieved.

2 THE MARKETING MIX

Price, though important, is only one of the 4 Ps in the marketing mix which the marketing manager can control. If the other three are not mixed in a way that supports the price, then the price asked may not generate the same volume of customers.

If, for instance, the product is presented to the market as 'unique', 'advanced' or 'exclusive' then the price set must communicate the relevant message to the consumers. A product presented as a 'genuine bargain', without any 'high quality' claims, may warrant a low price which will not adversely affect the product's or company's overall reputation.

A product only distributed through prestigious stores can generally command a higher price. A well designed product can usually command a higher price than a competitor's that does not have the same features. Therefore, if the other 3 Ps are not directed properly, the price expected may not be achieved and distributors may be left with stocks on their hands, which will affect the trading image of the company.

3 COSTS
Costs in general

It would be pointless to attempt to set a price for a product without allowing for the direct or indirect costs attributed to its production and marketing. Full recovery of costs and profit maximisation within a short space of time could be treated as a priority but it is sometimes impossible to achieve and sometimes sensible to accept a loss on a short term basis for greater medium or long term gain. Consider the situation where a large company is seeking consumer acceptance for a newly launched product. A price at cost may be set as a special introductory offer so that purchasing is encouraged. Once consumer acceptance has been achieved, the company may embark on a profit making price by letting the price float up until the right sales level and maximum profitability is obtained.

This idea of profitability from products is essential to understand. A company does not necessarily wish to sell as much of the same product as it can, unless of course it wants dominance in a market for strategic purposes. If a company can produce different products – with the same workforce and machinery – with each product returning a different level of profit the company will attempt to market varying quantities of their products in such a way that overall profits of the company are maximised. This may mean that although a company may be able to sell one million units of one product, it may sell only half a million of that product and ask a higher price so that production capacity is available for other products it markets that return good profits. How far it can accomplish this pricing mix will depend on the number of products it can make and market, the uniqueness of individual products and the demand for each product.

Marginal costs and contribution

All companies have to cover their total costs, i.e. fixed costs and variable costs, but once they have covered their fixed costs through the sale of a number of products, each subsequent product may be sold at any price above variable costs involved and still make a **contribution** towards profits, or for that matter, losses, if the company is not currently making profits.

Consider for instance, a company making cups. Let us suppose that once it has sold two million cups it has covered its total costs – costs such as rent, rates, heating, lighting, basic staffing requirements, etc. (its **fixed costs**) as well as the **variable costs** (costs that will vary according to the amount of cups the company produces). In more detail, variable costs are those costs which are not fixed but will vary according to the amount produced and will include materials, transportation, extra electricity, coal or gas and possibly additional labour.

If the company now has the opportunity to sell a further one million cups to a customer in another country but cannot obtain a price that will cover its total costs, it will still find it profitable provided the revenue from the sale covers the variable costs as any payment from the customer above the variable costs involved will be a contribution towards profits, as fixed costs have already been covered by the earlier sale of the two million cups.

The actual percentage profitability will vary from situation to situation. However, the major lesson here is that marketers should closely consider costs, but without allowing them to dominate their marketing approach or the price they will set. Many products have been costed and a price set that is unacceptable only to find that the product can be produced in another material at much lower costs that make for an acceptable price. Chrome and wood used on most cars have in many cases now been replaced with plastic fittings doing exactly the same job.

If you are directly involved in pricing, do make sure that you allow for wastage that occurs not only in production but in distribution e.g., breakages; selling e.g., unsold perishable items such as bakery products; after sales e.g., returns by customers due to failure of the product.

4 ATTITUDE OF SENIOR MANAGEMENT
Sometimes the attitude of senior management such as the chairman and managing director are inconsistent with that of the marketing dirctor. It may be that the company has an outlook that is more concerned with the intrinsic value of the product rather than the price the market is willing to pay. It may also be that the marketing director is reluctant to set the price he or she should because the company does not have an integrated marketing approach. Therefore, the worry is that backup services will not be in keeping with promises offered to consumers or the channels of distribution.

Invariably there is internal conflict when a price is being determined, much of which is fully justified. It is up to the marketing director, like any other director making a proposal, to prove his/her case and obtain the commitment of the board of directors, but it does help if management at all levels appreciate the problems involved in asking a price from a market.

5 RESOURCES
The price a company can ask for a product is not always solely based on the product itself. The price that can be asked may be determined by the level of after sales services provided: the length of time of guarantees offered, the guarantee of consistent quality and the speed with which the product can be delivered. To be able to offer these extra services a company needs to be sure that it has the quantity and quality of human resources (necessary staff), and equipment and sufficient finances.

External factors

6 CONSUMER PERCEPTIONS AND EXPECTATIONS

As indicated earlier, the price of a product is a major communicator within the company's marketing mix so special attention must be paid to the way consumers respond to specific prices. Consumers may already have perceptions and expectations that will need changing if the price the company will ask is to be accepted.

Price will not act by itself, it will need to be supported by other factors like the usefulness of the product, the reputation of the company, distributor recommendations, etc.

Advertising campaigns are often used to justify the prices set for products and create a favourable consumer attitude. Long life batteries, for instance, may cost twice as much as standard batteries so advertising campaigns concentrate on informing the general public that they may last three or four times as long as the standard ones cutting down the amount of times they need replacing and/or the need to carry a number of extra batteries. Value for money is, therefore, communicated, and hopefully, a favourable reaction from the market is achieved.

7 DEMAND

General

This influence usually has a direct link with the cost factor. As demand grows for a particular product, the cost of producing additional numbers of units may be reduced. Economists refer to this phenomenon as **economies of scale** and it can be justified by the fact that as production output and sales grow, fixed costs will be absorbed by a greater number of units. In other words, each unit sold will be contributing less towards fixed costs. Consider a situation where a company faces a total fixed cost equal to £500 000. If it manufactures and sells only 500 000 units, each unit needs to contribute £1 towards these fixed costs. If the demand for the product grows to 2 500 000 units, and the company can accommodate such an increase without any additions to fixed costs, then cash flow into the company will be improved and each unit will need to contribute only £0.20 to the fixed costs, i.e. £500 000 divided by 2 500 000 units. This reduction offers the opportunity for a higher profit margin, or even a lower price, where a lower price becomes necessary for meeting growing competition or for restimulating demand.

Don't assume, however, that economies of scale are automatic. Sometimes as demand grows so does competition causing a company to spend some of the money saved on extra promotional efforts.

Derived demand

On the other hand an increase or decrease in demand may result from the activities of other industries. This is referred to as **derived demand**. If the car industry is producing and marketing successfully, then companies mainly producing parts and machinery for the car industry should find that their sales increase. The opposite may be the case if the car industry is not doing well. Hence the need for a company to have alternative customers and products to ensure production levels should demand from one of the markets they serve decline.

8 COMPANY REPUTATION

Many products are sold at a higher price than normally would be expected on the strength of the reputation of the manufacturer or retailer. The price set does not necessarily relate to the true quality of the product; it simply allows for the extra price that may be asked due to the favourable or élitist image of the company in question. Psychologically, most consumers feel there is less risk of purchasing an inadequate product from a company with a good reputation: Hoover is an example in the case of vacuum cleaners and Sellotape in the case of sticky tapes. When such companies produce different products that are related to their current product(s) their favourable reputation enables them to ask a little more for their new products.

9 SEASONAL FACTORS

Demand for certain products is affected by the time of day, weather conditions, national festivals or religious occasions. In other words the demand for such products is seasonal. As a result the companies marketing products associated with such occasions need to introduce a range of prices for different periods for the same product which will enable them to achieve the maximum possible total revenue. During periods of high demand a higher price may be obtained than in periods of relatively low demand. An airline ticket to a specific holiday resort may cost twice as much during the peak holiday period than it would during the off peak months. A day return rail fare is much cheaper when the rush hour is over as are telephone charges out of office hours. Some companies trading internationally may choose to overcome the loss of income from seasonal factors by switching their marketing efforts at certain times of the year to other countries. After all, when it is summer in Europe it is winter in Australia and vice versa.

10 COMPETITORS' ACTIVITIES

Companies often use the price of their products or services to gain advantage over their competitors. Airlines trying to win business from each other on various international routes are often involved in intensive price competition which leads to extensive cuts in air fares. Since flying for most people represents a means to an end, the end being rapid travel to a preselected destination, it is possible to have a situation where selection of an airline for travel is based solely on price.

This not only applies to airlines, but to most situations where the market is very sensitive (reacts rapidly) to price changes.

When companies in fierce competition continually undercut each other's price the result is sometimes termed a **price war**. Consumers may at first gain from such undercutting of prices, but finally a more limited supply of goods and services may result and possibly high prices as a few companies ultimately gain control of the market. Continuous price wars, therefore, rarely benefit anyone, and companies determined not to be pulled into a price war will use methods other than price, such as new distribution methods, changes to their product or introduce sales promotion campaigns in order to keep the same price and thus the same level of revenue.

Sometimes, however, a company may have to lower its price, possibly offering discounts for a short period, until competition has slackened and the company can return to its original policies on pricing.

11 LEGAL CONSTRAINTS

Consumer prices for certain products are positively and/or adversely affected by government interference. Consider, for instance, petrol, cigarettes, cigars and alcoholic drinks. The price consumers pay in many countries includes a high level of tax; a relatively small percentage of the price paid is received by the manufacturers who are not in a position to overrule such decisions by the government. For the general health of the population, for raising finance, or for political reasons a government may regularly change the tax on such products, thus causing a change in the price.

The products which are affected by tax impositions are often in a fairly **inelastic demand situation**. Inelastic demand contends that a very small change in demand will result from a significant change in price. With cigarettes or alcoholic drinks, for instance, a ten per cent increase in price may only cause a one per cent drop in demand, thus giving more tax income to the particular government.

It is possible to witness some significant changes in demand immediately after such price changes but demand usually returns to its previous position, or very near its previous position, once the price changes have been accepted by the purchasers affected by the change.

On a more positive note, it is possible to find products which are supported by government actions, so that prices are kept at relatively low levels. A government, for example, may subsidise some basic foods and/or not tax them so that the price is affordable by all people in the country, especially families with young children using the product extensively.

12 THE ECONOMY

The state of the economy will generally affect the amount of money in the country for buying goods and services. A strong currency will improve people's ability to pay for overseas holidays or imported goods while a weak economy will have the opposite effect.

13 INCOMES

The current as well as the projected level and distribution of incomes within an economy will often limit the size of the market for a product and the amount of money purchasers can afford to pay. A socio-economic class in one country may be large but earn relatively low incomes and, therefore, members of that class are unable to purchase a particular product such as a television. In another country the size of the same socio-economic group may be much smaller but its members receive higher incomes which enable them to purchase such a product.

We have just touched on some of the major internal and external factors that can affect the price that may be asked for a product. When a company is going to market overseas it would have to consider these factors and many more before committing substantial sums to the venture.

Nevertheless, even a person starting in business for the first time on a home market should at the very least consider **costs**, **competition**, **resources**, **expected demand**, **legal restraints** and of course the mix of the 4 Ps.

■ 4 PRICING POLICIES

Having analysed and evaluated the affect of each influence, the marketing director must propose a pricing policy to adopt. Pricing policies do not represent a **specific price**, they simply identify the **type of pricing approach** which may be necessary to achieve defined marketing objectives. As each policy is considered you are encouraged to consider carefully the situations which favour the application of that policy.

Although there are several pricing policies that may be adopted by companies they may in effect be categorised into three areas which are:

1 *Market orientated policies*: policies determined as a result of market conditions and/or expectations.
2 *Cost orientated policies*: related to the integral cost of a product.
3 *Competitor based policies*: revolve around competition between buyers, competition between sellers, or both.

1 Market orientated policies

MARKET PENETRATION/SATURATION PRICING

In market penetration pricing the object is to saturate the market with sales of the product as quickly as possible in order to gain a major foothold in the market or gain brand leadership, thus making it exceedingly difficult for possible future competitors to enter the market. Because of the costs involved this pricing method, when applied nationally, is usually undertaken by large companies. Once brand leadership has been obtained the price may be allowed to float up – provided brand leadership is maintained – until maximum total profitability is obtained, even if this causes a fall off in the number of units sold.

The same technique, linked with substantial trade and quantity discounts, may also be used in the channels of distribution. Large quantities of the product are sold into the channels of distribution prior to the launch. The idea is that wholesalers and retailers, holding large amounts of one product will not then buy more from other suppliers until they have lowered their enormous stock levels. Thus, tactics by competitors to spoil the launch of a company's latest version of a product can be minimised.

As indicated this method is more suitable for large companies in a market or large market segment where:

(a) the market is very price sensitive
(b) economies of scale can be enjoyed through larger levels of output, thus producing larger profits
(c) a low price can discourage actual and potential competitors
(d) product demeaning (loss of perceived product quality) through low price does not occur
(e) the company is mainly geared for large scale production

New brands of toothpaste, chocolate and instant coffee would be products that may attract this policy nationwide, i.e. low priced products in mass markets. However, having made this general statement it should be noted that the approach may be used in other circumstances. The Amstrad Computer Company, for example, are brand leaders in several European countries having followed such a policy in their market segment, i.e. low price, the right benefits, a strong promotional campaign and good distribution.

Market skimming and **hit and run** pricing methods are both used for short term profit maximisation.

SHORT-TERM PROFIT MAXIMISATION PRICING
Market skimming pricing
This policy requires the setting of a high price in order to obtain large profits in, what may be, a short period of time. Pricing this way may be considered in two situations.

Where there is a need to obtain revenue quickly for further investment in the development and/or marketing of the product. The product may be developed further (new sizes, new appearance, etc.), or introduced into new markets in order to maintain steady growth. The initial high profits are used to support the future development of the product and marketing activities such as entry into other markets where purchasers cannot afford to pay the price that was asked for the product when it was initially launched. A drug company, for example, may need high initial returns on a new drug to develop a less expensive version for sale to larger markets. It is a method that can readily be used where the company has exclusivity or a patent for its product. For example, a book may firstly be sold in hardback at a high price to those in a market that are not price sensitive. This will ensure high returns and will test the market and create awareness of the book ready for the paperback version coming out at a later date.

The need to make satisfactory profits before large competitors produce another version at a price which is lower than that with which the company may be able to compete. For instance, some years ago an American company first introduced ball point pens and sold them at $12.50 as an unusual gift, but it had to abandon the market within six months due to new competition from the large pen and pencil producers. Nevertheless, the company by then had obtained profits of $1 500 000 for an investment of $26 000. Therefore, the high price that was set was adopted because there was uncertainty regarding the future life of the market.

Market skimming derives its name from skimming the cream off milk. As applied to marketing it means choosing to market to the most profitable segment of a market before marketing to other segments at lower prices with the same product or a modified version developed to be sold at a lower price.

Hit and run pricing
Here the need is to obtain satisfactory profits while there is a rare or limited opportunity for a product that will not have lasting demand, such as unusual consumer products at celebrations that only come once a year. The price set will depend on what the supplier believes can be asked and may change nearing the end of the celebration. This is not the same as market skimming where the future is not certain and the supplier is aiming for the top end of a market first before supplying other levels with what will invariably be a modified version.

Product line pricing
This form of pricing has become extremely popular in the retailing field. It involves determining what profit is required from a range of goods and then using some of the goods to entice customers to buy other goods in the range. As an example, a supermarket may offer a regularly purchased item such as sugar or tea at cost in order to encourage customers to enter the supermarket where they will probably buy other, more profitable, items while they are there. The product(s) sold at cost are generally referred to as loss leaders and are positioned at points that will force customers to walk past other items in the store which are profitable. It is a method preferred where the pricing of individual products may favourably affect the sale of other product lines.

Prestige pricing
Prestige pricing is predominantly used by suppliers whose name carries a certain prestige, such as Gucci shoes and Cartier jewellery. These types of companies can and do ask a higher price for their products to keep their name prestigious as well as obtain relatively high profits. Exclusivity, uniqueness, status and perceived quality in the minds of customers seem to be the main areas of justification for prestige pricing and companies use this knowledge of some people's status needs to encourage potential purchasers to accept the price asked.

DISCRIMINATORY/DIFFERENTIATED PRICING
The final three policies **discriminate prices** on the basis of time, product or place/market. Nevertheless, they are still subject to market forces and characteristics.

Variable pricing (or time differentiated pricing)

This is price variance or discrimination on a time basis as a result of the level of demand that exists at different times or periods. The objective is usually to increase total revenue by evening out the demand for products or services that are overstretched at certain periods of the day, month or year. Price discrimination on a time basis can be seen in our everyday lives: travelling cheaper on the railways in offpeak periods; electricity cheaper at night; telephone calls cheaper at night and weekends; cheaper holidays in low season, etc.

Product differentiated pricing

This amounts to discrimination of the price as a result of slight changes to the basic product, like a car being made to appear different by adding small embellishments such as reclining seats, heated rear window, chrome wheels, etc. It is still the same basic car but different prices can be charged due to the embellishments and the fact that certain segments of the total market are willing to pay considerably more because of the small additions. It is therefore, a useful method where a basic product can be made to appear significantly different through the addition of a mix of accessories, e.g. a basic car having certain extras added may be named the 'Executive' version, and with more extras still the 'Statesman' version. A book that has just been published may be simultaneously sold in hardback as well as softback in the knowledge that the slight addition of a hard cover will cause the book to appeal to different markets. Of course the publisher will ask the higher price for the hardback version – even though the content is the same – thereby obtaining more profits.

Market differentiated pricing

This represents price discrimination due to differences in markets (the place). Sometimes companies use different prices in different markets because of the level of demand in the different markets or the level of disposable incomes. Hence, a company trading internationally may charge different prices in two or more countries for the exact same product because of the levels of demand that exist in the various countries.

Likewise, there may have to be discrimination in the one market place to maximise revenues because some segments of the total market may not be able to purchase at the standard price. Hence, old age pensioners and children are charged much less if they travel, and parents travelling may be charged the full price but will only have to pay for one of their children, even if all their children travel with them.

The price that can be asked for ice cream by a corner shop in a major town is invariably considerably less than the price that can be obtained by an ice cream kiosk at a fun-fair or 'once-a-year' special event.

2 Cost orientated pricing

In marketing, cost orientated pricing methods are sometimes frowned upon as it takes no account of the value that the market places on the product or service. For instance, if through market research we discover that the market is happy to pay £2 for a product that costs £1 to make, it is sensible – from the producer's point of view – to sell at £2 and not at a set 20 per cent mark up on costs which would only come to £1.20.

If a company designed a new machine that can produce items at twice the speed of current machines it would probably not be acting sensibly if it sold the machine to its industrial purchasers at the same price as the current machines. If it did it could mean that the purchasing companies may make double profits from its use while the company selling the machine makes the same profits as before after doing all the research and designing.

Nevertheless, a 'cost' approach is still widespread and the following are the major methods employed.

'MARK-UP' OR 'COST PLUS' PRICING

Mark-up pricing has its origins in the product orientated days as it concerns itself more with the cost of producing a product rather than the price consumers are willing to pay. The cost of each product made is determined and the percentage profit required is added. For example, if the cost is £1.00 per unit and the profit required 20 per cent, it will be sold at £1.20. This form of pricing is still very popular with companies supplying industrial users as it is easy to understand and apply.

It is also extensively used by retailers in determining the profit they will receive. The retailer may have to sell particular products at around £1 each. Therefore, the immediate concern is with the cost of the product as the mark-up to be added on to costs can only be determined after adding a percentage to cover operating costs and the value added tax or sales tax that has to be passed over to the tax authorities.

This method of pricing can prove problematic if different retailers expect and apply substantially different mark ups for the same product being sold to a price sensitive market. In this situation customers may start to shop at the outlets where the product is cheaper, possibly believing that their usual retailer is asking an unreasonable price. The result may be a loss of confidence by many customers in their retailer and many retailers overstocked with items they will find difficult to sell and impossible to return to the manufacturer (unless they were purchased on a sale-or-return basis).

For this reason manufacturers give retailers an idea of the price at which the product should be sold – a suggested retail price – leaving the retailer to determine the price he can reasonably ask from the customers to whom he sells. Likewise, large multiple retail outlets may inform manufacturers of the price which they can ask from customers leaving the manufacturers to determine if they can supply at a price that ensures an adequate mark-up for the retailer.

SATISFACTORY RATE OF RETURN PRICING

This form of pricing is often referred to as **target pricing**.

Basically it involves the supplier in determining an acceptable rate of return on the capital invested, over a period of time. If the expected capital and operational investment over a year is £1 000 000 and a company expects a minimum of 10 per cent (£100 000) return on its investment, the price of the product(s) or services(s) will be set to ensure that this return on investment (£100 000) is achieved.

The advantage is that the company has a pricing target for which to aim to ensure satisfactory profits. The disadvantage is that it is necessary to keep a close eye on demand and costs throughout the year to be sure that the return on capital can be achieved.

The popularity of these cost-orientated pricing methods exists mainly because:

- They offer simplicity to the administrators of pricing in a company.
- Some jobs are non routine, such as the production of a batch of items or even just one item like a particular piece of machinery, and it is difficult or impossible to cost them as if there were a continuous market.
- They guarantee a profit assuming that the price(s) set is competitive enough to generate demand.

3 Competitor based approaches

The price a company can ask for its product is sometimes strongly affected by and related to the prices asked by competitors, as illustrated in the following methods.

GOING RATE PRICING
Where there are many other suppliers to compete with in a market that is very price sensitive, a company's price for its product may have to be set around the price (going rate) its competitors are charging. To avoid this as much as possible a company will try to amplify the advantages of its own product, or try for brand leadership.

This approach is often preferred where:

- Acceptance of the existing average price range charged by competitors in the industry is the most effective means of reaching and convincing a target audience to purchase.
- Competitors' reaction to an independently set price may be a problem and cannot be exactly assessed, i.e. a possible price war between competitors (as has happened between petrol companies) takes place, which may only result in damaging the company's trading position.
- In some situations it is often the case that a company will gain little or nothing if it raises prices when demand is sensitive to change as there may be a significant fall off in demand and possibly total revenue. Alternatively, if a company lowers the price in an inelastic demand situation then again it may receive less total revenue as sales may not drastically increase. The company may also precipitate a price war costing it time, effort and revenue.

CLOSE BID PRICING

This form of pricing is normally found where it is required that companies tender a bid for work, such as work for a government or a state or local authority.

Usually a company will submit a price in confidence that it considers to be competitive in order to obtain the work. However, a high price may also be submitted where a company does not want the work at the time but does not wish to be forgotten – and at any rate could sub-contract the work under its control if its high price is accepted.

Conversely, if a large specialised company is aware that its few competitors are already overloaded with work it may submit a high price in the hope that the contract may prove rather problematic for other companies bidding for it due to their current commitments. Any bids submitted need to be considered very carefully because once they are accepted they may commit the company to the price for a specific period of time. Any unexpected changes in costs or availability of raw materials may lead to heavy losses or legal proceedings against the company if it fails to supply the products or services within the agreed price and time.

OPEN BIDDING

This form of bidding is usually associated with auctioneering companies acting as agents for the seller although bidding does apply in many other situations. Potential purchasers openly bid against each other (compete) to purchase the item in question and the auctioneer accepts the highest price offered provided it is above any reserve price that may have been set indicating the minimum price the seller will accept. This is a usual form of arriving at a sale price in the sale of second hand industrial and trade goods, the sale of farm animals, world commodities, second hand cars, antiques, etc.

NEGOTIATED PRICES

Sometimes a pricing policy that will apply to all sales cannot be predetermined and so a price has to be negotiated with customers or the price is reached through a form of bartering between the buyer and seller.

Prices often have to be arrived at through negotiation between buyer and seller where the products are very expensive, have to be produced to the customer's specification, after sales services may be involved and there is competition for the order. For example, the supply of jet engines for a new fleet of aircraft may need to be negotiated before production starts.

The buyer wants the lowest price in keeping with quality and expected delivery times. The supplier wants to obtain the maximum price but also has to set a competitive price in order to obtain the order. The supplier will also want the maximum price to allow for unfavourable cost changes that may occur during the execution of the work and to allow for any payment necessary if a penalty clause is attached penalising for late delivery or faults with the product.

Understandably, therefore, senior personnel negotiating prices have to be very skilled in their work.

Negotiation will also have to be used where **counter** (**reciprocal**) **trading** is needed for a sale to be made. In most cases counter trading takes place where a company in a country that has little foreign currency wants to purchase goods from a company in another country. As the company cannot obtain the appropriate currency to purchase the goods it wants, it offers goods in return for the goods it needs.

If the supplying company agrees to this method of payment negotiations will take place to determine the amount of goods each company should provide. It may be necessary for the supplying company to use the services of a 'factor' who will purchase the goods that the supplier has accepted or arrange for their purchase. Otherwise the supplier company will have to sell the goods it accepted, by itself.

As the goods that have been accepted for payment may have to be sold in smaller quantities to a number of customers the supplier company cannot be certain of the total money it will finally receive. It could be more, or it could be less, than anticipated, unless the factor has guaranteed a price.

To some degree prices that have resulted from negotiation derive from the old barter method of trading that started well before the advent of money when the exchange of goods and services was the only way to trade. Today, however, we associate **bartering** much more with a retailer offering a price and the customer almost instantaneously counter offering a lower price for the product. This process continues until the customer is satisfied at that moment with the price he/she will pay and the retailer can sell at a price that ensures a satisfactory profit. The problem is that customers not accustomed to this method of arriving at a price may pay much more than what could be considered a fair price. The whole process may involve the customer in hours of bartering with alternative retailers to find the lowest price and the retailer may waste considerable time competing for one customer with the result that other customers waiting may leave. Therefore, in economies that have a sophisticated marketing system this method of arriving at a price is a rarity.

■ 5 CREDIT

Credit involves a company in allowing a period of time for a customer to pay for the goods supplied. Suppliers today increasingly have to consider the credit facilities they will offer to purchasers if they are to maximise and/or maintain sales.

Selling without offering credit to industrial and reseller markets is virtually unheard of and even consumers are increasingly requiring credit in order to buy goods, hence the increase in credit cards and interest free, long term repayment facilities.

If a company allows its customers more time to pay, then it is in effect granting a form of loan to them. Although this may seem an attractive strategy, it costs money and it is often difficult to reverse the facility in periods when liquidity problems are being faced. If a company has a major user market customer who averages £200 000 in orders each year and it allows the customer one month credit, then the monthly average amount outstanding will be:

$$£200\,000 \div 12 = £16\,666$$

If the company allows an extension of the credit period to two months, because competitors start offering such credit facilities or because the customer is threatening to change to another source of supply, then the average monthly amount outstanding will increase to:

$$£200\,000 \div 6 = £33\,333$$

Such an increase may introduce extra pressure on the supplier's finances.

Leasing and hire purchase (HP) in which customers are allowed to purchase by regular payments over months or years is also a form of credit as is renting of equipment or items. Therefore, decisions regarding these forms of trading must be considered very carefully before they are adopted.

The decision to allow credit will depend on one or more of the following.

- The credit allowed to a company from its suppliers of raw materials, finished goods, etc. Companies are often trying to delay the time for payment of goods they have received while speeding up outstanding payments from their customers so they are generating money for their own operations.
- The opportunity to obtain insurance against bad debts or use of a debt collecting agency to collect bad debts.
- Credit facilities offered to other segments of the company's total customers.
- Importance of the customer(s) to the company.
- Credit period offered by the company's direct competitors.
- The possibility of using HP and leasing companies who will pay the supplier cash and then make profits as a result of interest payments customers pay in excess of the standard price.
- Liquidity situation of the company.
- Degree of reliability associated with customers – the more risk, the more bad debts.
- The possibility of setting a precedent which may create a future problem with other groups of customers.
- The amount of profits from sales to determine if there is plenty of room for offering credit terms.

■ 6 DISCOUNTS

Discounts are the amounts reduced off the standard price for certain categories of customers. They are essential to support most pricing policies and will definitely be required by organisations in any channel of distribution. Four main types exist, namely:

TRADE DISCOUNTS

These are normally offered to shops and other distributors, i.e. customers in a particular trade which forms part of the channel of distribution. Traders would include national and regional distributors, wholesalers and retailers in the resale channels of distribution. In service industries where there may be plumbers, electricians, builders, carpet layers, etc., people in these trades would obtain a trade discount at local parts' suppliers on evidence that they are in the trade in question.

QUANTITY DISCOUNTS

These are invariably available to traders to encourage large stocking and therefore, commitment to making sales. They are also regularly available to consumers, although the discounting element is not always readily apparent, e.g. buy a giant pack of washing powder and the price per measure of weight of the powder is reduced, or buy six rolls of toilet paper and the price per roll is reduced.

SETTLEMENT DISCOUNTS

These are given to ensure that debtors pay their account invoice on time, e.g. a five per cent reduction from the published price if the customer pays immediately, or within a certain period. This method however, is more widespread with customers in industrial and retail markets where each customer (company) purchases large quantities and is, therefore, owing the supplier large amounts.

SEASONAL DISCOUNTS

These are discounts offered at certain periods, such as

- January to encourage purchasing in a post Christmas period when purchases seem to be at a low level.
- At certain times of year to clear out-of-date or out-of-fashion stocks.
- End of week in shops that stock perishable goods so that the store does not have to stock some items which are starting to perish over a weekend.

Which pricing policy is chosen must of course depend upon the objectives and strategies of the company and the amount of resources that are at the company's command. Thus, pricing is often an integrated activity involving the skills of all marketing staff within the company. As an example, the market research team should help determine the right market price and the promotions department salesforce should communicate the right support ideas to the channels of distribution and consumers.

■ 7 SOME ADDITIONAL PRICING TERMINOLOGY

Often companies – particularly in the industrial market – will offer a price which directly reflects the additional costs involved in delivering the goods to customers. For example:

(a) *Ex-works*: a price offered by the supplier if the customer collects from the supplier's premises (works).

(b) *FOB (free on board)*: an FOB price is the price a supplier may quote to an overseas customer for placing the goods on a ship or aeroplane ready for the customer to arrange the rest of the transportation to his own premises.

(c) *CIF (carriage, insurance, freight included)*: CIF is generally applicable for quotes to overseas customers in which the supplier is stating a price that includes transportation and insurance of the goods to the overseas customer's premises.

(d) *Delivered*: the price if the supplier arranges delivery to the customer although this usually relates to deliveries within a home market.

The supplier may also demand firm payment immediately the goods are delivered i.e., *COD (cash on delivery)*. If payment must be made before the goods will be delivered, the supplier will send the customer a 'Pro-Forma invoice' which requests payment first, unlike the ordinary invoice which is sent after the goods have been delivered to request payment. If it is intended that the buyer does not have to pay the supplier until the buyer has sold the goods, and can return them if they are not sold, this would constitute goods supplied on a *sale-or-return* basis.

■ 8 DETERMINING A PRICE STRUCTURE

To conclude and consolidate what you have learnt from reading this chapter it seems appropriate to put some of the ideas discussed to the test by designing a price structure for a company that intends selling fresh orange juice.

Marketing research undertaken by the company has determined the following:

1 Consumers who like orange juice may purchase if the juice is sold in 70cl bottles at £1 per bottle.
2 To encourage companies in the channels of distribution to purchase and sell the juice, companies in the distribution channel need to purchase at the following prices.

(a) Restaurants, pubs, bars and retailers (shops, stalls and supermarkets) 60p per bottle – though they will purchase as a minimum one case of 12 bottles.

(b) Wholesalers and supermarket chains 40p and 50p per bottle respectively – but they are willing to purchase 100 cases of 12 bottles to obtain this price.

3 (a) and (b) require 30 days credit from date of delivery.

Without using research the manufacturer has decided not to trouble servicing export orders unless an overseas customer purchases one container load, which represents 800 cases, at 40p per bottle FOB. The result is the price structure shown in Fig. 5.1.

Fig. 5.1

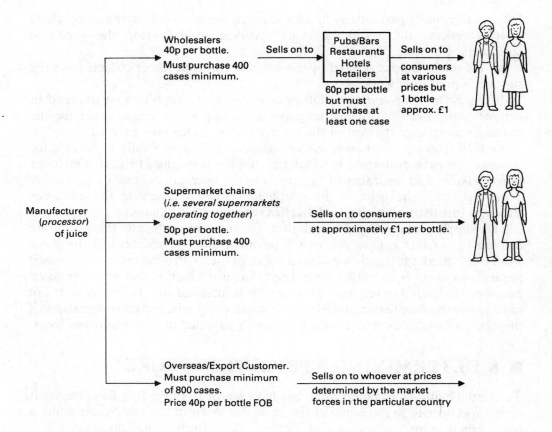

DISCOUNTS

To encourage wholesalers and supermarket chains to purchase larger quantities and achieve higher mark ups, the manufacturer may additionally offer them a quantity discount structure as follows:

Numbers of cases purchased	400	500	600	800
Discount from standard price*	0%	5%	10%	12½%

*40p for wholesalers, 50p for supermarket chains

The manufacturer is offering these discounts to encourage wholesalers to be more committed to the product and in the hope that part of these discounts will be passed on by the wholesalers to retailers, thus increasing overall sales. Additionally the manufacturer and in turn retailers may offer seasonal discounts in winter when people are drinking less juice to encourage them to drink more, or possibly consumer sales promotions may be introduced.

SUMMING UP

The illustration outlined is quite simplified. In the real life situation the producer would probably be supplying different sized packs of juice for different needs. For example, 25cl cartons for instant purchasing by children and workers at lunch time, 1 litre cartons, 2 litre bottles or cartons and 5 and 25 litre containers for restaurants and bars. This would obviously mean a more complex price structure but only an extension of what has been already illustrated. In fact many companies may have a large number of products to price and may use a different policy for each to market the individual products as well as help in the selling of other products in the company's product range.

But whatever the structure most of the aims will be the same, namely:

1 To encourage consumers constituting the market to purchase in sufficient quantities to encourage companies in the channels of distribution to hold stock.
2 To offer prices, discounts and credit to companies in the channels of distribution that will encourage them to purchase and sell on.
3 To ensure that individual quantities purchased from the manufacturer are of sufficient value to ensure acceptable profit levels.

Although this has been just one example, you should find that by the time you have fully read this manual your knowledge of pricing, market segmentation and distribution will help you to analyse most price structures no matter what size the company is or the type of products.

■ STUDY AND EXAM TIPS

1 Be prepared to discuss, in detail, the major influences on price setting. Examiners do not always set questions solely on pricing policies and methods.
2 Become familiar with the circumstances which encourage or allow for a particular pricing method.
3 Treat the price as an element of the marketing mix and always allow for the effect on price of the other three elements of the mix when discussing the pricing process.
4 Examiners may specify the pricing method(s) they want you to discuss. Do not waste time by writing everything you know about pricing; concentrate only on the pricing methods the examiner mentioned.
5 Try to give your own examples which highlight a particular pricing method. To do this keep your eye on the price of major goods in your local shops, markets and supermarkets and note the effect on price when sales promotions are used or products are updated in some way.

■ SELF ASSESSMENT QUESTIONS

Answer the following questions without reference to the chapter and then refer to the answers given at the end of the manual to determine the marks you achieved. Allow 1 mark for each complete question that you answer correctly. If you read the chapter effectively you should obtain 10 or more marks. Re-read those parts of the chapter which relate to the questions you failed to answer correctly.

1 Is pricing only concerned with new products?

☐ YES   ☐ NO (tick appropriate box)

2 Complete the sentence:
Pricing is the process of determining the _ _ _ _ _ _ _ _ that an organisation should _ _ _ _ _ _ _ _ from purchasers for the product or service it supplies.

3 Complete the sentence:
Price is the _ _ _ _ _ _ _ _ value attached to a _ _ _ _ _ _ _ _ or service at a particular point in time.

4 Complete the sentence:
Satisfactory rate of return pricing is also referred to as _ _ _ _ _ _ _ _ _ _ _ _ _ _ _ _ _ _

5 Complete the sentence:
In market penetration pricing it is not only the target market that should be saturated but also the _ _ _ _ _ _ _ _ to help prevent counter action by competitors.

6 Complete the sentence:
Loss leaders are usually a part of _ _ _ _ _ _ _ _ _ _ _ _ _ _ _ _ pricing.

7 One pricing policy that is cost orientated is satisfactory rate of return pricing. Name another.

_ _

8 Bid pricing is one form of pricing based on competitors. Name one other.

_ _

9 One type of discount is a settlement discount. Name two others.
(a) _
(b) _

10 Two major influences on the price that may be asked are the state of the economy and the other 3 Ps of the marketing mix. Name three more major influences on the price a company may ask for its products or services.
(a) _
(b) _
(c) _

11 Complete the sentence:
Marginal costs are the costs incurred when we make and sell an extra unit or batch of units. If we sell items just above marginal costs then the money obtained makes a _ _ _ _ _ _ _ _ towards profits or towards minimising _ _ _ _ _ _ _ _ _ _ _ _ _ _ _ _ _ _

12 Policies of pricing may be categorised into three areas, one of which is market orientated policies. Name the other two.

(a) _____

(b) _____

13 Complete the sentence:

The prime objective of pricing is to maximise profits in the short, medium or long term or/and minimise the risk of _____

■ **EXAMINATION QUESTIONS**

The Institute of Marketing

1 Distinguish between market skimming pricing and market penetration pricing and discuss the factors which will tend to favour each of these approaches to pricing.

2 Set out the elements of a typical price structure and distinguish between a wholesale 'mark-up' and a wholesale 'discount'.

The Association of Business Executives

3 Write notes on FOUR of the following:

(a) Mark-up pricing.

(b) Target pricing.

(c) Price discrimination.

(d) Loss leaders.

(e) Prestige pricing.

4 In addition to cost considerations, what other major factors might a marketing executive take into account in making pricing decisions for his products? Explain the significance of each factor identified.

5 Your company meets with competition in the form of 'price cutting'. How would you deal with this situation?

The Institute of Commercial Management

6 Distinguish between 'Market Skimming' and 'Market Penetration' approaches to pricing new products. What circumstances would tend to favour each approach?

6 Distribution policy

Physical distribution is about getting the right product, to the right place, in the right quantities at the right time!

■ INTRODUCTION

How many times have you come across an appealing advertisement, relating to a product or service which you have considered very interesting and exciting, at a price you can afford but you were unable to purchase the product because it was not available through the shops or supermarkets at which you normally buy? If this has happened to you, then you are in a good position to appreciate the importance and value of **distribution**. A company may have developed a good product, priced it correctly, presented it effectively through appropriate communication channels and generated enough interest – but failed to get the actual product to the interested parties because the distribution network was not properly set up or developed or because the company itself could not effect the physical distribution of the product on time.

The aim of this chapter is to explain the main issues associated with distribution and to identify the main techniques which can establish or improve the overall physical distribution and distribution network that a company uses. In order to cover the main areas in a logical and effective manner, the subject is presented in five parts.

1 defining distribution and distribution channels
2 key ingredients of distribution
3 direct marketing
4 selection of distribution channels
5 distribution strategies

1 DEFINING DISTRIBUTION

Distribution – the final P in the marketing mix – may be defined as:

'all the activities necessary for ensuring the transfer of products or services

from the supplier to a place of the purchaser's choice or to a place where potential purchasers may readily purchase them'

The letter 'P' for *place* refers to the market place and, therefore, indicates that distribution is about delivering products and services to the place where the market exists.

In the case of user markets most goods that are supplied are delivered to the premises of the purchaser although this is not always the case. For example, an overseas dealer may purchase but have the goods delivered to a customer, or the head office of a chain of supermarkets may purchase but expect the deliveries to be made to the individual supermarkets in the chain.

In consumer markets, the majority of goods are purchased and collected by consumers from retail outlets but a small percentage may be delivered by the seller direct to the consumer's home, e.g. washing machines or refrigerators. Some too may be sent by post, particularly where a customer has ordered by post.

The way in which products may be physically distributed is not always appreciated by the newcomer to marketing although most methods we see or experience regularly in our everyday lives. These methods include road transport, rail, water (sea, lakes, rivers and canals), air (aeroplanes and airships), wire/cable (for electricity, telephones, telexes), pipelines (e.g. for gas, oil and water), by hand (letters and newspapers), or, as is often the case, a mix of two or more of these methods.

But getting products to customers is not simply a question of physical distribution. The organisations who are part of the distribution network, such as retailers, have to be selected carefully, encouraged to become part of the network and motivated into promoting the sale of a product if the manufacturer is to obtain satisfactory sales levels for the product.

The channels of distribution may be defined as:

'the network of distributive organisations through which goods or services are transferred from the supplier to a place nominated by the purchaser or a place where they may be readily purchased'

A publisher, for instance, specialising in business education textbooks will need to seek a number of bookshops whose owners are interested in stocking the books on offer by the publisher. The bookshops on the other hand will have to be in a position to attract current and potential students and tutors to their premises so that they can interest them in the range of books on display. The bookshops represent just one form of **distribution channel**: a route to a particular destination. In our example the destination is business students and tutors.

A number of different terms are used to describe individuals or organisations who purchase goods for resale, the most common ones being **middlemen** or **intermediaries**. Generally speaking, there are three major types of distributors extensively used in the marketing and distribution of finished products for consumer markets:

(a) agents and brokers
(b) retailers
(c) wholesalers

Agents and brokers

Agents and brokers are business units which specialise in and concentrate on negotiating purchases or sales on behalf of a **principal**. The principal is usually the person or organisation selling something, but it can be the case that the agent is acting on behalf of the purchaser as in the case of advertising agencies who buy advertising space for their clients.

An estate agent, for instance, will act for a person selling a property and attempt to find purchasers for the property. The agent will provide advice to the principal (the seller) whenever needed and if a sale is successfully completed, a commission based on the value of the sale will be received by the estate agent from the seller.

Since there is no transfer of ownership of the goods to the agent the principal has adequate control of the sales process.

Agents are preferred when their expertise can help an individual or a company establish market contacts, e.g., an overseas agent acting for a company wishing to export.

We have already listed many of the agents that exist in Chapter 2 and will consider them in greater detail in Chapter 9. We are here simply re-inforcing their importance as a part of certain distributive networks.

The role of brokers may not be as well known as the role of agents, but we come across brokers, e.g. insurance brokers, in our everyday lives and they are often at work where large purchases of world commodities such as tea, coffee, sugar, etc., are taking place.

Retailers

Retailers are *resellers* dealing directly with the ultimate consumer. They have established distribution outlets (shops, street stands, stalls in markets, etc.) and they can help a manufacturer to reach consumer markets with large numbers of purchasers who may be widely dispersed yet also concentrated in certain areas such as cities and towns. Consider how many people drink tea in the UK. The number obviously runs into millions, so tea manufacturers will have to use thousands of retailers in order to reach the potential consumers of the product.

The major types of retailers, defined along the guidelines issued by the

European Economic Community, are listed below with comments regarding their trading characteristics.

Department store
A large retail establishment with at least 2500 square metres of selling space, selling at least five different groups of products (of which one group must be women's attire) in separate departments. Often individual departments are franchise operations. Department stores tend to concentrate on the more highly priced products, e.g. shopping and speciality goods, to cover high operating costs. They are not as numerous or widely dispersed as supermarkets.

Multiple shop organisations
Organisations operating ten or more retail establishments (not including consumer co-operatives, departmental and variety stores). A group of specialist shops dealing in one group of products such as electrical goods or DIY. They expect low prices from suppliers and may buy direct from manufacturers, e.g. they may import wine and have it bottled themselves.

Retail buying group
Sometimes referred to as a 'retail co-operative'. These are groups of retailers who have agreed to purchase a substantial amount of their supplies in common and to participate in other joint activities such as promotional activities to reduce costs and buy at better prices to compete more effectively with supermarkets.

Supermarkets
Retail establishments selling mainly foodstuffs by self-service, with a minimum of 400 square metres of selling space. They tend to deal in convenience goods, large volume of sales and fast moving lines. When part of a chain, they buy centrally. They expect low prices, may often buy direct from manufacturers (rather than wholesalers), and there is a tendency towards 'private branding'.

Consumer co-operative societies
Organisations engaged in retail trade that operate on co-operative (shared ownership) principles. For many years co-ops experienced slow growth due to their inability to change rapidly to meet changing competitor and market conditions. Now, however, they have made immense progress in their market effort and should be considered in a similar way to supermarkets regarding method of trading and purchases.

Superstore or hypermarket
Retail organisation with at least 2500 square metres of selling space, selling by self-service a wide range of goods of which half is food. Three times the store area may be provided for customers' car parking and the stores are invariably located on the outskirts of the centre of towns or cities. They usually operate over 15 checkouts. Speciality goods may be sold. Their advantage is that they offer consumers a convenient means of shopping for most of their requirements.

Variety chain stores

These operate ten or more establishments and sell a wide range of goods. Woolworths is an example. Again there is a move towards private branding so many manufacturers may have to be prepared to place the store's brand on products. Nevertheless, there are opportunities for selling own brands. Centralised buying predominates but is not necessarily the case.

Voluntary wholesale chains

Where one or a number of wholesalers operate with retail members in both buying and retailing activities. The retailers will operate under the same name though each retail outlet may be independently owned. Their operation is similar to a retail buying group.

Wholesale buying group

Wholesalers in the same trade co-operate in buying and join together in other activities to combat the rise in the purchasing strength of supermarket chains. By joint purchases they are able to keep the costs lower for retailers purchasing from them.

NON SHOP RETAILING

Not all methods of retailing take place through shops, stores and supermarkets. In the retail category may also be added street market traders, mobile shops, street stands and vending machines, e.g. for cigarettes, chocolates and now many other items including food. Other methods of non shop selling are covered later in this chapter when direct marketing is discussed.

Wholesalers

Wholesalers (sometimes referred to as **jobbers**) are business units which buy, resell and deliver to other intermediaries such as smaller wholesalers or independent dealers, but in the main their business is with retailers. They invariably purchase large quantities from manufacturers and break them down into quantities suitable for retailers who wish to purchase lesser amounts. They reduce the costs associated with the physical distribution of consumer products as they are usually situated close to market concentrations and they contribute to the expansion of a manufacturer's distribution network. This category of wholesaler represents the usual and main body of wholesalers.

It can be, however, that the wholesaler is a **national wholesaler** (often referred to as a **national distributor**), which is likely where they are acting for an exporter to an overseas market. In these cases they may also be a wholesaler and agent for a particular region of the country so that they are aware of the problems that the local wholesalers or agents they supply may encounter and be able to offer them expert advice.

If a company is manufacturing three different products which must be distributed in varying quantities to a large number of retailers, then the operations of a wholesaler can prove extremely valuable in expanding the distribution channels for a manufacturer as indicated in Fig. 6.1. Large quantities of all three product lines can be delivered to the warehouse (storehouse) or a wholesaler who, by being in a particular region, can supply retailers at the times they require and in the smaller quantities demanded by them. In reality the wholesaler would probably be purchasing the lines of fifty or more manufacturers.

Wholesalers may deal in a range of unrelated products but it is more usual that they specialise in particular lines such as electrical equipment, clothing, furnishings, etc.

Fig. 6.1

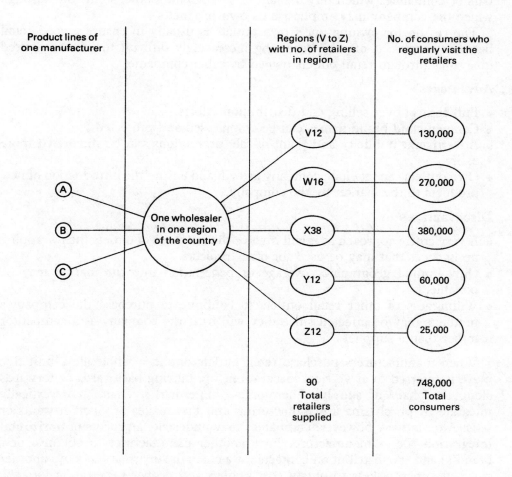

There are also **cash and carry** wholesalers who are prepared to sell to anyone – trade or consumer – provided that they purchase an adequate amount, collect the goods themselves and pay in cash or by credit card.

Advantages and disadvantages of various distribution channels

Marketing companies attempt to combine the distributors in a way that will offer them an effective marketing approach. Before a combination is sought, one must consider the relative advantages and disadvantages of the major distribution alternatives.

OWN RETAIL OUTLETS

This method of distribution is usually used by companies that can offer a complete range of products, such as breweries owning off-licences and pubs and bars or companies which buy a chain of shops selling other items but through which the company may emphasise its own product(s).

The reason for owning one's own outlets is usually to ensure a good retail network because it may be becoming increasingly difficult to sell the desired quantities through retail outlets owned by other companies.

Advantages

- Full control over selling and distribution efforts.
- Company and brand names can be emphasised and protected.
- Advertising, publicity and point-of-sale promotions can be integrated more easily.
- Own outlets can facilitate company growth and ensure the introduction of new products to the market by the company.

Disadvantages

- A very costly approach as it will involve the purchase of outlets thus wrapping up finances that may be used for other projects.
- Only limited geographic coverage or penetration into the market may be possible.
- Willingness of other retail outlets to continue to purchase the company's products may be affected since they will treat the company as a competitor rather than a supplier.

When manufacturers purchase retail outlets or/and a wholesaling unit this move is referred to as **vertical integration**, i.e. moving backwards or forwards along the chain of supply. Therefore, a supermarket chain may vertically integrate by purchasing a manufacturing unit that makes products it wants or sells. Alternatively however, companies may undertake a process of **horizontal integration**, i.e. a manufacturer buys another manufacturer to obtain a new brand(s) and the distribution contacts, or a chain of supermarkets buys another chain of supermarkets to obtain cost savings and deeper penetration into the market place.

USE OF WHOLESALERS

We have briefly outlined the advantages of using wholesalers but it will not hurt to reconsider the advantages in a list form and add some disadvantages.

Advantages

- They break down the bulk supplies that manufacturers like to deliver to keep their transport costs down.
- They can help the manufacturer cover a vast geographical area.
- They offer an established selling and distribution network (wholesalers and retailers jointly constitute the main distribution outlet for goods).
- Their own promotional activities can support or improve market performance of a manufacturer's product.
- They offer expertise.

Disadvantages

- They are profit making organisations and tend to pay attention to high profit or fast turnover goods.
- They may not provide adequate promotional attention to a company's product, treating it just as another one of its many lines. They may even threaten to cease selling and distributing if they do not obtain the terms they would like from the manufacturer. Hence, some manufacturers will prefer to sell direct or deliver to retailers themselves.
- Loss of company prestige that may be suffered by individual wholesaling organisations may have an effect on the image of individual products they handle.

Some companies whose product is in regular high demand may dispense with wholesalers by setting up their own warehouses (stocking centres) throughout the country from where their own vans and lorries will deliver to local retail outlets thus cutting out the wholesalers' profit and retaining control of the market.

USE OF INDEPENDENT RETAILERS
Advantages

- They offer extensive geographic coverage.
- They offer a shop window/shelf display of a company's product to consumers.
- Their own promotional activities can induce adoption of a manufacturer's product.
- Retailer acceptance can often lead to consumer acceptance of a product since many individual retailing organisations have an established image in the market (Tesco – value for money; Safeway – availability of alternatives; Sainsbury – quality of food).

Disadvantages

• The disadvantages that one can list about retailers are the same as the disadvantages mentioned about wholesalers (see earlier).

AGENTS AND BROKERS

As indicated earlier, agents operate in home markets but they are also important for exporting companies. Their advantages and disadvantages will be discussed in Chapter 9.

FRANCHISORS

Franchising offers a compromise for a company providing highly marketable products between owning its own outlets and selling through the outlets of others. However, many franchising companies are marketing wholesalers who buy in bulk from manufacturers and then sell to their distribution network (the franchisees) who in turn sell to the final purchaser. Therefore, they offer a channel of distribution for some manufacturers, though they do not form a distribution network suitable for most manufacturers.

Because the Americans initiated the franchising movement its purpose and advantages and disadvantages in distribution will be discussed in Chapter 9.

MAIL ORDER HOUSES

As mail order houses operate in a similar form to direct mail undertaken by a manufacturer or wholesaler/retailer, their value as a means of selling can be compared with the advantages and disadvantages of direct marketing discussed later in this chapter – in particular catalogue selling. As a channel of distribution for most manufacturers' goods, mail order houses still represent a minor outlet dealing in particular with shopping and the lower priced speciality goods.

OTHER DISTRIBUTION SITUATIONS

It is not always the case that distribution channels currently exist. This is often the case with non profit making organisations, such as charities wanting to distribute to the needy and starving in an underdeveloped country. In such situations the charity may have to establish or encourage the establishment of channels for distribution which may include the services of the donating country's airforce, the establishing of local agents and the mobilising of the benefactors to transport supplies themselves, etc. So if obtaining intermediaries for a commercial product seems formidable to you, spare a thought for those who do not have ready distributors at hand.

The movement of goods and services via the major distribution channels is illustrated in Figs 6.2 to 6.5.

Fig. 6.2 *Zero stage marketing channels*

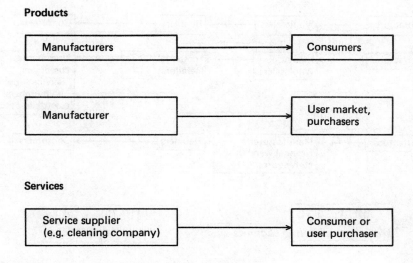

Fig. 6.3 *One stage marketing channels*

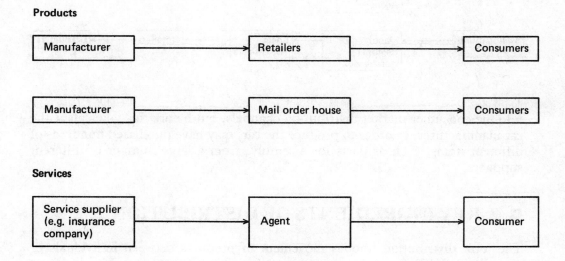

The zero stage method of selling (Fig. 6.2), which eliminates intermediaries, we will consider later under direct marketing where a company promotes, sells and delivers direct to potential purchasers.

Note that in the above examples we have started with manufacturers. A variety of distribution activities may have taken place even before the manufacturer produces the product. For example a car manufacturer will send finished cars

Fig. 6.4 *Two stage marketing channels*

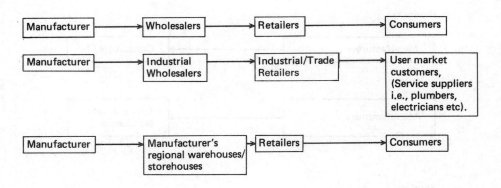

Fig. 6.5 *Three stage marketing channels*

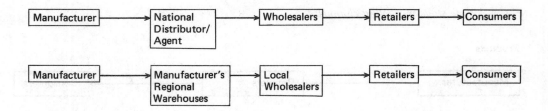

into the consumer market distribution channels, but before this takes place the car manufacturer, in order to produce the car, may have purchased hundreds of different items, such as parts for assembly, from a large number of different suppliers.

■ 2 KEY INGREDIENTS OF DISTRIBUTION

The term distribution implies movement of products between individuals or organisations. When, for instance, a manufacturer delivers some of his products to a shop via a wholesaler, there is a movement of products from the stores of the manufacturer ultimately to the shop of the shopkeeper. The products will be subsequently bought by consumers, and a further movement from the hands of the shopkeeper to the hands of the consumer takes place.

This example highlights a simple distribution network for the distribution and sale of a product involving a manufacturer, a wholesaler, a shopkeeper and a consumer, which can only come into operation – no matter what the distribution network – when four ingredients are present.

1 The **provision of information** to the final purchaser and organisations making up the channel of distribution.

2 The **physical delivery of the product** to a member of the channel of distribution or direct to the purchaser.

3 The **payment for the goods** by the units constituting the channel of distribution and the purchaser.

4 The **transfer of title** of the goods (ownership) through the channel of distribution to the final purchaser.

1 Information

The provision of information will involve those elements of the promotion mix of a company designed to build awareness of the product in the minds of final purchasers and intermediaries: induce trial, encourage repeat purchases, create enthusiasm and improve the overall exposure of products within a specific target market.

Potential intermediaries, consumers or user purchasers will have to be offered relevant information which will encourage them to consider the purchase of the product in order to satisfy a specific set of needs. In the case of intermediaries – particularly when first in the channel of distribution – it could be information regarding profitability from buying and selling a product, while in the case of consumers it could be the offering of benefits that fulfil particular personal needs.

Once information is provided to companies in the channel of distribution they will pass it on to others in the channel and to the final customers through their own promotional efforts.

Most manufacturers will attempt to adopt a 'sell-in' (push) and a 'sell-out' (pull) policy with their promotional efforts. The **sell-in** aspect is designed to influence the organisations in the channels of distribution to purchase and push sales of the product through to the final purchaser. The **sell-out** policy is aimed at final purchasers (such as consumers) to encourage them to ask retailers for the product, the retailer in turn asking the wholesalers if they have the product and the wholesalers approaching the manufacturer to purchase. Hopefully information will not simply flow from the manufacturer, it may also flow from the wholesaler to the retailer or/and from the retailer to consumer, and possibly consumer comments back along the distribution channel. The flow of promotional information to a typical consumer market is illustrated in Fig. 6.6 with the flow being towards the final purchaser.

Fig. 6.6 *Promotion flow*

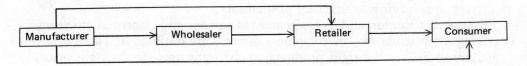

2 Physical distribution

Physical distribution relates to the actual movement of the products from one party to another. Physical distribution has attracted a lot of attention from marketing management in the last few years because of a number of elements which companies are seeing as increasingly important.

- By reducing the amount of intermediaries taking a profit and delivering more directly to purchasers (direct marketing) they may be able to reduce the price for the final purchaser, and thus hopefully improve sales.
- Reducing distribution costs while keeping the price the same earns more profits for the manufacturer, e.g. a considerable amount of oil is now delivered by pipeline instead of ship, thus reducing delivery costs per unit (barrel).
- Delivery of printers' plates, for example, can be speeded up by use of cable and sophisticated Fax machines over vast distances, rather than physically delivering by road, rail or air.
- Despite all the developments in transport, physical delivery still represents the major increase in cost for most companies over the last decade because of the increases in fuel costs. Therefore, companies have tended to take greater note of the savings that can be made through either changing the mode of transport, reducing the number of deliveries through encouraging the purchase of larger quantities or using better delivery methods, e.g. containers of uniform size for overseas deliveries. This helps a company to hold the price of the delivered product steady so that demand is maintained at current levels.
- To protect products and deliver them in a safer and more hygienic manner, companies are using a variety of packing materials and systems. For example polystyrene packing to prevent damage and vacuum packs for preventing contamination and decay.
- Companies would like to ensure that every purchaser can purchase exactly when they wish, but this is not possible as retaining stocks sufficient to meet this level of service would be extremely expensive for the manufacturer and all organisations in the channel of distribution. To contribute towards achieving this situation manufacturers attempt to assess exactly the levels of stocks needed to maintain a predetermined level of customer service. This also requires the efficient planning of deliveries.

If we consider physical distribution from the aspects of cost and efficiency, we can identify five key areas where improvements may be possible: storing, handling, despatching, transportation and documentation. For many products distribution and physical delivery represents a higher cost than producing the product. Therefore, cost-effectiveness in physical distribution will contribute positively to achieving satisfactory profitability.

Physical distribution and its main areas of savings and improved efficiency in servicing intermediaries – or customers direct – are outlined in Table 6.1.

Failure to deliver the right products, at the right time, to the right place, in

Table 6.1

Marketing element	Physical distribution element
The right product in the right quantities	**Selecting or making the exact product the customer ordered requires:** • The right production processing system, i.e. linking sales forecasting with the production process so that forecasted demand is met on time. This will involve production, which reinforces the need for an integrated marketing effort involving all departments. • Right stock/inventory levels. • Right order processing system. • Right collection and packing system.
to the right place at the right time	**Delivering the product to the customer's nominated premises requires:** • All of the above, plus • Right delivery note and parcel labelling system. • Using a reliable carrier, unless the company is using its own transportation.

the right quantities can seriously affect customer relations and the reputation of the company and its products. In addition, if the products are not delivered when they should be, the customers expecting the supply of these products may switch to other brands and the cost and effort of regaining them as customers could be formidable. Figure 6.7 is a typical representation of the physical flow of finished goods to a consumer market.

Fig. 6.7 *Physical flow*

Manufacturer → Wholesalers → Retailers → Consumers

3 Payments

Physical distribution concerns the actual movement of products from one party to another along the channel of distribution to the final purchaser. When such a movement is achieved then payment for the goods must take place. This aspect of distribution relates to the movement of cash or other forms of payment in exchange for goods received or sold, and it tends to follow the opposite direction to the physical flow. Goods move forward along the channels of distribution, payments move backward in exchange for the goods. Payment may be immediate, e.g. customers paying cash, by credit card or HP, or after a credit period, e.g. wholesalers given one month to pay the manufacturer for goods received.

This is just as important as the channels chosen and physical distribution for ensuring the supply of goods, as the payment will imply the profit made by organisations in the channels of distribution and therefore influence distribution. The typical payment flow of finished goods for a consumer market is shown in Fig. 6.8.

Fig. 6.8 *Payment flow*

4 Title of goods

This aspect of distribution relates to the passage of ownership which could result from ordering, receiving, accepting and paying for products. It is worth remembering that ownership is only passed on in the case of products and that it does not take place in the case of services as the provider of the service retains his/her service skills and knowledge. The passage of ownership is an important element of physical distribution as we need to be sure that we will own an item before we are willing to pay for it. Figure 6.9 shows the title flow.

Fig. 6.9 *Title flow*

We can now define the supplier's role in ensuring distribution through the chosen channels of distribution as:

the marketing activity which involves the provision of relevant information, which can facilitate acceptance and physical movement of products, in

*return for a satisfactory payment which could lead to the passage of
ownership for a particular product*

Whatever method of distribution a commercial company selects to use to
distribute and sell its products, the ingredients identified will be present and
failure to execute them effectively may result in a partial or total breakdown of
the company's system of distribution.

■ 3 DIRECT MARKETING

Direct marketing refers to the marketing operations where a sale is made directly
to the purchaser without any conventional distributors being involved. It can be
defined as:

marketing of products without using intermediaries

Applied to consumer markets, direct marketing refers to consumers being
able to order products from their own home and have them delivered to their
home. It is with consumers that we will begin considering the topic of direct
marketing.

Direct marketing may involve a number of different methods which can be
used in order to reach, communicate, interest and encourage consumers to buy.
The most popular methods are:

- direct response advertisements
- direct mail and mail drops
- personal (direct) selling
- catalogue selling

1 Direct response advertisements

Advertisements are placed in the Press, on TV or radio and consumers are
encouraged to order directly by telephoning or writing to the supplier of the
goods or by filling in a coupon which may be incorporated in a Press
advertisement. 'Off-the-page' purchasing of this nature relies on impulse, and
there is a need to present an attractive proposition in order to get people to view
the offer favourably since they are being asked to spend money through the post.
The advertisement used must be informative enough to enable the potential
customer to make a decision to purchase. Alternatively the advert may invite the
potential customer to write in or phone for a catalogue or leaflet listing the full
range of products. This is usually the approach where a company wishes to make
additional sales.

Advantages

- It can help reach a widely dispersed market whose characteristics are unknown. For example, a company may advertise in several magazines to reach potential customers for their product. The company may not know which people might wish to buy the product and therefore may have difficulty in obtaining a list of potential customers. By advertising in magazines, customers may be generated and a mailing list for future reference compiled.
- It dispenses with having to allow for profits to intermediaries.
- It can be used where distributing via intermediaries may be more difficult, e.g. with a product which would only sell through limited outlets and not be given considerable attention by retailers stocking it.
- It allows the company, when it sends the potential customer promotional information, to present an extensive message in its own way.

Disadvantages

- Promotional and delivery costs in relation to the amount of final purchases is high, thus requiring most products to be highly priced within the price band of like products.
- Consumers may be suspicious as they cannot evaluate competitors' brands and they may believe that the product must be available in shops at a much lower price.
- Many companies marketing relatively low priced products this way usually need a range of products to generate sufficient customers to make the effort adequately rewarding.

2 Direct mail and mail drops

Direct mail involves the posting (mailing via the normal postal service) of promotional literature, designed to sell a product or service direct to a potential customer's home. **Mail drops** on the other hand are where the delivery of promotional literature to potential customers is undertaken by agents of the company. It may involve posting through letter boxes, handing promotion literature out in the streets, or even placing literature under the windscreen wipers of cars.

Advantages

- It can help a company reach a widely dispersed target market.
- It can help a company present its message in a very personalised way, by addressing letters directly to potential buyers.
- Consumers may treat it as something specially selected for them or for their needs.
- Measurement of direct response is possible, because orders received will be linked to specific individuals or consumer groups.

- It can offer economies of scale which may not otherwise be available to a small company.
- It offers the opportunity of informing consumers in detail about the complete product range offered.
- It enables a company that is having, or will have, difficulty in using the normal distribution channels to market its goods.
- It often enables a company to reach a target market that is very small with extensive literature.

Disadvantages

- It is very difficult to purchase or create and maintain up-to-date, accurate and complete mailing lists which can be used to determine the correct people at which to aim direct mailings (direct mail shot).
- Too much direct mail is currently in use. Therefore, many people now see that it is promotional literature and immediately throw it in the dustbin.
- Due to the high delivery and promotional costs that may be involved, and the wastage such a method of contact is usually more useful for products returning a high profit, e.g. shopping and speciality items.
- The consumer does not have the opportunity to examine the product or for that matter alternatives of competitors. To overcome this problem to some degree consumers are offered the opportunity to examine the product for a few days and if not satisfied return it (sale or return).

Mail drops may obviously be more reliable than mailing lists as the people distributing can often see if a person or house fits the description of people within the target audience, e.g. they can distribute only to women who look under the age of thirty. However, they have a major drawback in that there is a considerable cost involved in recruiting and paying reliable people to distribute what is simply a promotional leaflet. Therefore, while they may be very accurate, they may also prove costly if not well planned and targeted.

3 Personal (direct) selling

With door-to-door selling a salesperson may simply make himself or herself known by knocking on the door. This is sometimes referred to as canvassing for orders. Alternatively he/she may call in response to the consumer's request, i.e. the consumer first responded to an advertisement or was telephoned by a salesperson asking if they would like someone to call and discuss the product/service.

Sometimes the salesperson may hold a party at a house to which consumers will be invited. At the party the salesperson will demonstrate and sell the items that they have for sale. This is often referred to as party selling or party planning.

Advantages

- It offers the opportunity of having complete control over selling and distribution activities i.e. the salesperson often delivers the product.
- Local agents (salespersons operating independently) on a commission basis can reach target audiences that are widely dispersed at convenient times, i.e. in the evening and at weekends, e.g. people selling Avon or Tupperware products.
- It is a popular method when the products in question cannot sell themselves, i.e. there is a need to explain technology, show the product in action, demonstrate number of applications, etc.

Disadvantages

- Unsolicited visits are not welcomed by most consumers.
- If a company uses its own salesforce, high profits are needed in order to cover travelling and selling expenses as well as the salaries and commission of their sales staff.
    Note: Companies marketing to industrial and reseller markets extensively use their own salesforce (see **Summary**).
- If a company uses local agents it needs to allow for damaged goods, bad debts, delayed payments, etc.
- Agents may not have adequate selling ability with the result that they earn little commission and may soon become despondent and cease selling.

4 Catalogue selling

The outlet for communicating and selling in this case is a producer's own catalogue of its products, or it may be a marketing organisation (a mail order house) using catalogue selling. A range of products is included in the catalogue and people can study them, inform their friends, order the products they want or even become commission agents for the company operating the catalogue selling activities.

Catalogues have to be kept exciting and they should be able to appeal to highly diversified audiences with ever changing needs. They may sometimes be added to by simply sending pages with additional products for sale to the customers who have already received the initial catalogue.

The catalogue may be offered through an advertisement or obtained through a person already acting as a commission agent for the company who visits the consumer's house.

General considerations

All the approaches of direct marketing outlined above summarise a very modern way of selling products to consumers, but at the same time they involve costly, risky and complex operations. Success in this area of marketing will depend on efficient organisation and control of all the operations. The following must be considered:

1 The product has to lend itself to direct marketing. Although many products are now sold by direct marketing methods, breaking into this area for the first time can be difficult if manufacturers do not closely consider the product they are offering. The main factors which need to be taken into account are that the product should:

- be new in concept to catch the recipient's attention, particularly if an advertisement in the media is used to generate response.
- be exclusive to the customer. Customers should feel that there is a good reason why they personally have been sent direct promotional literature.
- look good in presentation and be exciting to write about.
- have a high profit margin to cover the high costs of promotion, high costs of maintaining an effective mailing list and high cost of packaging and delivery.
- appear to be good value for money.
- appear to be from a reputable supplier.
- **not** attract only a small and virtually indefinable market.
- **not** be a failed retail product.
- **not** need demonstration for adoption (except in the case of personal selling).

2 Prices must be set correctly bearing in mind that as much as one third of the selling price may be taken up in advertising costs.
3 Sufficient stocks must be available to despatch within an acceptable period or the customer may cancel the order.
4 Depending on the product, a company must be prepared to have to replace damaged goods and also allow for returns by dissatisfied customers.
5 If a company is selling on credit or on free approval bad debts are likely to occur. The company has to decide in advance whether to credit check customers.
6 Credit card facilities can be offered to increase the number of orders and the value of a company's cash flow.

Reasons behind the growth of direct marketing

All changes, developments, improvements or disappointments in the field of marketing can be attributed to some changes in the marketing environment. Direct marketing has been aided greatly by a number of technological, economic and social developments which are likely to accelerate its growth even further in the next few years.

The main reasons behind the growth of direct marketing include:

(a) Changes in consumer attitudes towards shopping through the post. In the recent past, for instance, consumers perceived purchases through company's catalogues as an activity confined to consumers who could not afford to purchase the goods they needed from shops where full payment was expected. Buying through catalogues enabled them to pay for the goods on a weekly basis. Attitudes have now changed and if one examines the pages of popular newspapers and magazines one can find a variety of products aimed at all social classes and all income groups within a national market. More importantly, consumers are willing to accept this method of selling and now believe that most products sold this way are value for money as they are usually sent on a trial period basis, e.g. books or records from specialist clubs.

(**b**) A higher proportion of women are entering the workforce and pursue long term careers. As a result, they have less time for shopping. Direct marketing represents an acceptable alternative means of shopping for speciality products, such as records, radios, TVs, sun lamps, china, etc.

(**c**) There is increased demand for speciality products and services which are often hard to find in shops or shopping centres. An item such as a cane rocking chair might not be sold by local furniture stores. However, an examination of catalogues may reveal that the product is widely available on a direct marketing basis.

(**d**) Increased ownership and acceptance of credit cards and bank accounts offering cheque book facilities have also contributed to the growth of direct marketing because consumers can order and pay for the products from their own home. A cheque can be posted to the supplier or the credit card number can be given over the telephone.

(**e**) Improved transportation and postal systems make deliveries of goods easier, safer and quicker.

(**f**) The legislation covering direct marketing offers extensive protection to consumers and as a result there is less suspicion and/or anxiety when purchasing products this way. To advertise in the national press and the local evening papers in many countries it is now necessary to obtain clearance through a newspaper publishers association or similar body and pay a fee to a fund to indemnify readers of the newspaper against loss due to the default in the supply of goods.

(**g**) Some media owners have also contributed to the growth of direct marketing by showing a willingness to offer free advertising space to advertisers in return for a pre-agreed percentage commission on the sales generated through the advert. This approach – forming part of direct response advertising – is called **per item advertising** and the general idea is very simple. An advertiser can obtain free advertising space (which the media owner could have sold). All orders generated are sent to the media owner. The media owner will forward the orders to the supplier having full knowledge of the number of units ordered and of the commission owed. Small companies lacking the finance to advertise nationally – often involving the expense of colour – may have the opportunity to do so by this method, and media owners, through their commission, may be able to generate a far greater revenue from advertising space than they could have from selling the space at a set price. Bear in mind, however, that it must be a good sales idea for the media owner to accept a per item advertising proposition.

(**h**) A major boost for direct marketing has also been received from a rather surprising source: distributors themselves. When a marketing trend is established, organisations need to adapt to it or face the consequences. A major lesson can be found in the USA which is likely to apply to many other countries in the very near future. Consumers are sent an in-home video display catalogue which they can use to order products from a retailer. Television is also being used to encourage direct purchases. In Britain records and cassettes are often sold this way, but in America the system is used for many more products.

(i) Finally, consumers seek increased leisure time and they have less time to spend shopping or travelling to shopping centres to seek out – in particular – unusual speciality goods, especially if they live in remote areas.

It would appear that direct marketing will evolve further, and certain products which do not lend themselves to it today could prove ideal in the future.

Summary

Advantages of direct marketing

- It is an alternative when there is difficulty in using the more usual distribution channels or where distributors are not making enough effort to sell the product or service, e.g. selling double glazing services can be difficult through DIY stores.
- It is useful when there is the need to examine or explain and/or demonstrate a product. A house, for instance, would need examining before it could be fitted with double glazing and direct marketing allows for calls from sales representatives. Few user purchasers – in particular industrial buyers – would purchase without a detailed examination and possibly the opportunity to talk with other companies that have purchased.
- User markets encourage the use of visits from salespersons due to the high value of their purchases, their concentration in geographical areas and the need for technical advice. The normal situation in industrial and reseller markets is that the sales representative regularly visits customers to promote sales and resolve problems, but the customer orders direct from the supplier, as and when needed, and the goods are delivered against a telephoned or written order.
- The avoidance of high profits required by intermediaries may also make direct marketing a sensible alternative.
- Difficulties with deliveries by intermediaries or lack of retail outlets, particularly where consumers are widely dispersed, often living in remote areas, is a situation that encourages direct marketing.
- Direct marketing can be an extension of current activities to broaden the market and reach people who are likely to purchase if they are regularly informed, e.g. book clubs and record clubs or a chain of shops selling books. Usually the books sold through the club will be the higher priced books.

Disadvantages of direct marketing

- Considerable capital is needed for door-to-door selling to provide sample goods for salespersons as well as to pay the salesforce. It is a lot less expensive to send one or two representatives to convince wholesalers to stock and sell. Direct mail and direct response advertising is not always an adequate alternative to personal selling. High priced complex items will not be purchased simply as a result of receiving promotional literature.
- There are high costs of promotion, packaging and delivery. These apply more to consumer markets where customers are widely dispersed and are usually purchasing just one item. Delivery costs to industrial and reseller customers is generally lower per item as they are regularly purchasing higher quantities.
- Marketing direct to consumers has difficulties in identifying potential customers/audience/readers. The normal methods are:

  (a) *Direct response advertising*: The media owners (press, TV, radio) will provide details of the socio-economic groups who use their media, the numbers viewing/listening/reading or circulation figures and often demographic information such as age and sex.

  (b) *Direct mail*: Mailing lists may have to be purchased that provide the names and addresses of individuals constituting the target audience, e.g. car drivers, investors, people in a certain occupation. If this option is not possible then the company may have to devise its own list which can be very difficult except in the case of industrial and reseller markets where there are usually trade directories that may be used to locate potential customers.

  (c) *Personal selling to consumers and mail drops*: Direct observation may also be used. For example, personal sales representatives selling double glazing may select areas where older houses exist that may be needing their windows changing and then visually identify houses that could represent potential customers. With mail drops certain types of people may be noted and the drop, for example, might be done by slipping promotional literature under the windscreen wipers of cars that are over three years old.

- Direct marketing may be frustrated by a lack of marketing knowledge. Defining the target market, arranging promotional literature, answering enquiries, planning media coverage and/or obtaining mailing lists takes some marketing skill which the newcomer to business rarely appreciates. A way around this problem for a small business is for the proprietor or manager to read a book on the subject of mail order and/or use the services of a small advertising agency.
- People being solicited by direct marketing may often resent the method, whereas people visiting a shop show some interest in purchasing.

When supplying **industrial and reseller markets**, direct (personal) selling is the most common method, although catalogues for selling office, educational and light service equipment are often used. In consumer markets over 90 per cent of distribution is through wholesaler, agents and retailers, and they will probably always represent the main method of distribution – though direct marketing is still continuing to grow.

BASIC RULES OF DISTRIBUTION
One needs to bear in mind some basic rules which ought to govern decision making on distribution.

- (**a**) Offer the right product in a way which is acceptable to the target market.
- (**b**) Make evaluation, selection and purchase as easy as possible.
- (**c**) Supply the market and channels with the right quantities at the right time.
- (**d**) Maintain satisfaction of all concerned by offering satisfactory profit margins to distributors and adequate information and the right benefits to the final purchasers.
- (**e**) Integrate distribution with the other elements – price, promotion, product – of the marketing mix.

■ 4 SELECTION OF DISTRIBUTION CHANNELS

Decisions about the best channels of distribution to be used can only be reached once the following have been considered.

PRODUCT CHARACTERISTICS
Size, price, perishability, status attached to the product, nature of benefits offered by the product, etc. must all be taken into account. Perishable goods for instance will need a short speedy distribution channel and stocks need to be kept low. Impulse purchase items usually require shops that sell low price items for display. Does the product require distributive outlets that have staff that have experience with the product, e.g. cameras, or staff who can supply after sales service?

MARKET CHARACTERISTICS
These include size of target market, profile of potential buyers, geographic dispersion of market, customer expectations, etc. For example, high socio-economic groups purchasing speciality items will probably buy from departmental stores or speciality shops. A large widely dispersed market often requires the use of wholesalers/retailers for distributing or, possibly, direct marketing.

COMPETITOR METHODS
The types of distribution channels used by competitors and the geographic spread of their operations should be considered closely, although one should not be completely led by what competitors are doing.

FINANCIAL POSITION OF THE COMPANY

Consideration of the ability to supply the required quantities, offer adequate promotional support and supply at a price acceptable to the channels used, may limit the company to distributing solely in a segment or specific geographical area of the market.

ECONOMIC CONDITIONS

Declining economic conditions may cause a company to start to sell abroad in countries where the price can be maintained.

SEASONAL FACTORS

If products produced on a seasonal basis cannot be fully sold within the season, refrigeration facilities of particular wholesalers and retailers may be needed so that the product may be sold at other times of the year or the product may be sent for sale in other countries.

AVAILABILITY OF AN ADEQUATE NETWORK

If an adequate network does not exist or cannot be entered, due possibly to competition, then a company may have to consider direct marketing.

MARKETING OBJECTIVES BEING PURSUED

If early market saturation is needed to obtain a firm foothold in the market then the company may need to use as many outlets as possible.

DISTRIBUTOR RESISTANCE

This may cause a company to buy its own outlets, i.e. vertical or horizontal integration.

LEGAL RESTRICTIONS

The channels that may be used may be limited by legal restrictions. For example, certain drugs will have to be distributed via pharmacists on the written authority of a doctor.

■ 5 DISTRIBUTION STRATEGIES

The choice of strategy will be influenced by the number of intermediaries the company wants to use, the degree of market coverage sought and how exposed the company wants its product to be. There are three main distribution strategies/policies.

1 Intensive distribution

Companies selling convenience goods and in particular everyday foods, regular domestic purchases, sweets/candy, cigarettes, etc. will usually seek to sell through as many outlets as possible within a given area to ensure that the market place is fully covered and to obtain every sales opportunity. This may even involve the use of street stands and vending machines, depending on the product.

2 Exclusive distribution

A supplier offers exclusive rights to very few carefully selected intermediaries without causing conflict of interest between them. The company may try to create or protect the product image through the intermediary's image, e.g. through Harrods, Macy's or Selfridges. Alternatively the company may encourage certain well chosen distributive outlets to stock a new product on the promise that they will be the only ones selling in the area.

The tendency for some shopping and speciality goods being sold in this way is increasing, as in the case of designer clothes and fashionable domestic products. The company will usually attempt to obtain high street outlets that are speciality shops or departmental stores.

3 Selective distribution

Selective distribution is a half way house between intensive and exclusive distribution and may be used for a whole variety of products. The manufacturer will attempt to gain adequate market coverage by selecting appropriate (but not necessarily exclusive) outlets through which the product or product range may be sold, e.g. solely through variety stores, hypermarkets and supermarkets, but any combination may be arranged in relation to the particular product and market.

■ CONCLUSION

We will conclude this chapter by using one product to illustrate a variety of distribution channels that may be used to distribute and sell. Figure 6.10 illustrates the distribution channels that may be used by a German producer marketing German white wine. The company sells to four countries: Germany (the home market), the UK, Austria and Denmark.

Fig. 6.10 *Distribution network of a German wine producer supplying Germany, Austria, UK and Denmark*

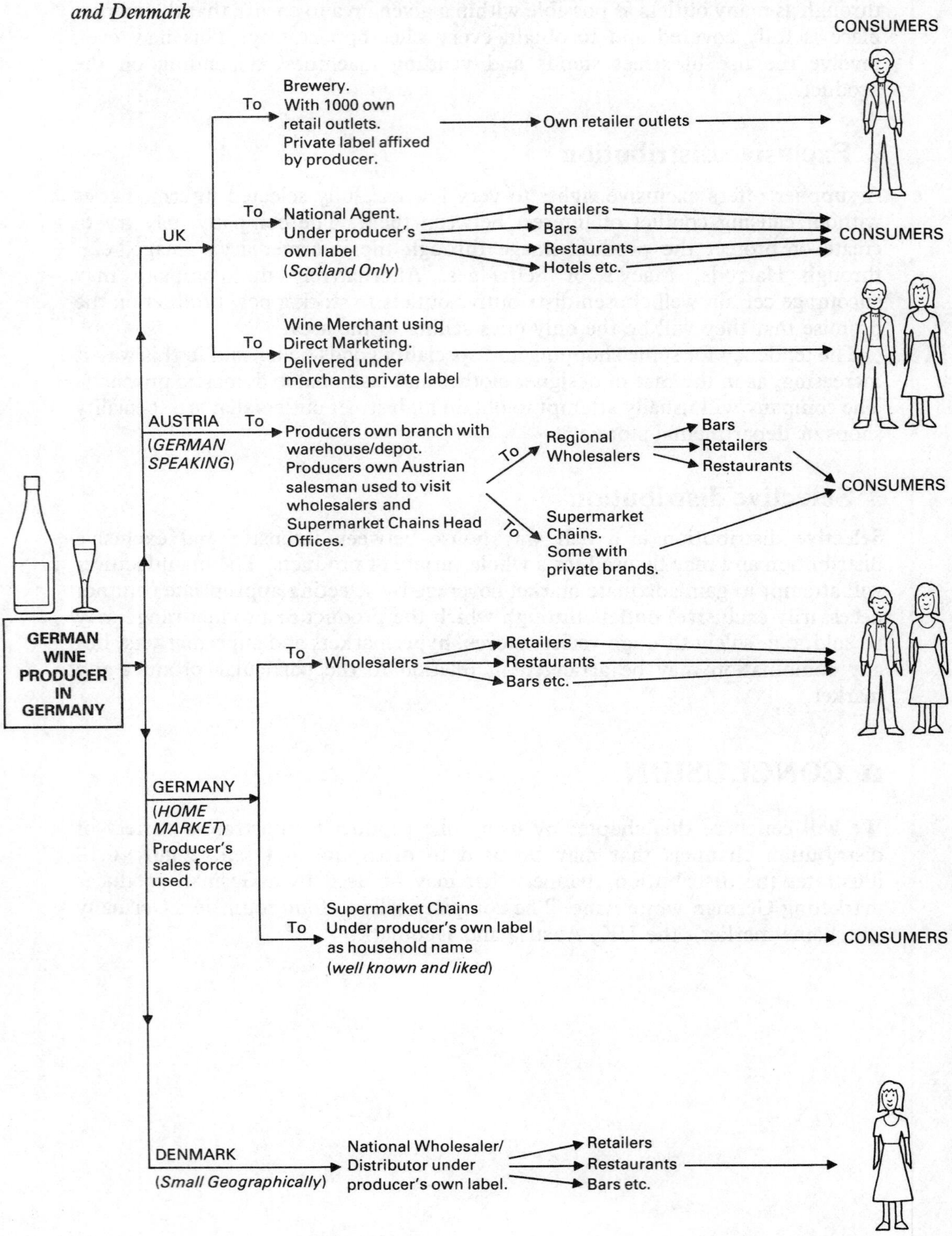

■ STUDY AND EXAM TIPS

1 Familiarise yourself with the major selection criteria to be used in assessing distribution alternatives. What is right for one product may be totally inadequate for another.

2 Direct marketing involves a series of distinct activities. Distinguish between the main alternatives and be prepared to discuss the major qualities of each alternative.

3 Remember to represent distribution as a marketing activity which is designed to achieve and maintain consumer satisfaction, not simply a method for a company to get its goods to purchasers. This will often require distribution being analysed in relation to the other 3 Ps in the marketing mix.

4 Examine closely the major reasons behind the growth of direct marketing. Most of us have already purchased something through the post, so the reasons behind *your* purchase could prove an ideal example or justification to be used in the examination.

5 Do not confuse **distribution channels** with **distribution strategies**.

■ SELF ASSESSMENT QUESTIONS

Answer the following questions without reference to the text and then refer to the answers given at the end of the manual to determine your score. Award yourself 1 mark for each complete question that you answer correctly. If you scored 7 or more you are reading efficiently. Where you answer wrongly check back in the chapter to see what the answer should have been.

1 Define distribution as defined in this chapter.

_____

_____

2 One of the three major types of organisation in the channels of distribution for consumer goods and services is agents or brokers. Name the other two.

(a) _____

(b) _____

3 Name the major direct marketing method used to sell to industrial and reseller markets.

_____

4 When a manufacturer sells to a wholesaler who sells to a retailer who sells to the consumer, how many marketing stages are involved?

_____

5 One key essential ingredient for ensuring distribution of a suitable product is the physical delivery. Name three more.

(a) _____

(b) _____

(c) _____

6 Complete the sentence:

Effective physical distribution relies on delivering the right product in the right quantities _____

7 One method employed in direct marketing for promoting goods which subsequently will be sent direct is **catalogue selling**. Name three more.

(a) _____

(b) _____

(c) _____

8 Name three methods of non shop retailing mentioned in this chapter.

(a) _____

(b) _____

(c) _____

9 One factor in deciding on a choice of distribution channels is the product. Name four more.

(a) _____

(b) _____

(c) _____

(d) _____

10 One distribution strategy is **intensive distribution**. Name the other two.

(a) _____

(b) _____

■ EXAMINATION QUESTIONS

The Institute of Marketing

1 Using examples, discuss the factors which would influence the choice between intensive, exclusive or selective distribution.

2 How do you account for the growth in interest in the management of physical distribution?

What factors should be considered in designing the physical distribution system?

3 For what reasons might a company consider limiting the number of retail outlets it will supply?

The Association of Business Executives

4 What factors influence the choice of distribution channels?

5 When developing distribution plans, management will need to consider what degree of market exposure it will utilise in marketing a product. Identify the three different types of distribution strategy and suggest under what circumstances management may choose to use each of them.

6 Identify and discuss the distribution alternatives that a manufacturer might employ to effectively serve a consumer market (ignore physical distribution). Identify the influencing factors you will consider before selecting the most attractive distribution alternatives.

Institute of Commercial Management

7 Direct selling is the most expensive method of establishing contact with the potential customer. Explain why this method is so widely used in the selling of products and services to industrial customers, but is used much less in consumer selling.

8 What are the advantages of direct marketing and what factors might affect response rates? How are readership classes normally defined?

7 | Personal selling

The best advertisement is a good product
Alan H. Meyer

People often confuse marketing with selling or vice versa. Many believe that a salesforce cannot be marketing orientated due to the nature of their function which fundamentally is to make sales. People feel that a salesperson will try to achieve a sale irrespective of a customer's needs or wants, and as a result of this the marketing orientation of a salesforce is challenged. This view is extremely short sighted, because salespeople represent a vital tool of marketing and therefore, a marketing orientated organisation will attempt to ensure that salespeople operate within the marketing and sales policy of the company. The marketing orientated company will also try to minimise the amount of forceful selling needed by producing a product that the market – or a segment of the market – needs.

Seen in this context it is understandable that the salesforce are not simply there to sell but to transfer the company's philosophy to the marketplace, communicate important issues to selected audiences, aid consumer decision making, explain and possibly demonstrate the product(s), protect and enhance a company's reputation, collect information, solve customer problems, remove anxieties and also act as an integral aspect of the promotion mix.

Selling, therefore, is a function of marketing which must be fully integrated with all other marketing functions present within the organisation.

We see salespeople when we go shopping, we may have had a salesperson try to sell to us over the telephone or at our door, but the salespeople that we do not often see are those who make appointments with and travel to visit customers. The reason for this is that they are usually visiting industrial or reseller purchasers. It is this latter type of salesperson that we will consider in this section as they are probably the most skilled in negotiating sales with professional buyers. Salespeople that travel out from the company to visit customers are referred to as 'field salespeople'. Elements of much of their work, nevertheless, often apply to many other types of salespeople.

Throughout this book we are using the term 'salesperson' and 'salespeople' in recognition of the fact that many more women are now entering the field of selling. The male gender terms 'salesman' and 'salesmen' have therefore become unrepresentative and inappropriate.

The aspects of sales we will consider in the three parts of this chapter are:

1 role of the sales manager and the structure of the sales organisation and salesforce
2 role of salesperson
3 recruitment and selection, training and personal characteristics of salespeople

■ 1 ROLE OF THE SALES MANAGER

Sales managers, the people in charge of the sales department, are by and large just like any other manager. They must fulfil the functions of management with regard to their department, namely set objectives, plan, organise, direct, co-ordinate and control the human, financial and physical resources for which they are responsible (see Chapter 10). However, there are functions such as those that are detailed below that collectively distinguish their work from that of other managers. Sales managers should:

(a) **Plan and co-ordinate** and control activities of the salespeople by advising and deciding on:

- Number of customers to be visited on a daily, weekly or quarterly basis.
- Number of times to visit each customer in order to obtain repeat orders or in order to convince potential customers to buy for the first time.
- Average length of time of each visit, e.g., average time taken for the sales interviews plus travelling between customers.
- Routing decisions made by salespeople. It will be pointless to allow individual salespeople to waste a lot of time by choosing the wrong routes to follow when visiting their customers.
- The types of customers various members of the salesforce may or should visit.

(b) **Improve performance** of salespeople by devising attractive training or sales development programmes which can enhance the professional and personal skills of the salespeople.

The sales manager is the link between the marketing or sales director and the salesforce and is judged by the success of the salespeople.

There are four main ways of ensuring that the salesforce perform their functions effectively:

- Consider the **personality of individual salespeople** and allow for it in any development programmes used.
- Examine the **level of technical and selling knowledge** of all salespeople employed and identify areas of possible improvement.
- Examine the **level of motivation** among salespeople by considering levels of pay, working conditions, training needs, attitudes towards management and personal expectations.

- **Sales manager's own style of management.** Salespeople must be clear about and in full agreement with the tasks they have been set. The sales manager must be able to define and explain the task/s and discuss any problems or ideas presented by the salespeople.

(c) Be directly **involved with recruitment and training** of salespeople. These tasks will be discussed in detail in later parts of this chapter because any mistakes in these areas will lead to extensive problems in relation to the overall effectiveness of the salesforce.

(d) Develop **efficient organisational and co-ordination procedures for the salesforce and the sales office.** In some companies the sales office will come under the control of the sales manager. In others it may be the responsibility of a commercial manager. The salespeople must feel confident that orders they obtain will be processed correctly by the sales office and will be delivered on time. After all it is often the case that the salesperson has to take the brunt of complaints by customers concerning delivery.

(e) Co-ordinate **post sales services.** Many products require services like maintenance, repairs, training of purchaser's staff on the use of the product, etc. It may be the duty of the sales manager to ensure that these services are carried out efficiently, on time and at a pre-agreed cost, so that complaints are not generated and good relations with the customers are maintained.

This function may alternatively be the responsibility of a separate maintenance or customer services manager, but if it is not done well it will make subsequent sales to the customer(s) difficult for the salesforce to achieve.

(f) Help in achieving the **marketing objectives** of the company, as expressed in the marketing plan, which could revolve around growth, profitability, survival, new product introduction, maintenance of product and company reputation and, most importantly, maintenance of good working relationships with current customers.

(g) Ensure **efficient budgeting**, which seeks sales maximisation at the lowest possible cost.

(h) Seek **consistency with advertising, sales promotions and public relations campaigns** undertaken by the company. As we have already seen, personal selling also plays a vital role in the promotion mix, and total consistency and co-ordination beween the promotional assets is essential.

Which of the above functions the sales manager would be responsible for would depend more on the way the company is conducting its marketing effort than what the sales manager chooses to believe he or she should be responsible for.

Sales organisation structures

Every department of an organisation must be structured in a way which allows the people involved to maximise their performance so that they can contribute positively to the overall goals of the organisation.

This idea applies equally well to the sales function of an organisation and every sales manager must seek to evaluate and employ the most suitable structure for the sales department. A poorly structured department cannot function effectively and frustrations, arguments, misunderstandings and poor performance will result.

New salespeople and sales office staff must be introduced into a **structure** which allows for the following:

- integration of effort
- clear identification of lines of authority
- ability to respond efficiently, speedily and accurately to market opportunities
- personal expectations, needs, wishes and ambitions
- effective communication of ideas and concerns

It should be remembered that the structure of an organisation or a department represents the basic skeleton upon which operations can be built. A poorly controlled system or inappropriate structure will be the equivalent of trying to build a castle on sand – sooner or later it will collapse.

Bearing all these factors in mind, we are now in a position to examine the different **types of sales department organisation structures** which can be adopted by companies:

(**1**) organisation by function
(**2**) organisation by customer
(**3**) organisation by product groups
(**4**) organisation by region/area
(**5**) compound/combined structure

Each type of structure will be favoured under different conditions.

1 ORGANISATION BY FUNCTION

In this organisational structure each section of the department deals with a separate function as illustrated in Fig. 7.1. This enables specialisation and,

Fig. 7.1

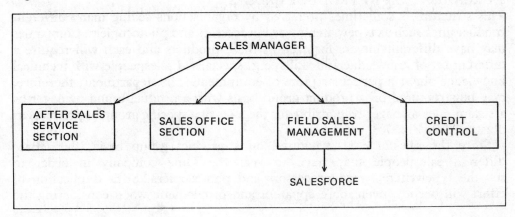

therefore, a build up of knowledge of specific functions, but it limits the amount of knowledge that people in certain sections have about the work of other sections.

2 ORGANISATION BY CUSTOMER (OR END USE)

Sometimes a company provides products that are purchased by large groups of customers that have different needs and possibly belong to different industries. To service these different needs the department may be structured according to the category of customer. For instance, an oil company selling oil, diesel and petrol may be structured as shown in Fig. 7.2.

Fig. 7.2

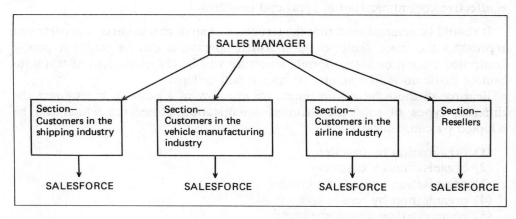

This has the advantage of building up knowledge of the needs of particular categories of customers and people working in the various industries may be selected and trained by the company for selling. If, however, operating costs are to be kept down it does rely on customers being many in number or located close together to keep travelling time and costs to a minimum.

3 ORGANISATION BY PRODUCT GROUPS

This structure is sometimes preferred by organisations selling many different product lines such as typewriters, word processors and photocopiers. Companies may have different buyers for each of these products and each will require a different set of knowledge and skills, e.g. specialised salespeople with technical knowledge about a particular piece of equipment. The department, therefore, may be structured on a product group basis with a product/brand manager or assistant sales manager responsible for the sales of a specific group of products as illustrated in Fig. 7.3.

Since the salesforce is structured on a product group basis, then three different salespeople may have to visit the same company in order to sell the typewriters, word processors and photocopiers. Such duplication of effort will become even more apparent and problematic when considering the

Fig. 7.3

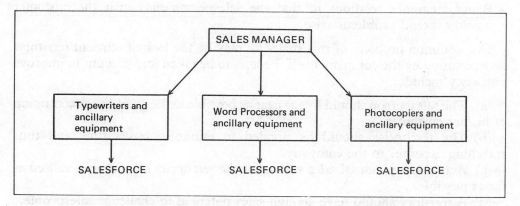

possibility of having to sell these products to many potential customers scattered throughout a large country. Salespeople may be experts on their products but they will have great difficulty in servicing large geographic markets. This problem gives rise to the importance of geographic areas as a means of structuring.

4 ORGANISATION BY REGION/AREA

This is perhaps the most common system used and it is preferred by companies which operate in large, geographically dispersed markets with a limited product range and where a regional sales manager can effect better control of the sales function in the regions. Figure 7.4 illustrates the structure.

Fig. 7.4

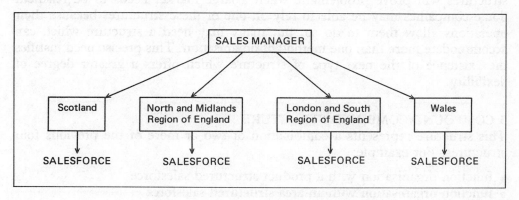

Where salespeople operate on an area basis, the advantages will include:

• Equitable work loads could result from efficient division of the market to be reached.
• Clear limits to each salesperson's operations are possible.

- Less wastage of time in travelling.
- Better customer relations in that the salesperson may visit the customer quickly should problems arise.

One common problem of this structure may be the lack of efficient territory/area planning by the company itself. Factors to be taken into account to improve efficiency include:

(a) The salesperson should live as near as possible to the greatest concentration of his/her customers.

(b) The territories should be divided to minimise travel time and thus travelling expenses to the company.

(c) Actual and potential sales volume of the territories should be equalised as far as possible.

(d) A territory should have enough sales potential to challenge salespeople.

This structure is very attractive when the company is offering similar products to a well defined geographic market and operates through regional wholesalers or company warehouses. It will prove problematic if many different complex products need to be marketed from one central point of distribution. Salespeople could be experts on a given area or product group, but they may find it impossible to handle a wealth of unrelated products.

At this point it is worth considering the relative advantages and disadvantages of the structures discussed. They all offer a specific area of specialisation (function, product, customer or area) but they all seem to suffer from certain limitations. The function and area structures cannot readily accommodate a wide range of unrelated products or markets, the product and customer based structures will prove problematic when a large market needs to be reached. Some companies may be able to rely on one of these structures because their operations allow them to do so, but many may need a structure which can accommodate more than one method of organisation. This precise need justifies the existence of the next type of structure which offers a greater degree of flexibility.

5 COMPOUND/COMBINED STRUCTURE

This structure represents a combination of two or more of the previous four structures. For example:

- function organisation with a product structured salesforce
- function organisation with an area structured salesforce
- product organisation with an area structured salesforce

Many more mixes may be arranged.

Each combination involves the basic areas of specialisation already discussed and helps individual companies overcome the limitations identified for each structure considered in isolation.

A product structured department with an area structured salesforce, for instance, will involve salespeople allocated to specific areas specialising in a specific range of products. Other salespeople, in the same area, may handle a different range of products which minimises any duplication of effort resulting from having to visit the same customers.

An example of a more complex structure (area – product groups – area) is shown in Fig. 7.5.

Fig. 7.5

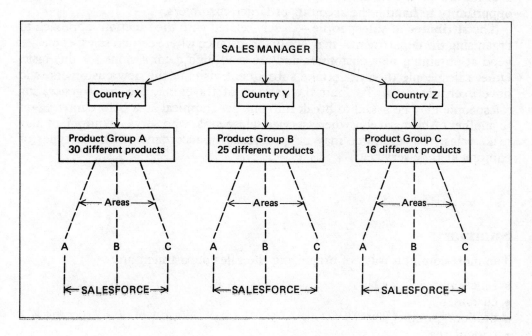

The actual decision on the structure of the organisation and/or salesforce will depend on the following issues:

- nature of the products
- number/variety of products sold. The greater the variety of products the greater the need for the product/area structure
- size and diversity of markets to be served
- resources available (human, physical, financial)
- company objectives

NOTE: It would be appropriate at this point to read once again the second part of Chapter 1 on organising the marketing department to identify further advantages and disadvantages of organising by function, product, brand or market.

Salesforce structure

As already indicated the work of the salesforce may be organised in a similar way to that of the sections of the department, i.e. by customer, product group or area but there are two other ways which are sometimes used, namely by **size/value** of customer and **attributes of the salesperson**.

When **size of customer** applies it is usually because the company believes their importance as a customer warrants a senior salesperson calling on them to ensure mistakes do not occur and the customer is not lost. However, this can be a disincentive to new salespeople who feel that they are not being given the opportunity to handle the accounts of larger customers.

The **attributes of salespeople** – closely related with the functions approach to organising the department – may apply for instance where certain salespeople are good at obtaining new customers and are paid high commissions for this task. Other salespeople then undertake subsequent visits to the new customers who have been obtained. To limit the amount of travelling, the order-generating salespeople may be asked to break into one geographical area before moving on to another. Alternatively, where service salespeople who service equipment also make sales, the salesforce may be structured in accordance with the types of equipment they service.

Summary

The most common ways of organising the sales department are:

- function
- customer
- product group
- region/area

or as is more usually the case, a

- compound/combined basis (mixture of two or more of the others).

The most common ways of organising the salesforce are:

- customer type
- customer size
- product group
- area/region
- salesperson's functions/attributes (see the section on types of salespeople later in this chapter)
- combination of two or more of the above five

The most common method probably tends to be organising by area/region.

■ 2 ROLE OF SALESPEOPLE

Basic responsibilities and/or duties of a salesperson

Salespeople are expected to perform a wide variety of selling and non selling tasks beyond their central purpose of making sales and the following list outlines the most important tasks (responsibilities and duties). A salesperson should attempt to perform the following:

(a) **Act as an ambassador for the company**. All salespeople represent their company in the market place and their approach and general behaviour will have a direct effect on the way people view them and their company.

(b) **Be a competent and helpful advisor** to current and potential customers so that questions are clearly answered, worries are removed, anxiety is minimised and confidence towards the product, the company and the salesperson is developed.

(c) **Plan the most profitable use of his or her time** so that many customers can be visited during the course of a working day.

(d) **Compile a record system** to facilitate forward planning of his or her sales work.

(e) **Act as a two-way communicator** between customers and the company.

(f) **Act as a reporter on the activities of competitors**.

(g) **Achieve personal sales targets** agreed with the sales manager which will invariably entail seeking out new customers as well as maintaining or improving sales to current customers.

(h) **Develop personal and professional skills** so that job and career goals are achieved.

(i) In some instances where products are small, **deliver the products**.

(j) **Become an effective organiser**, manager and administrator of clerical, statistical and correspondence procedures and responsibilities related to the work.

(k) **Show initiative and take both preventive and remedial actions** when problems become evident.

Collectively the salesforce as a whole also has these objectives and must blend in with the overall marketing aims of the company.

Types of salespeople

How many of these attributes the salesperson should have and which are the most important will depend on the type of salesperson and his or her level of responsibilities. The general tendency is towards **order (sales) makers** or towards **order takers** with the former enjoying more importance with most companies. The categories in which various types of salespeople may be placed may be identified by the following list. The types of salespeople that exist tend to relate to the main purpose of their work with the following five being the main categories.

(a) **Order makers** may be considered as the most creative salespeople because their main function is to obtain orders from existing or new customers. Their performance is evaluated in terms of actual sales. Typical areas in which order makers may be found include encyclopaedia, double glazing salespeople, etc., though they do exist in most areas of selling.

(b) **Order takers** are less creative than order makers because they mainly respond to orders requested by interested parties. Many sales assistants, for instance, rarely participate in the decision making process of customers unless a customer enters the shop and asks for information and advice.

(c) **Goodwill ambassadors** are the type of salespeople who try to maintain good working relationships with established customers. They attempt to retain customers by regular visiting and resolving problems customers may have. They tend to obtain additional orders or generate sales leads through existing customers.

(d) **Technical advisors** are specialist salespeople concentrating on explaining the concept of and technology relating to a product, demonstrating the product for customers, undertaking minor repairs, etc. They are mainly used for selling technically complex products which need detailed explanation in order to effect a sale.

(e) **Delivery people**. The importance of these salespeople is often under-estimated because a lot of their work is concerned with the actual delivery of the goods to the customer. Timing of the deliveries, accurate invoicing, and the general behaviour of the delivery person will have a direct effect on how customers perceive the company represented by the salesperson, e.g. bread and milk salespeople concentrate on efficient delivery while taking and sometimes making orders.

Those whose role is predominantly selling are usually referred to as salespeople; those who are mainly goodwill ambassadors are often referred to as sales representatives.

Prospectors also have a major role to play in the sales process. Their role is not to sell but to undertake that part of a salesperson's work concerned with identifying prospective customers and making appointments with them for a salesperson of the company to make a sales visit. They are not used in the efforts of every salesforce but where they are used they may save salespeople considerable time in hunting for new customers.

The sales process

It is appropriate to complete our examination of personal selling by considering the area which is likely to interest salespeople more than anything else – the **actual selling aspect** of a salesperson's work.

Selling can be very rewarding, interesting, unpredictable and challenging, but at the same time it can be extremely frustrating and hard work. Like any other walk of life, selling needs to be planned very carefully so that individuals involved in this area of business can reap the excellent financial rewards possible for their effort.

The prime objective is to examine the main stages which have to be considered in order to sell. Collectively these stages and the sequence in which they take place are referred to as the **sales process** or selling sequence. It consists of five distinct stages which can be summarised as follows:

(1) prospecting and the pre-approach
(2) the approach
(3) the presentation
(4) closing the sale (the close)
(5) the follow-up (keeping the sale closed)

The fifth is included, and justifiably so, where delivery comes long after the order is taken or/and if the customer is to remain a regular customer.

The recommended stages represent a logical and at the same time practical approach to selling and a basic understanding of what is actually involved during each stage is essential. Before we examine the stages, it is worth noting that the actual sequence and the activities which may take place during the stages may vary quite distinctly from situation to situation. Indeed it is often the case that some stages are not needed at all. For example a salesperson may simply respond to a customer's request to purchase a product. An insurance salesperson on the other hand may have to spend a long time trying to reach a potential customer, trying to make an appointment, explaining alternative insurance schemes and hopefully convincing the customer to buy.

With these considerations in mind we can now proceed to the stages of the sales process and identify the main issues which could lead to a profitable sale, and hopefully, a long term relationship with a new customer.

1 PROSPECTING AND PRE-APPROACH

This is the first stage in the sales process and is concerned with searching for and identifying potential customers (prospecting) and determining how individual prospects (potential customers) should be approached (the pre-approach). This will involve the salesperson in collecting relevant information about potential customers. The information could include:

Consumers

- Age group.
- Occupation and likely income.
- Geographic location.
- Ownership of related products (a houseowner for instance could be interested in double glazing or a fitted kitchen, etc.).

- Interest shown towards the product or service, either in the past or now, e.g. people who have dabbled in shares may be potentials for investment services.

User market purchasers

In the case of user market prospects we would be attempting to obtain information on such aspects as:

- Value of customer to the company.
- Location.
- End use to which the product would be put.
- Amounts the customer already purchases (where applicable).
- Current product supplied by competitors – its features and benefits.

A few of the ways by which prospects can be identified and selected include:

- Recommendations of existing customers, past customers, friends, business acquaintances and social contacts.
- Company records on customers may also provide clues as to potential customers for a new product.
- Telephone directories and, with user-market purchasers, trade directories, trade exhibitions and directories on professions are also sources. Advertisements encouraging suppliers to tender for work are worthwhile sources.
- Mailing lists sold by some companies identifying customers who buy similar products.

The basic objective is to develop an attractive list of potential customers who may be contacted either by the salesperson developing the list or by other salespeople selling the company's products. The quality of the list will affect directly the degree of sales success which can be achieved.

Three basic ingredients, however, must be identified before an individual or a company may be considered a prospect. They are:

(a) **Need**: If individuals identified do not need or are unlikely to need the product or service offered, then they cannot be considered as likely targets or prospects and they should not be considered.

(b) **Means**: A person may need something but cannot necessarily afford it. If affordability is a major constraint then an individual cannot be considered as a prime prospect.

(c) **Authority**: It is pointless seeking to contact people who do not possess the authority to buy something, e.g. a person under the age for making a legally binding agreement.

A good list of prospects should therefore consist of individuals who need something, can afford it and have the power to buy it.

PRE-APPROACH

The pre-approach is concerned with determining the information that is necessary to make the right approach to a prospect and, hopefully, exact a sale.

The following questions indicate just some questions whose answers will help in completing a satisfactory pre-approach.

(**a**) Why should the customer buy? For example, to what use will he or she want to put the pumping machine we have for sale?

(**b**) What particular benefits of our product should we stress in relation to his or her needs?

(**c**) Can we offer ancillary facilities that will help make the sale, such as leasing, HP or an after sales service?

(**d**) Do we have the necessary sales aids and could a demonstration be arranged if necessary?

(**e**) If an interview (visit) is allowed, how should the presentation be conducted?

(**f**) How should we contact the customer? For example a salesperson could write or telephone for an interview or make a cold call (visit without warning).

(**g**) What objections to purchasing may the customer put forward?

(**h**) Who constitutes the decision making unit (DMU) and who in particular is the influencer?

Only when this information is determined can we approach (visit) the customer confident that we have the basics for conducting a **sales interview**, which is the time spent with the customer attempting to obtain a sale and includes the approach, presentation and close-of-sale. The salesperson should finally write down the essential information needed when he or she visits the customer in order not to forget anything, and make certain that all the necessary sales aids are prepared.

2 THE APPROACH

The approach can be a difficult time for newcomers to selling as they are not quite certain how to open the sales interview. In fact, this is not too difficult a task if some basic rules are remembered.

One rule is **first sell the interview not the product**. Remember time is valuable to a buyer so he or she is first waiting to hear the reason for listening to what you have to say. If you immediately commence by attempting to push the product you may cause caution in the mind of the customer. Instead try to gain the chance of an interview by asking the customer a question the answer to which will be of particular interest. For example, instead of starting the interview with, 'I have come to see if you are interested in a new product we are marketing', you could start with, 'If I could show you a way to reduce breakages of your product during production would you be interested?'. Remember it is not what your product is that is important it is what it can do for the customer.

Once the buyer is willing to listen, **ask questions** the answers to which will give you a good idea which features of your product will be of greatest interest to the buyer. If you were selling a car for instance, one question you may ask is if the person has back problems as a result of driving.

Sell yourself as a **professional**. You should look presentable and not be a constant teller of jokes, especially with customers who do not know you well.

Treat the customer's problems as if they were your own. This will require you to listen carefully and note his or her concerns. A buyer is more favourably disposed to a salesperson who shows genuine care for his or her problems than one who is simply intent on making a sale.

3 THE PRESENTATION

Having obtained during the approach the necessary information for conducting the rest of the interview you must now **present your proposal** to the customer. This will require that you change **features of your product** into **benefits to the customer**. For example, 'This car has an adjustable back rest in the driver's seat (feature) which cuts down troubles that sometimes occur in the small of the back of drivers (benefit to customer).' Stress only major benefits that relate to the needs of the customer so that you have others you may call on should the customer require further convincing.

If it is a small product **let the customer hold it** while you highlight and illustrate features, so that the customer feels confident about using the product and is feeling that it already is his or hers. If it is a large product use sales literature, diagrams or/and a video to illustrate it.

Sometimes a demonstration may be needed to put the customer's mind fully at rest. If this is the case make certain that you have **surveyed the specific needs** of the customer, e.g. will the machine you are selling shake the foundations of the customer's floor to pieces? An effective survey and demonstration that a product can do what you promised is one of the finest and honourable ways of making a sale. Try to get all members of the DMU along when giving a demonstration so that you may make the sale on the spot. Leave the suggestion of the price until the end of your presentation. A customer cannot evaluate the worth of a product until being made aware of all that it can do to satisfy his or her needs.

Having made an effective presentation, given a demonstration and answered questions of the buyer, and possibly other members of the DMU, you may find that the customer offers to buy. On the other hand it may be that while generally satisfied he or she is hesitant and therefore, you will have to attempt to close the sale.

4 CLOSING THE SALE

This is the point in the sales interview when you have to try and obtain a Yes to purchasing from the customer. Remember you are there to try and sell your product which you believe suits his or her needs – in fact, the customer may want to buy but needs help in deciding.

Never try to force or rush a close or you may frighten the customer off the purchase. If you use **closes** (techniques for closing the sale), i.e. getting the customer to say Yes, choose the most appropriate to the situation. There are many to choose from. For instance, if the customer raises an objection, and objections are the most common way customers attempt to avoid purchasing, then you might try an **objection close**.

For example, the customer may claim the price is too high. If this is the situation and you can adjust your price a little ask the customer what price he or she expects. If you can meet the price do not accept immediately; instead act as though you cannot and ask if this is the only reason why he or she will not purchase. Believing you cannot meet the price suggested the customer may confirm that there would be a purchase if it were not for the price. Once it has been confirmed that this is his or her sole objection you can then, with reluctance, say that you will make an exception and sell it at that price as you wish to obtain him or her as a future customer. Then immediately start completing the order for the customer to OK. **Avoid asking customers to sign**. We are constantly told not to sign anything. Okaying something is not so distressful.

The **order book close** is one regularly used by salespeople who sell to companies through the company's storeman in charge of stocks. The salesperson suggests or asks what is needed and completes the order as the storeman replies. He or she then simply asks the storeman to OK the order. The purchasing office will then place the order as they believe that the storeman would not have signed if the goods were not needed.

The **alternative choice close** may also be used in which the salesperson simply asks a question such as, 'Which do you prefer – the red or the blue tables?'. Whichever the customer chooses the salesperson assumes he or she wants to purchase and starts completing the order for the customer to OK. If the customer answers neither, the salesperson will rekindle the conversation, ask questions to discover what is causing resistance to the sale and then try another close.

We have placed closing the sale at the end of the presentation but in many sales interview situations, the salesperson, by watching for indications that the customer is ready to purchase, may close the sale before completing his or her presentation. Therefore, **watch for closing signals** throughout the sales interview.

One final note on closing. Whenever you ask a question during an attempt to close, **remain silent**, and wait for the customer to answer. Silence has its own pressure and if you continue talking you will let the customer off the hook. Although you may not particularly like closing, you have to remember that many salespeople, like someone delivering bread with many calls to make each day, do not have time to waste, nor do most customers. Often customers who buy regularly appreciate a salesperson who understands their changing needs and moves the sales process to a prompt but satisfactory close.

5 THE FOLLOW UP (KEEPING THE SALE CLOSED)

If you have obtained an order remember that you may have promised delivery within a certain time or the service of having a machine fitted into place and left working properly. You can still lose the sale if your company does not hold by the promises you made. Therefore, check that everything is proceeding on time and keep the customer informed of any problems that may arise.

If you have promised to visit the customer in the future make sure that you do particularly if he or she is to become a regular customer.

Record essential details of the first sale and for that matter sales that follow so that you can progress the customer's order(s), become increasingly familiar with the customer's needs and have information such as the customer's likes and dislikes that will make further sales visits easier to make.

There is further coverage of the role of sales personnel in part 4 of Chapter 8 and under **Direct Marketing**, Chapter 6.

■ 3 RECRUITMENT, SELECTION AND TRAINING

Recruitment and selection

Recruitment is about obtaining an adequate supply of candidates for selection for positions with the company and ends at the point where the selection process begins.

The first step in recruitment is to be aware of your present or future estimated skilled staffing needs, and the technical qualities needed in the salesforce to keep up with technical changes that are beyond the scope of current salespeople. Recruitment may be necessary to meet the extra work arising from expansion and to replace inadequate staff or those who leave of their own volition.

Company policy will lay down certain guidelines within which recruitment will take place and it is likely that people from the company's personnel department will be brought in, particularly for the initial screening of potential applicants.

Recruitment of an adequate salesforce requires five essential actions.

1 PREPARATION OF A JOB DESCRIPTION

The job description is a document describing the post or job to be filled and it will include such features as the job title, the responsibilities and the duties involved, the skills and knowledge required in the work. Only when a job description is complete can the characteristics and abilities of a candidate to fill the job be undertaken.

2 PREPARATION OF A CANDIDATE SPECIFICATION OR PROFILE

This is a list of characteristics of the sort of applicant who would be ideal for the work as detailed in and made up from the job description, and it will include such factors as: age, general personality, experience, qualifications, achievement levels and possibly health, etc. Those persons responsible for recruitment and selection then have a clear idea of the kind of person they are seeking.

3 MAKING THE POSITION KNOWN

As many sources of potential candidates as possible need to be considered and companies tend to concentrate on the following areas for obtaining applicants:

- The company itself, i.e. considering internal staff for the position. This keeps morale high in the company but severely limits the choice of candidates and thus new ideas.
- Advertising in the media, particularly trade journals.
- Head-hunting in universities, colleges and schools for young salespeople new to selling.
- Although approaching salespeople of competitor companies is often frowned upon, it is a possible source of applicants.
- Recommendations from existing salespeople. Good salespeople often have a tendency to recommend good salespeople but the result may gradually be the forming of cliques with the same attitudes.
- Employment agencies or consultants may be used to find sales staff but their commissions can be very costly.
- Professional bodies, trade association, etc., are aware of potential salespeople seeking work.

4 ISSUE APPLICATION FORMS

Once applicants have applied, application forms for a formal and detailed application for the position may be issued, assuming of course that the applicant has not been rejected due to poor presentation of the letter initially sent when applying.

Application forms should be designed in a way which maximises information from the applicants as they will be used as a method of eliminating applicants who do not readily meet the criteria already set out in the specification.

Essential information that application forms should seek should include:

- Relevant personal and domestic particulars.
- Educational background.
- Selling experience.
- Experience in other, unrelated business areas.
- References.

5 OBTAINING APPLICANTS' REFERENCES

Character or professional references represent additional evaluation criteria and they serve as a means of checking the consistency of information provided by the applicant. Opinions and/or recommendations by third parties can prove extremely valuable but we should not use them as a replacement for our own assessment and evaluation.

Sometimes applicants with considerable experience will provide several previous references but if a salesperson is currently employed the potential employer will invariably have to wait until after selection to obtain a reference from the current employer.

Selection of salespeople

Short-listed applicants (those selected for interview) will be invited to attend a series of interviews and/or tests used by the company.

Good selection techniques can help in identifying competent individuals, produce a highly skilled and self motivated salesforce, reduce labour turnover, reduce training costs and increase sales volume and profitability.

THE SELECTION PROCESS

The selector(s) must try to **predict** the applicant's level of performance in the job. This is always difficult so the following selection process is recommended – though it would need to be adapted to different companies' policies on selection.

The initial interview

Only one or two members of the personnel department may be at the initial interview which should be standardised to ensure uniformity of interview. It is a step which is intended to screen out unlikely candidates.

The candidate should be encouraged to talk freely, a relaxed atmosphere should be created, important issues in the application form should be thoroughly perused and an overall assessment made. The initial interviews should seek to reveal the following:

- Personal characteristics and abilities of the applicant exhibited in the interview situation.
- Whether the applicant's qualifications, experience and personality match the job being offered.
- The applicant's attitude and opinion regarding the job.
- Information which can enable the interviewer to compare all the applicants, such as dress, general appearance, arriving on time for the interview, etc.

Following this initial interview a short list of the most promising applicants will be compiled ready for the sales manager, possibly with one or two other staff, to hold the final interview with each applicant on the short list.

Final interview

The final interview again should also be standardised to ensure relevant topics are considered regarding the applicant's suitability for the post, but it will also have a full ranging aspect in order for the interviewers to evaluate the ideas of the applicant with regard to the function of selling. In this regard the sales manager will invariably play a major role.

Preparation of profile charts and the selection

Using the data collected in the previous stages, the selector(s) can construct a **profile chart** on each short-listed applicant, covering certain vital criteria such as:

impact on others, natural abilities, motivation, adaptability, suitability for position, etc. Each applicant should be graded according to the evaluation criteria applied (whether subjective or objective), the final selection of an applicant made and the person selected informed of his or her success in obtaining the position.

When the person selected does not perfectly fit the specification, then some initial training may be needed before he or she acts as a salesperson for the company.

The final task is to ensure that all unsuccessful applicants are informed that they have not been selected and thanked for applying.

While we have concerned ourselves here with the selection of salesmen the same principles would, of course, apply to selection in other areas of the company.

Training of salespeople

As products become more complex, competitors more competitive, purchasing officers more professional and consumers more demanding, the need for effective salespeople also becomes greater, demanding both initial and continuous training.

The total training – continuously or intermittently undertaken – by a company must:

- Generate the wish to improve in trainees.
- Enable salespeople to achieve a high standard of performance.
- Improve performance of non selling tasks.
- Reduce the amount of supervision required.
- Lead to increased earnings and higher job satisfaction.
- Reduce selling costs.
- Prepare new salespeople for their role and introduce the newcomer to the structure of the company and the sales department, the products sold and the market and customers supplied.

Lack of efficient training will lead to a general malfunction in the salesforce. Danger signals that may indicate that training is needed include:

- Salespeople are becoming merely order takers.
- No new accounts are being obtained.
- Limited or no prospecting is being carried out by the salesforce.
- Higher selling expenses are witnessed.
- Customers are dissatisfied with presentations and product knowledge shown by salespeople.
- Discontent, high staff turnover and low morale.

The total training need of a salesforce at any one time may be represented by the equation:

future salesforce performance needed − current performance = total training needed (training gap)

The training need of the individual – current or new to the company – may be expressed by the equation:

skills and knowledge needed to do the job − current skills and knowledge = training needed (training gap)

DETERMINING THE DETAILS OF THE TRAINING NEED

To evaluate the future training needs in greater detail we must identify key areas where training may be needed for individual salespeople as well as for the force as a whole.

The object is to define standards of performance which need to be achieved and check how they differ from current standards. This may, in some instances, involve the sales manager in travelling with salespeople to evaluate their work. The four key areas to evaluate are listed below.

Quantitative

- Marketing and sales objectives in relation to salesforce performance
- Personal sales quotas agreed against those achieved
- Personal budgets/expenses agreed with those actually resulting
- Levels of prospecting required to ensure new customers

Qualitative

- Appearance of salesperson
- Manner
- Speech
- Attitude
- Personality, etc.

Knowledge needed

- The product, its application(s), features and benefits
- The territory to be covered
- The industry in general and current and future developments
- The company's sales policy regarding price, delivery terms, services, etc.
- The sales process
- The needs of customers and benefits sought

Skills needed

- Ability to carry out prospecting
- Making successful contact with customers
- Presenting the sales proposition
- Identifying customer requirements
- Demonstrating the product
- Using sales aids

- Handling objections
- Closing the sale

TRAINING METHODS

Once the training need has been established an appropriate method of training may be devised to achieve the desired ends. This may be undertaken at the company or externally depending on the training required. The following indicate some training possibilities.

(a) *Demonstrations*: Trainers attempt to show and to explain what they consider the best methods of selling particular products that the company produces and they encourage discussions on the techniques they employ.

(b) *Lectures*: on specific or general topics of relevance to the training programme(s) often presented at local colleges as part of a course.

(c) *Tailor made courses*: designed to help salespeople improve their selling techniques.

(d) *Role playing*: This technique involves trainers and trainees acting as customers and salespeople. Mistakes in the overall approach of salespeople are identified, possibilities for improvement are suggested and corrective actions are discussed.

(e) *Workshops or seminars*: on the theory and techniques of selling.

(f) *Travelling*: with competent salespeople to see what they do, how they plan their daily activities and the methods used in approaching current or prospective buyers/customers, then advising them on better methods.

The training programmes are usually undertaken by the company's trainers at the company, by outside consultants at the company or outside by sales consultants, running training courses for specific industries.

Once training is complete, re-evaluation of performance must be undertaken to check how far training has been successful in achieving its aims and new training gaps identified. Therefore, training (while never representing the whole of a sales manager's work) should, nevertheless, be seen as a continuous process.

PERSONAL CHARACTERISTICS

Well designed training programmes or demonstrations of popular training techniques do not in themselves guarantee results. A number of **personal qualities** must be present in a salesperson attempting to develop within a company's salesforce, a few of which are listed below:

- An adaptable nature to meet changing circumstances and see the viewpoints of others – particularly customers.
- Able to command respect.
- Manner and dress must be appropriate to the position.
- A pleasant personality.
- Self-confident and self-motivated.
- Capable of decision making.

- Enthusiastic and prepared to sell.
- Integrity and regard for the customers and the image of their employer.

If most of the above personal qualities are evident when selecting, then a new salesperson may have been appointed.

A PERSONAL NOTE

More newcomers to marketing obtain work in personal selling, in a shop, over a telephone or as part of a field salesforce than in any other area of marketing. Therefore, it is appropriate to conclude this section with some personal advice on the subject.

Selling provides golden opportunities for advancement and teaches the newcomer a lot about persuading others: skills that will always prove useful for progression in the world of marketing. Selling can also, however, confront people with personal, moral and ethical problems that they may find difficult to resolve. It may be that a salesperson has the opportunity to sell a product that he or she does not believe is right for the potential customer. It may also be the case that a salesperson finds he or she feels that the selling methods of the organisation are unethical. Providing answers to these situations is impossible without knowing the exact circumstances, but some general guidelines may help.

Firstly, ask about the selling methods that a company uses when being interviewed. Do not simply accept any job.

When you start selling analyse the benefits of the product you sell against those of competitors' products. This will give you a good idea of the type of person or organisation your product is right for and the benefits you should stress. Remember you have every right to try hard to sell your product if you believe it is an ideal product for certain people, so do not feel shy about making a sale.

If you have concerns, discuss them with other salespeople to hear their opinions: bring your concerns to the attention of the sales manager. You yourself have to contribute to improving situations; do not simply leave decisions on moral and ethical issues to others. You do not win respect and promotion by sitting on fences. Honest, diplomatically presented, healthy criticism – including praise – can help most organisations develop from the inside.

If we intend buying a product such as a television set we appreciate and respect a salesperson who can properly explain the features of each set in relation to our own particular needs. It makes us feel more sure that we are taking the right decision and more desirous of being served by competent salespeople who have the necessary product knowledge.

■ STUDY AND EXAM TIPS

1 Treat personal selling as an essential function of marketing and in particular the marketing mix.

2 Do not confuse sales organisation structure (see Q4, Exam Questions) with salesforce organisation (see Q6, Exam Questions).

3 Try to remember two or three major aspects of each stage of the sales process as well as the reason for each stage.

4 Remember that a successful salesperson will need to prove him or herself in a number of non selling activities like administration, marketing, intelligence, customer relations, etc.

5 Recruitment and selection, training, the sales process, the tasks of salespeople and the salesforce organisation are five areas of the subject that regularly appear in examinations — so keep testing yourself on these topics.

■ SELF ASSESSMENT QUESTIONS

Answer the following questions without reference to the text and then refer to the answers given at the end of the manual to determine your score. Award yourself 1 mark for each complete question that you answer correctly. If you score 7 or more you are reading efficiently. Where you answer wrongly check back in the chapter to see what the answer should have been.

1 One of the five main functions a sales manager undertakes in his post is planning, co-ordination and control of the salesforce. Name three more.

    (a) _____

    (b) _____

    (c) _____

2 One method of sales organisation is by function. Name two more.

    (a) _____

    (b) _____

3 One way in which the salesforce may be organised is by salesperson's selling attributes. Name three more.

    (a) _____

    (b) _____

    (c) _____

4 Two of the responsibilities and/or duties of a salesperson are to act as an ambassador and to be a competent and helpful advisor. Name three more.

(a) _____

(b) _____

(c) _____

5 Complete the sentence.

There are order takers and order _____

6 One stage of the sales process is the follow up (or keeping the sale closed) stage. Name the other four.

(a) _____

(b) _____

(c) _____

(d) _____

7 One of the three key ingredients for determining if a prospect could translate into a potential customer is need. Name the other two.

(a) _____

(b) _____

8 Recruitment involves five essential actions, one of which is obtaining applicants' references. Name three more.

(a) _____

(b) _____

(c) _____

9 One of the three stages in the selection process is the preparation of profile charts and selection. Name the other two.

(a) _____

(b) _____

10 Complete the equation. Skills and knowledge needed to do the job − Current skills and knowledge = _____

■ EXAMINATION QUESTIONS

The Institute of Marketing

1 Outline and discuss the major steps involved in any effective sales process.

2 Discuss the tasks which the sales representative undertakes in the course of his/her contact with customers.

The Association of Business Executives

3 As the sales manager of a recently established company selling technical products into a competitive market, you are involved in setting up a pro-gramme for the recruitment and training of salesmen. Identify the main features you would consider significant in such a programme, giving reasons.

4 Suggest three different ways in which a sales organisation may be structured and outline the potential applications and likely problems of each.

The Institute of Commercial Management

5 (a) Why is the recruitment and selection of sales staff so critical to a company?

(b) What factors would you consider in recruitment and selection of sales staff?

6 Describe the functions generally performed by salesforces. In what ways may salesforces be organised?

8 The promotion mix

*Advertising is what you do when you can't go
to see somebody*
Fairfax Cone

The provision of information through **promotional methods** assumes great importance in the work of a marketing manager because one of his or her priorities is to inform particular consumer or/and user markets about the benefits of purchasing the company's products or services. Promotions, therefore, attempt to persuade people to respond in a manner desirable to a company and to accomplish this aim a wide variety of communciation methods are used. It is the study of the way in which the methods of promotion available to the marketing manager are mixed that provides us with the term **the promotion mix**. The object of this chapter is to identify and discuss the wide variety of promotional methods available to marketing management in order to maintain its commitment to the marketing plan.

Some writers prefer to use the term the **communication mix** rather than promotion mix, but we tend to follow the view expressed by Kotler that *many* aspects of marketing communicate. For instance, if a high price is set for a product and it is distributed through prestigious retail outlets, there is an implied message that the product is of high quality or prestigious in some way, but this is not an expressed promotional message. Therefore, the word *promotion* will be used and it is defined in the following way.

promotions encompass all the tools in the marketing mix whose major role is persuasive communication

Developing products or introducing services which satisfy needs and wants is of prime importance but it does not automatically lead to sales. The target market has to be informed, encouraged and motivated to purchase through logical, honest, interesting and financially attractive presentation of the product's or service's benefits. To do this we have to determine what the major message is we wish to communicate to a target audience (the reading, viewing or listening audience in the target market the advertiser wishes to reach) and by what method of communication we should communicate the message. The message may, for example, be in the form of an advertisement and the channel of communication commercial television – but there are many more as you will shortly discover.

Four methods of promoting form the promotion mix, and these will constitute the first four parts of this chapter. These are:

1 advertising
2 sales promotions and merchandising
3 public relations
4 personal (direct) selling

We illustrate their relationship in Fig. 8.1.

Fig. 8.1

After considering each of these methods in relation to their value in communications we will consider three other aspects of communications.

5 determining advertising budgets
6 advertising and society
7 promotion mix and plan

■ 1 ADVERTISING

Introduction

Advertising can be defined as:

> *a paid form of non personal presentation of ideas, goods or services by a clearly identified promoter*

Invariably the promoter will be an organisation advertising goods or services to achieve a predetermined goal. That goal may be ultimately to make a profit – as with commercial companies – but it may be to achieve a non profit goal, such as encouraging people to donate to a charity or a political party.

In the case of commercial companies – which are the ones which we will predominantly consider – they mainly advertise to promote their product or service or company (corporate) name to potential customers. Corporate advertising is advertising that attempts to create and/or maintain a favourable image of the company which in turn will reflect a favourable image on all the products the company (corporation) sells. Companies such as ICI, BP, Shell and Esso have regularly used corporate advertising to promote their name and thus their products.

Advertising will generally lack the persuasive power of effective personal selling and is concerned in the main with a one way message going out to potential purchasers. It has, however, a few distinct advantages which are:

- The same essential promotional message can be communicated to a large concentrated or widely dispersed audience at regular periods.
- Images, drama and atmosphere useful in promoting the product, that is not possible with other promotional methods, may be created.
- Customers may be persuaded without pressure.

In the case of marketing to consumer markets, advertising tends to be prominent as a promotional tool whereas when marketing to industrial and reseller markets personal selling becomes more prominent. Nevertheless, advertising is still important particularly for supporting the efforts of salespeople by making the market more receptive to the sales efforts of the salesforce.

Advertising may be divided into two distinct areas:

1 Above-the-line media/advertising refers to advertising carried out through the use of the conventional advertising media, e.g. commercial television, commercial radio, posters, cinemas and the Press (newspapers and magazines). The word *above* has come to indicate that it is an open form of advertising to mass audiences that possibly anyone could see, and that the advertising is done through an independent media organisation such as a newspaper which the advertising company does not control. If a company uses an advertising agency to book the advertising in the media on its behalf, the agency will receive its payment for its work in the form of commission from the media owner unless the amount placed is very low, in which case the agency may make a small charge to the company.

This kind of advertising is used extensively where it is necessary to advertise to a mass of people who are well dispersed in order to reach the proportion of that mass who may be potential purchasers. Because of its wide coverage it is often referred to as **blanket advertising**. In other words, like fishermen, the advertiser casts a wide net in order to get a catch – i.e. the attention of a quantity of those purchasers who form part of the total market.

It may be that a company cannot reach the target audience satisfactorily by other promotional methods. For example, we cannot know the names and addresses of potential purchasers of tins of beans to advertise to them by mailing to their homes. Even if we could, the low price of the product would make posting the adverts (and possibly the tin of beans if they purchase) uneconomical. But by using the media we can instantly advertise to millions in the knowledge that a million or more people who purchase beans will read our advertisement.

2 Below-the-line advertising is a catch all phrase used in advertising to refer to advertising undertaken that is not carried out through the use of the commercial media, but instead through methods over which the company has considerable control, such as exhibiting at trade fairs and exhibitions, point of sale advertising, direct mail, merchandising, etc. We will shortly consider these various promotional methods. The word *below* indicates that there is not an independently owned mass media directly involved and not every one may always have the opportunity to see or read the promoter's message.

These promotional methods are of immense value where the target audience we wish to reach is known or can be selected. For instance, most people visiting a motor show are interested in cars and may purchase. Therefore, if a company exhibits at the show it has the opportunity of promoting and selling to visitors interested in cars. Alternatively, if we obtain a list of members of a national automobile club we can send promotional messages by post to their homes in the knowledge that they own at least one car. If a company is using an advertising agency for arranging its below-the-line activities then the company will have to pay the agency for its work unlike above-the-line advertising where the media pays the agency commission for placing advertising with them.

We can encapsulate the various elements of these forms of promotion in Fig. 8.2.

Fig. 8.2

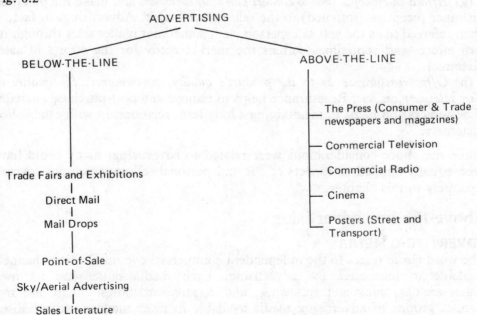

ADVERTISING

BELOW-THE-LINE

ABOVE-THE-LINE

The Press (Consumer & Trade newspapers and magazines)

Commercial Television

Commercial Radio

Cinema

Posters (Street and Transport)

Trade Fairs and Exhibitions

Direct Mail

Mail Drops

Point-of-Sale

Sky/Aerial Advertising

Sales Literature

Objectives of advertising

Many advertising campaigns involve above- and below-the-line methods of advertising, but whatever the methods chosen as part of the campaign each will be required to fulfil several or all of the following objectives if it is to be effective in obtaining and/or retaining customers.

(a) *Reach the target market/audience*: which may be geographically dispersed or difficult or costly to reach by other means of communication, such as the use of door-to-door salespeople.

(b) *Develop awareness of the product, service or organisation*: which could lead to trial, evaluation and, hopefully, a sale (adoption).

(c) *Increase understanding of the product, service or organisation*: by explaining the benefits, applications and other issues of importance, so that customers feel more confident about their selection.

(d) *Act as a constant reminder of the product, service or organisation*: Reminding encourages existing customers to remember the product and re-purchase, and may convince potential customers to purchase for the first time.

(e) *Draw the market to sales places*: e.g. shops, supermarkets, stores etc. where the goods or services are available. Advertising designed to draw potential customers to the place of purchase is referred to as a pull or sell out policy.

(f) *Push the product through channels of distribution*: i.e. encourage wholesalers, retailers, etc. to purchase and resell. This form of advertising is referred to as a **push** or sell in policy.

(g) *Afford salespeople time to contact potential customers* and make the potential customer receptive (softened) to the salesperson's visit. Advertising, in fact, is often referred to as the soft salesperson, as it sometimes makes sales through its own efforts and sometimes softens the market ready for the efforts of sales personnel.

(h) *Offer reassurance as to the product's quality, performance, the quality of after sales services, etc*: Reassurance helps to remove any post-purchase anxieties of customers and helps in maintaining a long term relationship with established customers.

While the above considerations were related to advertising, many could have been equally applied to aspects of PR and personal selling which are covered separately in this chapter.

Above-the-line advertising

ADVERTISING MEDIA

The word *media* refers to the independent commercial communication channels available to marketers for advertising. Each media outlet has its own characteristics, consumer following, and creative attributes. There are five distinct groups of advertising media available in most modern industrialised countries.

1 commercial television
2 commercial radio
3 the Press (newspapers and magazines)
4 cinema
5 posters

Each has its own characteristics and within each there is variety: for example, quality daily newspapers have different characteristics to popular daily newspapers and appeal to different reading audiences.

1 COMMERCIAL TELEVISION

Advertising on television is initially a costly form of reaching the market as production and screening costs are very high, and so too are transmission charges, particularly at peak viewing times.

Once the programme schedules are known, advertisers or advertising agencies can apply for the most attractive times for the presentation of their advertisements, although the times they have selected may not always be available.

Products for the mass markets, e.g. toothpaste, may be best advertised during the commercial break of programmes that have a large national audience – popular soap operas, films, etc. – while specialist products, e.g. sportswear, may be better shown during sports programmes.

Though initially costly, its effect in encouraging purchases may make its cost per sale generated relatively low. The medium is extremely flexible. Programmes operate throughout most of the day appealing to many sections of the population including children, housewives and pensioners, as well as adults going out to work. There is a tendency for the main audience of commercial television to come from C2, D and E socio-economic groups, which makes it useful for reaching mass markets but not quite so useful for reaching A, B and C1 socio-economic groups.

Television has strong visual impact, even more so with most countries now having colour television. TV audiences are virtually captive as they intend continuing to view in order to watch the programme in which they are interested. For this reason many adverts attempt to be interesting or humorous to retain the audience during commercial breaks.

In some countries the company wishing to advertise sponsors the whole programme and, therefore, has considerable control over the amount of advertising time that will apply to any programme and the type of programme that will be shown.

Advantages

- Advertisements are presented in the home to what is almost a captive audience.
- Pictures can often tell more than words.
- Movement and sound attract attention.

- Moving colour pictures of actual scenes, people and products have a realism not possible via other media.
- Hardly any effort is necessary for a viewer to absorb television advertising.
- A television advertisement can be timed to the hour, day, week or programme.
- The advertisement can be repeated every few hours, daily, weekly, etc.
- Campaigns in TV regions can be linked with advertising undertaken in other media.
- Merchandising facilities are usually available (see the section on merchandising in this chapter).
- Audience viewing figures are available.
- Resellers also see television, i.e. members of the channels of distribution, and they too may respond favourably to a product or company.
- Economical in relation to audience size.
- Colour aids brand and pack recognition.
- Less expensive spots are usually available to local advertisers on regional channels.
- Useful for reaching young children who often could not read a publication.

Disadvantages

- Advertisements that need much complex and technical information to be shown cannot be used.
- Television production and transmission costs are high – although per sale obtained it could be less expensive than other methods.
- Television advertising can sometimes be doing more entertaining than selling.
- It is a transient medium. The message is over in seconds and cannot be shown to others.
- There is a similarity in the products advertised, i.e. convenience goods predominate, although shopping and speciality goods are advertised.
- It is difficult to attract enquiries.
- There is a long time gap before purchase is possible – major viewing is at a time when shops are closed, i.e. in the evening.
- Television can be watched while doing something else, and therefore concentration may be lost.
- Bookings are inflexible and take some time to book.
- TV lacks mobility unlike newspapers and magazines which may be carried by the purchaser.

2 RADIO

Radio obviously lacks the visual dimension of television. The key to success of advertising messages on radio seems to be the use of appropriate voices which transmit desired images about the product or service. Popular musical themes, familiar sounds and simple descriptions are often introduced in an effort to facilitate understanding and information retention.

Commercial radio is mainly used as a support medium by major advertisers. It has been shown that commercial radio appeals mainly to 15–34 year olds in C2,

D and E socio-economic groups. Compared with television, there are many more local radio stations through which an advertiser can advertise. It often has larger daytime audiences than television as many people can use radios at work, or at home while working, and today many young people have personal radios with headphones which can be listened to in most situations.

Local businesses may use local radio advertising quite extensively for announcements of special offers and services, end of season sales in stores, recruitment, etc.

However, as noted for TV, the message is short lived, cannot be physically passed to another person and cannot be studied in depth or at a convenient time. Therefore advertisements tend to emphasise main themes leaving long advertising messages for selected posters, direct mailings and, in particular, the Press.

Advantages

- National and local advertising is possible.
- A variety of voices and sounds can be used in order to dramatise the presentation of the product or service in question.
- Radio advertisements can be inexpensive to produce.
- Useful for appealing to specific types of listeners.
- Large and small audiences can be reached.
- Excellent for reaching young audiences.

Disadvantages

- There is no visual effect and some commentators have irritating voices.
- It is a transient medium, i.e. the message cannot be physically passed on or re-read.
- Like TV, it may sometimes do more entertaining than promoting.
- Radio can be listened to while doing something else, therefore not gaining the full attention of the listener.

3 PRESS (NEWSPAPERS AND MAGAZINES)

The Press represents a very complex but extremely popular area of advertising. Newspaper reading in most developed countries is an habitual activity, with approximately 70 per cent of the adult population reading at least one publication every day.

Most of us will advertise in a newspaper or magazine at some time in our lives to sell, buy or exchange our car, some furniture, hi fi equipment or TV, sell our house or even to meet a friend. The advertising that we place will normally be of the **classified** type. Classified advertising is presented in the typefaces normally used for editorials by the publication and will come under a particular heading to which the advert relates such as 'Houses for Sale', 'Cars for Sale', etc.

On the other hand Press advertising placed by companies will usually be in the form of a **display**. Display advertising means that the advertisement will be in a design and typeface(s) determined by the company advertising and may be surrounded by a line (boxed) to distinguish it from the text or advertisements around it.

Newspapers offer geographical flexibility in that there are hundreds of regional and local newspapers in addition to the daily nationals. Permanency of adverts applies as the advert lasts as long as the reader retains newspapers or magazines. There is a variety of editorial themes and the possibility of placing adverts at relatively short notice, such as within one or two days in some local or national newspapers.

Magazines, on the other hand, tend to reflect life styles and subsequently have their own demographic and psychographic profiles. They offer high reference value as copies are often kept or collected for future reference. Readership build-up is possible as publications are often passed on to friends or relatives particularly within a family and there is a wide geographical coverage as well as a defined editorial emphasis. Therefore, plenty of opportunity exists for advertisers to reach their target audience and deliver extensive messages, such as those advertisements detailing the technical aspects of a car, recruitment adverts or financial and banking services adverts.

Newspapers and magazines also represent a rapidly changing area of communications with growing trends including:

- Specialist publications concentrating on hobbies, general interests, social causes, sports, computing, DIY etc.
- Growth of freesheets or magazines distributed door-to-door or to the public in the streets. These publications are free and relate to specific geographic areas.
- Expansion of regional dailies or weeklies. These publications must not be confused with the previous group of media because although they relate to specific geographic areas, such as towns, cities or conurbations, they are not offered free.
- Expansion of professional and trade publications.
- Continuing growth of Sunday colour supplement magazines. Most Sunday newspapers in the UK include a colour magazine which offers an ideal opportunity for advertising in the Press products that gain from colour displays.
- Opportunities for inserting 'flyers' (loose leaf advertisements) in newspapers and magazines is continuing to grow.

Advantages

- An enormous variety of products and services can be advertised, e.g. convenience shopping and speciality goods as well as services such as travel insurance, jobs, investment, charity donations, etc.
- Special circulations exist – national, regional, local.
- Advertisements may be placed at short notice.
- It is one of the cheapest means of advertising to a large audience at a particular time.

- There are newspapers or magazines to suit most readers' tastes whether for social or work purposes.
- Sufficient space can be taken to convey the whole message.
- The message can be re-read.
- Replies and other responses can be encouraged through the length of the message.
- Reply coupons/addresses can be coded to determine area/market response levels.
- The reading public places great faith on the integrity of the Press.
- Advertisements can be illustrated.
- Many publications are bought regularly enabling repetition of the same message.

Disadvantages

- There are many advertisements, so impact of individual adverts may be low.
- Figures quoted by the media owners can be deceptive.
- There are rarely any special inducements to read advertisements.
- A Press advertisement is static.
- Colour is available only in a very limited way.

4 CINEMA

Cinema is a medium which has suffered a tremendous loss of popularity over recent years. Research figures have shown that average weekly cinema admissions have dropped dramatically in modern industrialised countries although there is now a gradual resurgence.

This decline can be attributed to the growth in ownership of video recorders, rising admission prices, increasing popularity of television, changes in consumer lifestyles, growth of other outdoor activities and even, perhaps, to the uneven standards of the film industry.

As a medium for advertising, it has strong impact and the ability to effectively hold audiences' attention, due to the size of the screen, the isolation of the audience and their willingness to watch as they are already at the cinema. Many advert variations can be introduced and, in particular, adverts for local businesses can be accommodated: a local restaurant, for instance, may encourage the audience to have an enjoyable dinner after the film.

The opportunity of the advert to reach a large audience relates directly to the popularity of the film. Cinema advertising has proved to be very useful for reaching 16–34 year old consumers as these are the main cinemagoers, but when children are on school holidays, films for children are shown and there arises the opportunity to reach children as well as their parents.

Advantages

- There is a captive audience.
- There is a very large screen improving impact.
- Advertisements can be seen in full colour.

- Whether film or cartoon, there can be movement, music, commentary, sound effects.
- Local advertising is possible, e.g. a standard film on Indian restaurants in general can have a verbal message superimposed (voice over) giving the address of the nearest Indian restaurant to the cinema.
- Regional advertising is possible.
- There is effortless acceptance of the message.
- Seen in a pleasant atmosphere.
- Only a small number of different advertisements.
- Young audience – approximately 85 per cent are 16 to 34 years of age – making it an excellent medium for products predominantly purchased by young adults.

Disadvantages

- The same advertisement can suffer from the monotony of repetition.
- Items advertised tend to be limited in range of subject.
- It is a transient medium.
- Repetition is impossible until either attending another cinema in the area that week, or visiting the same cinema.
- No guarantee of consistent audience figures, as these strongly depend on the film being shown.

5 POSTERS
Posters appear in the streets, on tube stations, outside and inside many shops, on vehicles, etc.

Transport or street posters (billboards) vary greatly in size, position, colour and cost. In most instances they do not carry long messages as people in vehicles or pedestrians have only a few seconds to read them. In fact, it is estimated that a motorist driving at a modest speed only has enough time to read six words on a poster, hence only the main theme of a message tends to be displayed, like the Coca Cola advert which simply said *It's the real thing!*. Because of the shortness of the message, posters are often a 'support medium' – supporting the longer message on TV or in the Press. Individual poster sites must be evaluated in terms of:

- *Size*: the larger the poster, the more visible it will be.
- *Number*: of people and/or vehicles passing by.
- *Visibility*: of the site by all types of traffic.
- *Noticeability*.
- *Positioning*: A poster site near traffic lights will be a very attractive advertising medium, because the traffic will often be stationary and people in vehicles will have a better opportunity to see and read the poster in full.
- *Cost*: of individual sites. This is likely to be affected by all the above factors.

Individual posters are comparatively more expensive than one small advert in the Press with a very large audience, but posters may be placed to target closely a particular audience, e.g. on the back of buses to reach motorists or on bus shelters outside supermarkets to reach shoppers.

Advantages

- The size and dominance of posters and bulletin boards on the streets.
- The position. Can be positioned where a particular sector of the community pass, e.g. for motorists going to major areas of work, pedestrians at bus stops, etc.
- They can be in full colour, two colours, three colours or simply black and white.
- Long life and exposure. They are usually booked for a minimum of one month.
- Repetition value. They are constantly in the same spot where the same main audience passes.
- Geographical flexibility is possible. Only one or two posters may be used in a key location for a local advertiser or thousands nationally for a large company.
- Complement to national Press or television, i.e. good support medium.
- Useful medium for helping to launch a new product to obtain the additional coverage of the market.

Disadvantages

- The message – the copy – has to be brief.
- The poster audience is usually a moving one.
- Posters are subject to vagaries, such as the effects of the weather or graffiti.
- Colours may fade and pictures become distorted.
- Suitable only for short term campaigns as message is ignored when people continually see it.

There are special considerations which apply to posters that move, e.g. inside or outside of buses and taxis, or in underground or overground trains, etc. (i.e. transport posters)

Advantages

- Carried from one audience to another.
- People are attracted by moving objects.
- Many passengers on buses, etc. will tend to read anything to occupy themselves.
- A more detailed poster may be used for travellers. As people are in the same position for some time, copy can be lengthier.
- Advertisements can be placed on certain routes.
- National or local campaigns are possible.
- A very large number of people use public transport.

Disadvantages

- Big fluctuations in numbers of passengers.

- There are not sufficient numbers of poster positions available.
- Posters can very quickly become dirtied or vandalised.
- Inside transport posters are limited to those who use transport.
- Interior advertisements are small.
- Advertisements on tip seats in taxis disappear when the seat is used.
- Not entirely a captive audience.

Below-the-line advertising

Although below-the-line advertising does not operate in the same way as the established mass advertising media, its elements are nevertheless media for advertising (making known) products or services particularly to smaller closely defined audiences.

DIRECT MAIL

Offers and special invitations (usually in the form of a lengthy advert) are sent to potential and/or actual customers through the post. If the customer wants the product he/she would then purchase by post or telephone and the product would be delivered by post.

The popularity of direct mail has grown tremendously over the last few years and it has become an important element of the promotion mix of many companies. Direct mail – and mail drops – forms a part of direct marketing, and hence the topic has been covered in Chapter 6 on distribution.

POINT-OF-SALE

Point-of-sale advertising refers to advertising taking place at the point, or near to the point, where the product is sold.

Probably the most important advertising taking place at the point where the product is purchased is on the pack in which the product is contained.

Many products that are not advertised in any of the media still make sales in the shop, store or supermarket simply because of the design of the pack and label and information carried on the pack. The next time you are in a supermarket just take a look at the products that you have never seen advertised in the media. You will possibly find a hundred or more.

The purpose of the pack at the point-of-sale is to encourage purchasing by attracting the **attention** of passers, raising their **interest** in the product through the information provided on the pack and the **desire** to purchase and, finally, the **action** of purchasing. These are, in fact, the intentions of most full advertising messages: **AIDA** (Attention, Interest, Desire, Action).

Of course, every company would like to claim that its product has a **unique selling proposition**, USP (something worthwhile and totally different to offer purchasers in the way of a benefit), but in many cases there is little difference between products, e.g. petrols and sugars. Therefore, through PR, personal selling and advertising – particularly on the pack – the producer will attempt to create a USP in the minds of potential customers.

In many instances, the pack will also enable the producer to carry sales promotions to consumers which may not be possible by other means. For instance, some stores may not allow tastings, but the producer may attach to a current product a small sample of a new product for consumers to taste. Most breakfast cereals have sales promotional material on or inside the pack such as gifts for children.

There is, however, much more point-of-sale material that can carry advertising messages of which the following are but a few.

- *Display stands*: in which the product may be displayed and a message appears on the stand itself, e.g. display stand holding several copies of a new book on the market.
- *Posters*: in shop windows.
- *Beer mats*: with the name of the beer or brewery.
- *Dump bins*: in which the product is placed. The dump bin is usually in a central position, thus providing unique display as well as intimating that the product is on special offer.
- *Show cards*: which are a form of cardboard poster that can be hung over the product like mobiles or be free standing in the shop window display.
- *Plastic shopping bags*: carrying the name of the retail outlet.
- *Calendars, wallcharts and office presents*: sent to buyers for use in their office with the name of the producer on the item.
- *Catalogues*: which illustrate products, their benefits and prices (see catalogue selling in Chapter 6).

Of course most producers would like plenty of sales literature beside their product at the point-of-sale but understandably retailers do not allow too much point-of-sale – other than the pack – in their store, as it may reduce the image of the outlet to resembling a stationary street carnival.

SKY (AERIAL) ADVERTISING

Sky writing by planes using smoke trailers to advertise and sky advertising banners pulled behind planes or adverts on airships or hot air balloons are little used today because of costs and legal constraints to ensure safety in the air. They are useful for short messages, but have the disadvantage of relying on people looking in the air at the time, and of course the message is short lived.

EXHIBITIONS AND TRADE FAIRS

These are forms of promotion that may be used to sell to consumers, the general reseller trade or to industrial customers. They have the advantage of actually illustrating many aspects of a company as well as its goods and services at a point where actual and potential customers can visit. For this reason senior managers, production and technical personnel of the company may be present, not just sales staff. The Ideal Home Exhibition, the Motor Show and the Office Automation exhibitions are examples of popular and well attended exhibitions in the UK. Trade fairs and exhibitions take place in most countries.

They may provide the following promotional services to the companies that use them for projecting the right image of the company and/or making sales.

(a) They can be used to announce a new product or service, such as a newly designed car or a new advisory service to small businesses.

(b) They can bring new business that could not be obtained without an actual demonstration. This is particularly important where a travelling salesperson cannot provide a demonstration due to the size of the product or complexity of the service, such as large farming equipment.

(c) They can help in increasing commercial links with existing customers, e.g. farmers visiting an agricultural trade fair may have the opportunity to express their views to the managing director of a company. In addition the customers are likely to be in a relaxed mood, treating the fair as a mixture of business and pleasure.

(d) They may offer the market in a specific area an opportunity to see, evaluate, try or discuss the product or service with technical experts and sales personnel.

(e) They can have (if successful) a favourable effect on the company's reputation, as the major work of the company may be on view and staff available for discussions and answering questions.

(f) They offer an opportunity for rival salespeople to meet and discuss current developments in the trade.

(g) They may help the company in obtaining orders, in appointing home or overseas agents, in obtaining new sales leads, etc.

(h) Exhibitions or trade fairs can also serve as an opportunity to test some of a market's response to a new product. A company can test an element of consumer or/and potential distributor reactions, before committing itself to selling in the market place, e.g. at motor shows there are trade days and days for visits by consumers.

Detailed planning and budgeting for a company's appearance at a trade fair or exhibition can only be implemented once decisions upon the promotional objectives, the target audience and the method of approaching the market have been made. Many companies do not effectively use exhibitions and subsequently receive very low returns for their investment. Thinking about the promotional objectives of entry as an exhibitor is vital if the exhibition or trade fair is to be treated as an integral part of a marketing plan. The following steps need to be considered if promotional and cost effectiveness is to be achieved when exhibiting.

- Let your target market know that you are taking part and ensure that you use words to maximum effect: 'See us on Stand 123 at the Interbuild Exhibition', etc.
- Focus a portion of the company's public relations activities on the exhibition to make certain the company obtains Press coverage and try to get influential people to visit the stand.

- Send tickets to existing and potential customers so that they are more likely to visit your stand, if only to thank you for the invitation.
- Brief staff thoroughly, and do it well before the event. Sales and senior staff need a stock of invitations to give personally to any current or potential customers they may meet.
- Make certain that you book a stand that is large enough to accommodate all the facilities you wish to have on the stand, and attempt to obtain a stand that will have a sufficient flow of visitors passing.
- Select a list of influential visitors. Research them well and invite them well before the exhibition begins. If they have not responded by the appointed time, phone to remind them even if it has to be from the exhibition.
- Make future appointments with potential customers who visit your stand during the exhibition and monitor extra sales following the event. Try to make sales from the stand itself so that you can also see the instant effect of the fair or exhibition.

Of particular interest to small unknown companies is the value of trade fairs and exhibitions for meeting major buyers in industrial and reseller markets and for projecting the idea that the company is already well established.

SALES LITERATURE
Sales literature may take the form of leaflets, brochures or simply single sheets to support the sales of products/services. We see sales literature in hotels (at receptions), in stores and many other places where products/services are sold, or where they can be effectively promoted. Sales literature is also carried by and used to support salespeople and will be considered later in this chapter under personal selling.

Media selection criteria

Having examined above-the-line media, the problem remains how to select the media appropriate for promoting a particular product or service. This is never a simple task and most companies often feel they could have got the mix better – hence they make changes every so often. There are some sound rules to selection that may be used which we describe below.

In the case of any advertising the following must be considered:

- need for colour
- need for sound
- need for movement
- need for size
- length of copy text required
- repetition of placement needed
- the characteristics of the people we wish to influence, i.e. target audience

Media planners in companies or advertising agencies must reach decisions on these points before they select the advertising media which can serve them most effectively.

As we have already established, advertising in the media is very dynamic, complex, costly and often confusing, so clearly established selection criteria must be adopted for media planners to pick the best combination of media to use in their advertising campaign. The most widely used criteria to arrive at a decision regarding the choice of media, include:

FREQUENCY/REPETITION

This consideration refers to the frequency with which one may advertise to obtain the repetition necessary for implanting the message in the minds of potential customers. It also relates to timing and changes to the advertisement possible. Can we advertise on the hour, the half day, daily, weekly, monthly, quarterly or only yearly (often the case with trade fairs and exhibitions)? How regularly can we repeat the advertisement – repetition is essential for effective advertising.

PENETRATION

This refers to the ability of the particular medium to reach the largest number of potential purchasers, not simply the largest number of readers, listeners or viewers. If people purchase a publication or make a determined effort to watch a particular TV programme then they are more likely to notice advertisements than when they receive unsolicited literature in the form of direct mail or free newspapers whose content is mainly advertising.

Two considerations must be made here when considering penetration. The editorial and entertainment emphasis offered by each medium and their relevance to the product or service to be advertised. The word *emphasis* refers to the overall tone and bias created by each individual medium as well as individual editorials or programmes within the medium. A comedy programme on radio for instance, will create a light-hearted situation which may not be ideal for advertisements relating to higher educational courses, while a quality daily newspaper could prove an ideal channel for communications associated with education. A magazine specialising on home decorations could prove ideal for advertising DIY items, while street posters could prove a very helpful support medium in promoting a new range of cars.

Creative dimensions offered by individual media must also be considered, as the creative dimensions of the advertising media can vary quite distinctly. Radio for example may be used for advertising holidays but the added dimension of colour showing the actual resort and movement would probably make TV a more useful medium for influencing the market for holidays.

Already mentioned but worth repeating: marketers need to decide what they want to say or show to their audience, how they want to say it and then proceed to the selection of suitable media which can communicate the intended messages effectively.

CIRCULATION

This refers to the audited figures of the Press regarding the actual number of copies sold. It is an indication of the number of readers and helps with advertising that is not only intended to reach potential customers but wishes also to build maximum awareness. Therefore, if there is a choice between two media with the same penetration and socio-economic coverage at similar costs, total circulation may be a firm consideration. If audited circulation figures are not available then the publication must be viewed with suspicion.

TV and radio companies provide figures on viewers and listeners, respectively, though the research is invariably carried out by independent research agencies whose figures will be accepted by advertising agencies and the companies who are advertising.

READERSHIP AND READERSHIP PROFILES

Readership refers to the total number of people who probably will read the publication. For example trade and technical publications are often read by people other than the purchaser at the purchaser's place of work. Sunday newspapers and colour supplements are invariably passed around the family for reading. Therefore, readership figures may be several times larger than circulation figures and help to tell us how many people may read the publication.

The readership profiles usually indicate the demographic characteristics of the readership, such as age, sex, income and, in particular, socio-economic grading of readers, quintessential to the effective targeting of a company's advertising. Readership figures and characteristics may be provided independently for mass circulation newspapers, but with trade and technical publications the advertiser may have to rely on the figures presented by the particular medium. Where concern exists regarding the suitability of a medium only one or two advertisements may be placed to test response before more regular advertising in the particular medium is undertaken. Again, figures for TV and radio are available.

PRIMARY AND SUPPORT MEDIA

All advertising selection involves choice between alternatives. Therefore, for maximum penetration it may help to select primary (first choice) media that interlock or cross support each other.

If deeper penetration into the same target market, for example, is required, then vertical advertising in the media that reach the same target market will be sought. For example, advertising on commercial television may be linked with advertising in the magazine that provides the programme schedules for viewers, or local radio advertising in an area may be accompanied by direct mail or press advertising. Alternatively, if the advertiser wishes to reach a broadly based market he may advertise in unrelated media that are reaching different target audiences (horizontal advertising).

Support media may also be a criterion. For example, it may be considered that the primary advertising media for the launch of a new product will be television and colour supplements that accompany the popular Sunday newspapers. But for in-depth coverage posters may be needed to ensure continuity and spread of the main message across the whole range of socio-economic groups and geographical regions. This would be an essential feature in countries where televisions and literacy are mainly confined to the major towns and cities.

SEASONALITY AND THE PRODUCT LIFE CYCLE

Most products have a seasonal aspect and at certain times of the year sales promotions (covered shortly) may be needed to support flagging sales. At the introduction stage in the product life cycle advertising and sales promotions may be needed as a joint effort to ensure the satisfactory launch of the product. Alternatively, sales promotions may be needed at the decline stage in the hope that they will aid the re-cycle of the product or to clear out remaining stock ready for the introduction of a new version.

NATURE AND SCALE OF COMPETITOR ACTIVITY

Consideration of the intensity and variety of competitors' advertising needs to be undertaken because if consumers are only exposed to competitors' advertising, the company's product may be forgotten or curiosity may lead customers to try alternative products which are well advertised. Competitors' advertising methods should not dominate a company's thinking but it should be considered in case they are using a method that would appear to have potential.

LEGAL CONSTRAINTS

There are many products which cannot be advertised on certain mass communication media because of religious or social reasons, or they are considered to be harmful to people in the short or long term. In the UK, for instance, cigarettes cannot be advertised on television because of their adverse effect on people's health, and similar bans are in effect in many countries throughout the world for other products as well as for cigarettes. Although the actual number of products banned from certain media is relatively few, it is worth considering the law as it affects certain products nationally and particularly internationally when marketing overseas, before the media to be used as part of an advertising campaign are selected.

A well planned application of these criteria will enhance the chances of advertising success, so prudent media planners will attempt to accumulate as much information as possible on all relevant media before deciding on appropriate channels.

In essence then, effective advertising needs to:

- *reach the right target audience*: by defining the target market and through selecting the right advertising media for reaching that audience.
- *obtain impact*: through the design and message of adverts and again the choice of media.

- *ensure repetition*: through the repeated showing of an advertisement by selecting a media channel and advertising mix that ensures the target market regularly receives the message.

These aims are often abbreviated to **TIR** (Target audience, Impact, Repetition).

Promotions are often relied upon as a means of establishing an advantage over competitors or as a counter measure against promotions or price cuts by competitors. However, such strategy can be very expensive, particularly if a company's product does not have a clear advantage over its competitors' which can be exploited when advertising.

And at the end of all this checking there must still be the final criterion, namely **cost effectiveness**. Therefore, marketers will firstly consider what is the best advertising mix to adopt and finally adjust the mix to correspond with the finances of the company and/or the production resources available.

■ 2 SALES PROMOTIONS AND MERCHANDISING

Sales promotions can be defined as

> *short term incentives offered to consumers, members of the trade or the company's salesforce in an effort to boost sales*

If used frequently in a user or consumer market over an extended period of time they may demean the product suggesting that the seller is over anxious to make a sale with the result that buyers may become suspicious.

Most of us have in fact been subjected to sales promotions, such as gift tokens at petrol stations, holiday competitions and free offers, but what we are rarely aware of is that industrial and reseller markets are also subject to sales promotions by their suppliers, as are sales personnel by their employers.

There are three kinds of sales promotions, which apart from increasing sales, may make additional contributions to a promotional campaign.

(**1**) Trade and technical.
(**2**) Consumer.
(**3**) Salesforce.

1 Trade and technical promotions

The term **trade and technical** (usually shortened to *trade and tech* or *trade*) refers to promotions directed at producers, resellers, professionals such as doctors, dentists, lawyers, teachers, and skilled technicians such as plumbers, electricians, hairdressers. However, we will concentrate on the trade promotions most companies supplying consumers are interested in – namely resellers – and list the following advantages of sales promotions directed at resellers.

- Contribute to increasing the levels of stock held by distributors.
- Increase the number of distributors handling the company's product(s)
- Improve display at the point-of-sale (actual place where the product is sold).

The purpose is not simply that resellers buy more, but they also sell more. Therefore promotions to resellers are often linked with promotions to consumers.

2 Consumer promotions

Sales promotions directed at consumers:

- Encourage or achieve product trial.
- Encourage sampling of the goods or service and/or achieve repeat purchases.
- Create enthusiasm around the product.
- May reward loyal users, by refunding some of their expenditure on the product(s).
- Attract consumers to specific outlets.

Table 8.1 compares some of the types of sales promotions which might be

Table 8.1 Common consumer (C) and/or trade and technical (T&T) promotions

Method/type	Explanation	Examples
Use of personalities (C or T&T)	Using people such as tennis stars to endorse a sports product or service	A certain film star will open our new store on such and such a day, and customers will have the opportunity to meet her and obtain her autograph.
Refund offers (C)	A monetary return to consumers obtained through proof of a certain number of purchases. This is a reward for loyalty.	If you collect 5 of our product's labels we will refund you £1.
Coupons (C)	A monetary saving on initial or repeat purchase	5p off first or next purchase of Silk Cut cigarettes.
Cross couponing (C)	One product carrying a coupon for the consumer to obtain a discount on another product or service free of charge	Collect 5 labels off Swiftrinse automatic detergent and you will qualify for a half price train ticket to a destination of your choice.

Method/type	Explanation	Examples
Free offers (C or T&T)	Gifts, banded packs, e.g. two for the price of one	'Buy the new Razorsharp shaving foam and you get a free disposable razor' or 'Buy 200 and we will give you an extra 20 completely free'.
Consumer competitions (C, occasionally T&T)	Raffles, draws, quizzes	Bensens cigars, £1m challenge.
Re-usable containers (C)	The product is in a re-usable container (jar, box etc.) that may be used by the purchaser for other domestic purposes	Nescafé's latest coffee containers can be used as storage jars once the coffee has been used.
Short term (possibly one month) quantity discounts (C or T&T)	An immediate saving in return for a higher value order. When used in this way short term promotions may be offered to both consumers and distributors	For this month only, buy a pack of 6 toilet rolls and you will receive 20p off the usual price.
Special credit terms for a limited period (C or T&T)	Customer can buy now but pay later. This encourages new distributors to stock and consumers to buy	'Buy a compact disc player this month and you can pay in 12 monthly instalments interest free. or Buy in September and you will not have to pay for 3 months'.
Sale-or-return offers (C and T&T)	Unsold products can be returned by the distributor to the supplier	Distributors may be encouraged to accept a range of toys for Christmas and only pay for the goods they actually sell.
Free goods/samples (C and T&T)	One or a few products are offered free of charge to resellers or consumers so they can assess the potential and popularity of the product. It is hoped of course that a purchase of large amounts will follow	Cans of paint or spray cans may be given to a reseller in order to assess the paint's quality. or A slice of a new type of cheese could be given to customers by the retailer so that customers can taste and therefore, hopefully, purchase the cheese.

consumer promotions and/or trade and technical. Remember that where the trade and technical promotions apply they may be used for industrial, professional and technical trade purchasers, not simply resellers.

3 Salesforce promotions

Sales promotions directed at the salesforce/team:

- Help in spreading a message directly by word of mouth by the staff involved.
- Help a company's salespeople to achieve or surpass sales targets they have been set.
- Motivate salespeople at times of the year when sales are expected to flag.

Sales promotions directed at the salesforce to encourage them to increase sales over particular periods would include:

- *Bonuses*: in addition to normal earnings for achieving sales targets for certain products over a limited period.
- *Contests*: between salespeople with a free holiday, car, etc., going to the sales team (or salesperson) that obtains the highest sales over a stated period.
- *Individually agreed promotions*: This is a situation where the sales manager may agree different types of incentives with different salespeople or sales teams that are in keeping with their personal wants or the particular problems they encounter when selling. Extra time off may be agreed with one salesperson who obtains a certain level of sales for a given period; another may be offered promotion to a higher position if he or she breaks into a difficult area of an industrial market or obtains a particular customer who would be of immense value to the company.
- *Sales meetings*: designed to stimulate the selling efforts of salespeople over the immediate period ahead, e.g. informing them of market situations of which they are unaware that will help them to increase their sales.
- *Training sessions*: to show them selling techniques that work with the sales of a particular product to re-motivate them into effective selling.

What sales promotion(s) to use will depend on the marketing problem the company is facing.

Sales promotions – no matter what the type – are usually undertaken for one of three reasons.

(a) To help with the introduction/launch of a new product.
(b) To support flagging sales at certain times of the year, as they may create new awareness of the product as well as offer incentives to purchase, thus maintaining production levels as well as, hopefully, increasing penetration in the market.
(c) At the decline period in the product life cycle to re-kindle sales or clear out the stock of an old version ready for the introduction of a new one.

Merchandising

Merchandising is the part of promotions which concentrates on:

> *obtaining maximum persuasion at the point-of-sale without personal selling*

Point-of-sale refers to the point at which a product for sale in a shop (merchandise) is sold. In the case of merchandising this concept is broadened to include the place in which the product is sold, i.e. store, supermarket, etc.

Several years ago considerable merchandising in stores was actually undertaken by manufacturers often emphasising their own product in an ostentatious fashion to the detriment of other products in the store, frightening customers away with sales pressure activities that were simply too much for the normal consumer to tolerate. Now stores tend to control their own merchandising and keep it in the style and atmosphere of the store.

Merchandising now is associated with the close focusing of essential retailing efforts and has grown in importance as a result of the growth in supermarket and selfservice outlets and as a result of the growing consumer awareness of products and/or services available at different stores. It has become very much a part of effective marketing within most major retail outlets, including supermarkets, variety and departmental stores.

The major objective of any merchandising effort by stores is fast stock turn-over, i.e. rapid sales, which will depend on:

- Predominantly stocking and displaying products which are in high demand.
- Allocating shelf space relating directly to the amount of sales achieved for particular products.
- Maximising the information given to potential customers of a retail outlet on products sold, the image of the store, special purchase opportunities, customer service available, etc.

Of course such merchandising would continually take into account slow turnover stocks that return high profits or products that encourage customers into the store when they may stay for some time and purchase other products. In order to attain the above, merchandising efforts should concentrate on four ingredients for success.

1 STAFF

Staff must be trained in all aspects of merchandising to improve customer service while efficiently controlling the stocking of product lines, effective store layout and consumer sales promotions.

2 STOCKS

Merchandising requires the best use of shelf space, filling up and the swift replenishing of shelves, allocation of product space according to speed of turnover, minimal stock holding in relation to the time needed for new deliveries and efficient re-ordering. These all represent key aspects of this area of merchandising.

3 STORE LAYOUT

The floor layout must permit maximum customer flow through the store, expose customers to impulse (spontaneous) purchases, allow for efficient counter service and present a professional, relaxing and informative environment. It is often the case that essential or popular items are placed to the back and sides of stores so that customers walk by other items, which they may purchase, on the way to the essential purchases.

4 STORE PROMOTIONS

Store promotions are designed to project the overall image of the store, both in the store and outside, to the residents of nearby communities and thus increase the number of customers (store traffic). They are likely to concentrate on three areas.

Out-of-store advertising

- Products offered: 'A wide variety to satisfy your needs'.
- Peripheral services, e.g. free parking, late opening, etc: 'Do your shopping after work'.
- Competitive prices: 'Better value for money' themes.
- Friendly staff: willing to advise and help customers.

In-store promotions

- Special offers: certain product lines offering attractive discounts.
- Free offers.
- Consumer competitions.
- Personality promotions.

The last three are similar to sales promotions considered earlier. Sometimes these are a joint promotion with the manufacturer of a product being promoted with the manufacturer carrying the main costs involved in order to obtain prime exposure in the particular part of the store.

In-store advertising

- Posters on the walls with the name of the store and its central advertising message to customers.
- Advertising the name of the store on plastic shopping bags given free to shoppers as a promotion/customer service.
- Staff uniforms and customer receipts carrying the name of the store.

Manufacturers, however, may still attempt some point-of-sale advertising/ promotions themselves through leaflets handed out in the store concerning their product, point-of-sale displays and in-store tastings, etc., but usually only with the permission and under the watchful eye of the store.

While we have concentrated on merchandising by stores, the fact is that many organisations which supply services are now using merchandising, for example, banks.

■ 3 PUBLIC RELATIONS

Public Relations is the deliberate, planned and sustained effort to establish and maintain mutual understanding between an organisation and its public.

Within this definition as applied to commercial organisations, however, is the aim to

enhance the image of the company and its products or services in the eyes of potential customers in order to improve sales

The company's publics may include the government, shareholders, local councils, potential labour, customers, etc. In fact, any individual, group or organisation that may affect the performance or image of the company.

Not all, but a considerable part of public relations (PR) activities are directed at obtaining favourable presentation of the company and its products or services. Whenever possible, presentations through independent third parties are sought so that the third party is acting to a degree as an endorsement of the company and/or its product(s).

PR activities may include:

(a) **Press release** – articles on the organisation or its products that the press may consider newsworthy, such as a new social use to which a product may be applied, e.g. a company's lorries/trucks have been chosen to deliver supplies to the starving in country X because of their ability to stand up to the rugged terrain.

(b) **Seminars, meetings, visits**, etc. such as escorted tours of the company and meetings with the chairman and managing director, for shareholders and financial journalists, to maintain goodwill with major shareholders and the financial world in order to keep share prices buoyant.

(c) **Press conferences**: announcing newsworthy events to journalists, such as the introduction of a new car, ship or service.

(d) **Local community relations and events** – maintaining goodwill with the local community and local organisations.

(e) **Donations to charitable causes** – such as for medical research, hospitals, voluntary organisations and charities, etc.

(f) **Testimonials from personalities** and/or satisfied customers to contribute towards a favourable brand or/and corporate image.

(g) **In-house journals** (in-company journals) to promote a team spirit, an integrated workforce and a sense of purpose.

(h) **Sponsorship**: A company may sponsor an event, a personality, an organisation or long running competitions in order to establish favourable associations and thus obtain editorials in the media as well as an opportunity for advertising at the event. For example, Embassy cigarettes sponsor the World Snooker Championship, JVC the Arsenal football club and Mars the London Marathon.

Having mentioned the regular activities of PR personnel it is also necessary to mention the work they undertake as representatives of a company in times of crisis, such as, after a plane crash when they help passengers on behalf of the company, or when the company is receiving unfavourable press due to an action it has taken. Figure 8.3 shows many of the publics with which PR may be concerned.

Fig. 8.3 *The PR function and its major publics*

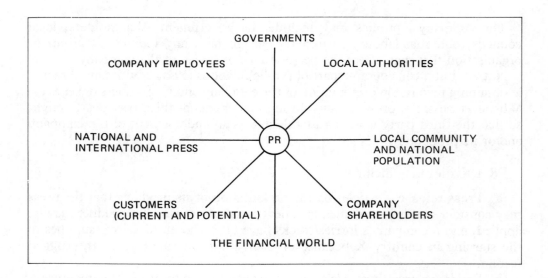

Publicity

Publicity may be defined as:

a non personal stimulation of demand for a product, service or business by offering commercially significant news about them to the media

Much of the work of PR is concerned with publicity, and it is publicity that is mainly associated with promotions, for it is a form of making something known to potential customers.

Newspapers, magazines, TV and radio stations may comment favourably or unfavourably on a company's activities or products as part of their usual reporting activities. Reports on companies may also be made by other parties, such as institutes, associations, government bodies, etc. and the general public may accept their comments as trustworthy, unbiased and credible. The nature of the comments will have a direct impact on consumers' perceptions of a company and its products. Therefore, the PR department will attempt to ensure that the media receive favourable information regarding a company and its products and will attempt to redress unfavourable press. In many large companies this task is so important that a publicity manager is employed specifically for fulfilling this aspect of PR.

Favourable publicity normally obtained through the PR activities of the company can make the following important contributions to a marketing communications campaign:

(a) Improve company image
(b) Improve product line/brand image
(c) Announce new products and encourage trial
(d) Encourage purchase of the product(s) or service(s)
(e) Add credibility to a company's own communications
(f) Overcome resistance by sections of the community to the company, and/ or its products or services
(g) Develop other aspects of the company, such as interest in the company's shares

It is essential, therefore, that PR personnel (like ambassadors) have and project an acceptable level of integrity.

■ 4 PERSONAL SELLING

Personal selling can be defined as:

> *the oral presentation of a product or service to one or more prospective purchasers with the purpose of making sales*

Personal selling comes in many forms, such as field selling (going out to potential customers), retail selling (selling in shops) or over the telephone (telephone selling), etc. The main purpose of personal selling is to make direct sales, but it is also part of the company's method of promotion with the object of:

(a) Creating awareness of the product/service
(b) Arousing interest in the product/service
(c) Developing product preference
(d) Explaining technology
(e) Building enthusiasm
(f) Encouraging trial
(g) Obtaining repeat orders
(h) Discovering new sales leads
(i) Offering reassurance to potential purchasers or current users
(j) In some instances, delivering goods to customers

Therefore, while advertising is a one way form of communication, personal selling has the advantage of being two way, allowing customers the immediate opportunity to ask detailed questions of the salesperson.

What sales personnel say and the promotional and technical literature they carry to show potential customers must be in keeping with the image the company wishes to project of itself and its products and the manner in which it wishes to sell. Therefore, sales personnel are a daily oral advertisement and envoy of the company.

The sales literature that salespeople carry with them will invariably be more extensive than that sent to customers and will usually cover such aspects as:

- The promotions – particularly advertising – being used to influence consumers and members of the distribution channel.
- Most of the benefits of the product, with major areas emphasised.
- Prices, discounts and delivery times.
- Detailed technical information on the product/service.
- Variations on the product/service possible.

What the salesperson chooses to show the customer will depend on the sales approach being used.

The more complex, highly priced or individual the product the more the tendency for the salesforce to gain in importance with regard to its position in the promotions mix, as detailed explanations of the product may be required before customers will purchase. This understandably means that personal selling is an essential part of the promotional efforts for most companies supplying industrial and reseller markets.

Due to the complexities of personal selling the activity tends to represent a separate function and section within the marketing department. A more detailed analysis of the selling effort can therefore be found in Chapters 6 (under Direct Marketing) and 7.

■ 5 ESTABLISHING THE SIZE OF THE ADVERTISING BUDGET/APPROPRIATION

There is no guaranteed system for setting the advertising appropriation which will produce a totally cost effective budget, but there are several common methods outlined in points 1–5 below.

1 Percentage of the previous year's sales

This method encourages marketing managers to allocate a percentage of the previous year's sales revenue or profitability to next year's advertising. It is regarded as being affordable, since expenditure should not exceed earnings achieved, and it is also very simple to administer.

Affordability and simplicity may seem attractive but this method tends to ignore or under-estimate the dynamic nature of the marketing environment. New product launches, market opportunities, changes in advertising tastes, changes in competitors' activities, new market entries, economic or technological developments and changes in consumer expectations cannot be accommodated effectively if one lets the past decide about the future. In addition, it tends to rely on sales results as a measure of advertising needs and effectiveness.

2 Percentage of future sales

With this method an estimate of future sales is used to determine advertising expenditure. The method relies heavily on sales forecasting, but the forecast itself may be little more than a subjective assessment. In many cases, sales forecasting is unfortunately used to justify preconceived attitudes or courses of action.

It may lead to overspending in markets which are expanding well and underspending in markets which are under competitive pressure. The method tends to treat advertising as a constant factor, but in reality new products require a higher proportion of advertising in order to reach and encourage a market to accept something new. Similarly, to increase market share of a current product a disproportionate increase in advertising may be necessary.

Limitations of the previous method apply equally well to this approach because sales revenue is directly linked to advertising expenditure. The previous method relied on revenue already achieved while this method relies on revenue which may or ought to be achieved.

3 Affordable method

This is a common method used by small companies where the basics of advertising are not understood or not appreciated as a prime promotional tool. It ignores competition and demand and only evaluates what the company considers affordable which may itself simply be a subjective judgement.

Such an approach tends to curtail the company's willingness to evaluate what is needed before looking at what can be afforded.

It is impossible to justify this method by the use of theories or empirical evidence.

4 Competitor parity method

This method uses competitor expenditure on advertising as the criterion for setting the advertising budget. The planned expenditure allows for competitors' activities but the following problems are likely to be encountered.

(a) Estimates of competitor levels of advertising are very difficult to determine.

(b) It takes a long time to respond to different levels of competitor spending. An increase in the rate of competitor spending may not be noticed for several months, and after analysis a reasonable response may take several more months to develop and implement. By this time the competition may have introduced new, totally different, advertising campaigns or have concentrated on other promotional methods, such as personal selling or PR, for influencing the market.

(c) Following competitors' advertising tactics implies that similar or identical marketing objectives are being pursued. Bearing in mind the fact that corporate and marketing objectives of competitors are not easily identifiable, how can one justify direct imitation of a competitor's tactics?

5 Objective and task method

The name of this method summarises the approach perfectly. The basic idea is to set the promotional objectives to be pursued in a clear, precise and sequential order and *then* to select the tactics which will best serve the attainment of these objectives.

This budget method evaluates the level of expenditure needed for a given plan of action to achieve a given objective. If it is not affordable, the production and marketing objectives set must be revised until the necessary tactics become affordable or perhaps a loan will have to be raised to achieve the objectives. It emphasises the need for the objectives to guide the plan of action and encourages marketers to utilise the ideas on advertising presented in this chapter.

This method is the one most favoured by the experts but it is also the one which is most difficult to quantify. Two major problems exist with this method:

(**a**) The nature of the objectives themselves cause problems. It is difficult always to relate specific advertising objectives directly with possible sales, so other measures may have to be used such as increased brand awareness or level of penetration into the target market.

(**b**) The second problem lies in estimating the methods needed to reach the objectives.

- What is the attention attracting power of the campaign as opposed to its persuasive power?
- Can we be certain that the advertising mix selected will reach the spread of the target audience as frequently as required?
- Do we need a similar objective for the whole of the country or must the campaign be weighted area by area or market by market?

All methods offer advantages but also suffer from major limitations. Solid theory and judgement, possibly backed by research findings, seem to be the answer to effective advertising budget setting.

Within the promotional mix, advertising, and the sums spent upon it, usually attract most of the attention, so that advertising is sometimes taken as a metaphor for the whole of promotions. There is an easy explanation for this which is that advertising is the most vivid, most visible and most noticed aspect of marketing. It is, therefore, the marketing director's role to ensure that, effective as an advertising campaign may appear, it only forms part of the total promotion mix needed for success.

■ 6 ROLE OF ADVERTISING IN SOCIETY

A discussion about advertising usually involves consideration of its advantages and disadvantages to society. These may not all be valid, but the main ones are probably those set out below.

Disadvantages of advertising

- Advertising is an added cost to marketing goods, for which the consumer has to pay.
- Advertising is wasteful as many people seeing or hearing advertisements do not intend purchasing.
- Advertising stimulates false demand for products and thus makes people more materialistic.

- Advertising tends to create oligopolies or monopolies because large companies can afford more advertising, thereby obtaining greater control of the market and restricting new companies from entering the market.
- Advertising makes the environment ugly by defacing buildings and transportation and, in the case of TV and radio, intrudes into the home.
- Advertising borders on propaganda as it impliedly supports capitalistic or mixed economy ideology.

Advantages of advertising

- Advertising makes consumers aware of the choices available to them so that they may make better purchasing decisions.
- Advertising affords small or new companies the opportunity of informing the market of its products nationally or locally.
- The subtle differences between brands are explained as consumers cannot always easily evaluate a wide variety of products themselves.
- Without advertising revenue, most newspapers and magazines would become extremely expensive or obsolete.
- Advertising revenue helps in providing free entertainment to society, in the form of commercial television and radio stations.
- The advertising industry provides employment to millions of people.
- Advertising makes our environment more colourful.

Advertising, like any other aspect of production, involves some waste. Advertisements are designed to reach specific consumer groups with specific communication objectives, but many other consumers may also see or hear adverts which may be of little value to them. This waste represents the cost of freedom of choice offered to companies and consumers in a democratic society. Constructive competition cannot exist without advertising (making known) and any criticisms aimed at advertising should allow for the fact that better consumer satisfaction, in a dynamic society, is usually achieved through competition, tempered by controls of the particular government.

At this point it may be worth reading once again the section on marketing and society (Chapter 1, p. 22) to see the proposed advantages in broader perspective.

■ 7 PROMOTIONS MIX AND PLAN

The mix

Before determining the promotions mix we need to determine the answer to several standard types of questions. Each of the questions that follow highlight a separate – but not exclusive – aspect of selecting methods of promoting, and yet they are all interrelated.

WHY ARE WE PROMOTING?

This is answered by determining the aims of the promotion, but companies do not always evaluate these aspects closely enough.

Some companies, for instance, have advertised extensively for extra sales at a time when their resources were too overstretched to accommodate additional orders. Therefore, fundamental to any promotional campaign is **determining if promotions** – in whatever form – **are truly needed**, and what their purpose is if promotions in addition to the current level are proposed.

WHAT ARE THE MARKETING AIMS?

These will usually be defined within the marketing plan for a specific period and will indicate the role of promotions within the marketing mix as well as define what each type of promotion – advertising, PR, personal selling – is supposed to achieve, e.g. deeper penetration of the market, role in launching a new product, change conceptions about the product, etc.

With regard to the marketing mix, management will have to determine the effect of each element of the mix on the other three elements and its importance in the mix that is finally determined. With regard to promotions for example:

● Is the promotional theme in keeping with the quality of the product and the price set?
● Are promotions to be designed to help distribution by pushing the product through the channels of distribution?
● Have promotions taken account of the position of the product in its life cycle?
● Could more discounts in the channels of distribution be more effective than increased promotions?
● Would a change in price create more revenue than an increase in promotions?

Determining the interacting effects of the 4 Ps on one another will require those responsible for each element to confer when marketing plans are being formulated.

WHOM DO WE WISH TO PROMOTE TO?

Having determined that promotions are needed it is essential to identify and describe the **target audience** we wish to reach. Once we have determined their age, sex, behaviour, likes, dislikes, reading, listening and viewing habits, we may then evaluate which method of promotion would be the best to use, taking into account cost considerations for reaching the target audience, e.g. advertising (above- and/or below-the-line), PR, personal selling, etc.

HOW CAN WE EFFECTIVELY INFLUENCE THE AUDIENCE?

Advertising, PR, sales promotions and personal selling may all influence an audience and most companies will use more than one of these methods.

Established companies who wish to continue to grow will usually choose promotional methods that enable them to repeat the message regularly as repetition is almost as important as the promotion itself. Research has shown that over 95 per cent of people forget the exact message of an advertisement within six weeks of seeing it.

WHEN TO PROMOTE?

Certain products have a seasonal pattern of demand and are, therefore, more effectively promoted through a medium that can accommodate this seasonality, such as poster advertising at holiday locations. Again certain events may indicate a time to promote, such as agricultural trade fairs when purchasers are interested in seeing the various new products or versions of products that are on offer.

WHERE TO PROMOTE?

Having defined our target audience the problem is determining where to promote to ensure that people have the **opportunity to see** (OTS). This is important with promotions, because the best promotions in the world are of little worth if they are not seen or heard.

The problem is that the target audience may be scattered throughout the nation and may not be identifiable. For example, we know there are millions of people who buy toothpaste but we do not know exactly which brand of toothpaste they buy or if they would buy our proposed new brand. To reach such people therefore, we may have to use above-the-line media such as commercial television or radio, the Press or/and posters. On the other hand, if we wanted to reach people in a particular trade or profession, and we knew they all had a particular interest, we may use trade journals, trade fairs, personal selling or even direct mail if they are few in number and we have their addresses.

Only when we have addressed ourselves to such questions can we determine the right promotional mix to adopt to achieve the promotional aims of the marketing plan.

The promotion plan

The **promotion plan** is a document compiled by a marketing or promotions manager which identifies clearly all the decisions reached on promotions to be used by the company for the achievement of specific objectives. It identifies and justifies the relative importance of promotions within the marketing mix and plan. Preparation of the promotion plan is a very complex exercise for which the following procedure is recommended:

(a) Define the target group(s) which the company is seeking to influence.

(b) Define or identify the type of information needed to influence the target group(s) selected.

(c) Determine the nature of messages to be made to the targets selected.

(d) List clearly the promotion objectives to be pursued.

(e) Identify the promotional tasks to be performed by each element of the promotion mix.

(f) Select the elements of promotions which can perform the promotional tasks most effectively, e.g. advertising, personal selling.

(g) Determine a method of monitoring promotion activities and a means of evaluating promotional success.

(h) Estimate the overall budget and identify its distribution over the elements of the promotion mix selected.

(i) Integrate the promotion plan into the overall marketing plan. (See Chapter 10.)

(j) Compile a promotion plan for the forthcoming year to which managerial staff in the department may refer, detailing the timing, quantity, cost and purpose of the major promotional activities/events.

■ STUDY AND EXAM TIPS

1 Remember most aspects of the promotions mix may be used for the purposes of profit as well as non profit making organisations such as political parties, clubs, unions, governments and by show business personalities, etc.

2 Do not confuse selecting advertising media with determining the promotions mix.

3 Try to use actual examples, wherever possible, as it indicates that you are interested and knowledgeable on the subject beyond the textbook. Study advertisements whenever you can and discuss their purpose with fellow students. In this way you will also obtain a feel for the subject instead of approaching it as if it were something that never changes.

4 Some examination bodies use the words 'marketing communications mix' instead of 'promotion mix' so make certain you check which terminology your examination body uses and what activities it lists under the various categories of promotions – in particular advertising.

5 In this chapter we have used the term below-the-line advertising to list all those elements that are not part of above-the-line advertising. However, some examination bodies prefer the words 'sales promotion' as a heading and, therefore, if you are taking examinations check the terminology used by the examining authority. It was decided that below-the-line would be used in this manual as this is the normal terminology used by advertising agencies.

6 Unless otherwise expressed in the question, examining bodies are usually referring to above-the-line advertising when they use the words 'advertising media'.

■ SELF ASSESSMENT QUESTIONS

Answer the following questions without reference to the text and then refer to the answers given at the end of the manual to determine your score. Award yourself 1 mark for each complete question that you answer correctly. If you scored 10 or more you are reading efficiently. Where you answered wrongly check back in the section to see what the answer should have been.

1 Define advertising as defined in this chapter.

_____
_____
_____

2 One advertising medium is posters. Name four more.
    (a)   _____
    (b)   _____
    (c)   _____
    (d)   _____

3 Which answer completes the following sentence?
Advertising is above-the-line or below-the- _____

| ☐ belt | ☐ media | ☐ line | ☐ promotion (tick appropriate box) |

4 Complete the sentence.
An opportunity for a company to display many of its characteristics as well as its products or services is at trade _____ and exhibitions.

5 What does TIR stand for?   _____

6 The use of coupons and trading stamps are two kinds of consumer promotions. Name three more.
    (a)   _____
    (b)   _____
    (c)   _____

7 Define sales promotions as defined in this chapter.
_____
_____
_____

8 Complete the sentence.
Merchandising is obtaining maximum persuasion at the point-of-sale without
_____

9 Merchandising campaigns in stores concentrate on four ingredients for success. One is staff. Name the other three.
    (a)   _____

(b) _____

(c) _____

10 Which of the following is **not** a method for determining an advertising budget/appropriation (tick the appropriate box).

☐ Percentage of previous year's sales.

☐ Percentage of future sales.

☐ Derived demand method.

☐ Affordable method.

☐ Competitor parity method.

☐ Objective and task method

11 Complete the sentence.

The purpose of public relations is to enhance the image of the company and its products and services in the eyes of _____

12 Complete the following sentence.

Publicity may be defined as a non personal stimulation of demand for a product, service or business by offering commercially significant news about them to

_____

13 Complete the sentence.

OTS stands for the opportunity _____

■ SPECIMEN ANSWER

When asked questions on promotions – particularly advertising – students often tend to simply regurgitate everything they can remember irrespective of what the question is asking of them. For this reason it was felt that to concentrate the mind of the reader on the different uses of advertising, we would conclude this chapter with a question that will review a major element of the chapter as well as provide an example of how to distinguish between the uses of different advertising media.

Question

A small company employing forty people produces a product for an industrial market and another for a consumer market. Discuss the ways by which it may advertise its products.

Answer

A company which employs only forty people will probably have certain limitations in so far as its ability to produce is concerned and also in how much money it has available to use on advertising. This means that the company will probably not be able to afford to launch a massive advertising campaign all over the country, or possibly abroad. Even if it did manage it somehow, it may not have the resources to cope with the large increase required in production and distribution that may result from such a campaign.

The product the company is manufacturing for industrial use would need to use specific advertising media and a selection of sales promotions in order to achieve optimum results. The appropriate media in which to advertise could probably be discovered by desk research or through retaining the expertise of an advertising agency. Whether or not an advertising agency was used the company would probably use above-and-below-the-line media such as trade journals, direct mail, trade fairs and exhibitions and perhaps the business sections in national newspapers. Advertisements used may show how the product the firm is making can benefit potential purchasers by improving efficiency, safety and hygiene, or increase profits.

A trade fair or exhibition, if available, would also be an ideal means to promote the company and sell, as potential customers may visit the company's stand at the exhibition. The promotional element comes from the company's very presence at an exhibition as well as editorial write ups and possibly an advert in the exhibition catalogue.

With a small firm of around forty people it is probable that a good personal selling service will be offered affording an added opportunity to provide potential customers with detailed sales and technical literature when sales personnel make sales visits.

A product for sale to a consumer market from the same firm would need a completely different advertising approach. Although the luxury of advertising research to determine the best methods may be too costly, the company itself, with the help of an advertising agency, would probably be able to decide on a suitable way of advertising the product.

If it is decided that national television advertising is out, and it usually would be, then there is the possibility of advertising on a regional television network or/and the national or regional Press. Advertising directed at the consumer, channels of distribution and salesforce may also help when sales flag.

The company may also consider direct marketing through direct response advertising, though for this method the product would need to have some unique quality and a good profit margin.

If its market is more localised, as is quite likely with a small firm, then the best media may be local newspapers, posters on local sites or possibly even advertising at local cinemas. Another possibility is mail drops through selected letter boxes in the immediate area of the business, which is a method often used by companies such as instant printers, garages, restaurants, etc.

Advertisements to a consumer market should generally contain less technical jargon but should emphasise the main benefits of the product to potential customers. Advertisements of the product to industry on the other hand can include more technical information as this is what the prospective industrial buyer may need for an effective assessment of the product's value.

The main considerations with advertising the two products to both the markets is what the company can afford in relation to what it considers to be the right advertising channels and what resources – human, financial and equipment – it has to meet the demand it wishes to generate.

Notes

1 This answer is around 2½ A4 pages of handwriting in length.
2 PR and personal selling were not examined as a method in the answer as they were not implied or mentioned in the question, i.e. the question was solely on advertising.
3 The answer was extracted and abridged from the book *How to Pass Exams* by W G Leader, also published by Hutchinson.

■ EXAMINATION QUESTIONS

The Institute of Marketing

1 Use examples to show how public relations might be used as an effective marketing tool.

2 Writes notes on four of the following:
   (a) The Marketing Communication Mix.
   (b) Merchandising.
   (c) Publicity.
   (d) Trade Promotions.
   (e) Advertising Media.

The Association of Business Executives

3 There are a number of different ways of deciding upon the appropriation for advertising. Examine critically those methods known to you and state with reasons which of the methods you would recommend.

4 Sales promotion is an important part of the marketing communications mix. Comment on its role and relationship to the other elements of the mix.

The Institute of Commercial Management

5 Using examples, discuss the use of sales promotion in each of the following categories:
   (a) Consumer promotion.
   (b) Trade promotion.
   (c) Salesforce promotion.

6 Critically appraise the various approaches to the determination of a budget for advertising.

9 International marketing

The world is a global village

In 1962 Marshall McLuhan had the foresight to see the world as a place where communications between people worldwide are as easy as those in a village when he commented, 'The new electronic interdependence re-creates the world in the image of a global village.' For companies considering marketing in other countries these words are even more true today as the dispensing of trade barriers and improvements in transportation seem to have kept pace with electronic developments.

Marketing products or services in many overseas markets used to be treated as an indicator of prosperous, large organisations which had outgrown their home markets. Nowadays, such a perception is misleading because involvement with markets is an option available to most companies.

Sophisticated communication and transportation systems, extensive consumer travelling, exposure to international media, removal of trading barriers between nations and changing consumer perceptions and expectations worldwide make international marketing a logical extension of the operations in the home market rather than an expensive luxury. Indeed governments within the EC (European Community) are currently promoting to companies in their own countries the idea that the whole of the EC should by 1992 – when the last trade barriers come down – be considered one whole home market, and that companies should be planning for that eventuality now by entering and building up markets in other European countries.

In this chapter we will examine the main opportunities, benefits and problems for companies of entering overseas markets and evaluate the most widely used methods by which companies can enter such markets.

A thorough examination of international marketing is beyond the scope of this manual, but a fundamental understanding of the main dimensions of the topic is a basic necessity to anybody studying marketing at this level.

Our examination will involve the following:

1 the reasons for marketing abroad
2 evaluation of an overseas market(s)

3 differences between exporting, export marketing and international business
4 methods of entering overseas markets

■ 1 REASONS FOR MARKETING ABROAD

What are the reasons for selling overseas?

Having considered some of the criteria involved in considering venturing abroad you may quite understandably conclude that there is no merit to selling to or marketing in another country. Fortunately, many companies do not arrive at this conclusion as you may appreciate when considering the following six reasons why many companies start to trade within or with different countries. Some of the reasons given indicate a positive desire to expand abroad/overseas while others reflect a no rational alternative situation.

SATURATION OR DECLINE IN THE HOME MARKET
This is one development which may cause a company to look abroad for expansion. Having considered the value of diversifying into new products, differentiating current products and changing the promotion mix to further stimulate a home market, a company may consider its best choice is entry into an overseas market where there is still potential.

MORE PROFITS ABROAD
Although a company may have excess capacity which can be used in the home market, it may consider it better utilised in a particular overseas market where purchasers are able and willing to pay more. It may find it less costly to sell across a nearby border than to the far corners of its home market. It may also find that labour costs are less when operating in another country and that it can export its product out of that country at a lower price than when it is made at home.

FEROCITY OF COMPETITION
A company in a highly competitive home market or about to be subjected to fierce competition may consider an overseas market an easier option.

RISK REDUCTION
Companies often go international to:

(a) Minimise the risk of a downturn in demand in one or more countries which will include their home market.
(b) At the moment operating production units internationally means that production at one unit, stopped through strikes or political instability, may be shifted to a unit the company owns in another country.

LEGAL RESTRAINTS

Legal restraints such as the banning of certain medical drugs, restrictions on the promotion or/and distribution of alcoholic drinks, cigarettes, etc. may cause a company to export to a country where there are fewer or no restrictions.

MARKET ACCEPTANCE

It may be that a company has developed a new product which it believes will be more easily sold in another country because of the attitudes of people in the home market or because the product is more suited for use in a colder or hotter climate, etc.

Whatever the reason(s) the prime objectives will be the same as for any marketing situation, namely to maximise profits while minimising the risk of losses.

Advantages and disadvantages applicable to most companies

Entry into a new market always involves a certain degree of risk and such a risk is obviously far greater when a totally unknown environment is faced in an overseas market. At the same time though, many opportunities can arise which may encourage companies to accept risks identified and help them in justifying their decision to allocate physical, human and financial resources to a foreign market.

ADVANTAGES

- Higher profit margins may be possible as a result of trading overseas/abroad. For example, increased sales volume may generate additional economies of scale which may reduce unit costs.
- By operating in many different markets, business risks – particularly those resulting from changes in the economy – are spread and a wider safety net is established.
- Products which have lost their popularity in the home market may be successfully introduced overseas.
- Success internationally may improve a company's or product's reputation.
- New business contacts can be established which can help a company's operations both at home and overseas.

DISADVANTAGES

- The level of risk associated with overseas market entry may prove unacceptable.
- Exchange rates may vary wildly and they may affect overall profits adversely.
- Additional investment is often required which may place too much pressure on a company's finances.

- Taxes imposed on imported products may make such products too costly in the eyes of overseas consumers.
- The product, brand and pack may have to be modified in order to be compatible with individual overseas market expectations and the required changes may prove too costly.

■ 2 EVALUATING AN OVERSEAS MARKET

In the study of international marketing, we operate on the premise that the entire world is a potential market, or series of markets. Arising from its own particular set of needs each country and region will offer a different range of marketing opportunities.

The analysis of these opportunities involves checks which evaluate the best chances for success, consistent with the company's resources and marketing capabilities. In this respect the analysis is obviously no different from the consideration of marketing opportunities that present themselves in the home as well as the export market. Fundamentally there is no difference.

There are, however, differences in approach, differences of language, culture distribution, advertising media, etc. There is also a difference that is not so obvious, and it relates to the fact that all people tend to see things from their own viewpoint based upon a particular cultural background which is sometimes referred to as the **self-reference criterion**. If we wish to carry out an unbiased analysis and make meaningful decisions about an overseas market it is necessary to be aware of this and attempt to see our product through the eyes of the consumer. To do this we must screen the characteristics of the proposed market within its national setting to make certain that selling or marketing our product would, or would not, be a success.

Screening overseas markets

When multinational companies are considering expanding into other countries they devise a checklist to screen out unsuitable countries until they arrive at a shortlist of countries to consider, or just one. From a multinational to a sole proprietor, any business considering operating in a country other than its own should use a set of criteria/considerations/checks to evaluate the overseas marketing opportunity.

Each company would have its own checklist relating to its own mode of operation, its resources and product(s) and/or service(s) it offers. For our general purpose we will use six criteria/checks which are **legal**, the **market**, **political**, **economic**, **social** and **technological**. An easy way to recall these six criteria is by remembering the phrase '**The legal, market PEST**' – PEST standing for Political, Economic, Social and Technological. In most cases the checks used will apply to user or consumer markets and to products or services.

1 LEGAL

Legal seems the logical one to start with because legal constraints may preclude any assessment of a market. For example there is little point to pushing alcohol in many Middle East countries as its sale is illegal. Some other legal considerations would be:

- Can profits be repatriated?
- What are the currency controls in operation?
- Are trade barriers and tariffs so restrictive for the product that they make exporting to the country a virtual impossibility?
- Can a foreign company only set up in the country under a joint venture agreement or through using a guarantor resident in the country, thus curtailing the usual mode of operation as well as causing profits to be shared?
- Are there severe restraints on advertising in the established mass media channels? Russia is just starting to allow advertising on television. Other countries will not allow some products to be advertised in certain media (cigarettes in UK) or the product used in certain places, e.g., public services in many countries now forbid smoking when using their service.
- Are the commercial laws, particularly contract and agency, the same as in one's own country?
- What levels of indigenous labour must be employed?
- Does the product, pack, package have to be changed in any way to meet legal requirements, e.g. cars and certain children's toys to meet national safety requirements?

2 THE MARKET

- How large is the market and are there substantial segments?
- What is the value of the target market to the company?
- What is the competitor situation? Do a few companies have control of the market?
- Does the product, pack, brand, packaging need changing in any way to suit the needs of the market or to meet legal requirements? Often international companies will have to slightly change their product, e.g. taste, dimensions, colour, texture, strength, etc., and significantly change their brand pack and promotions to serve the needs of particular markets and to influence markets in different countries (see Chapter 4).
- What is the trend in the market for similar products (if they exist)?
- Is credit and after sales servicing required?
- What price structure is needed?
- What promotions tend to be used to influence the market?
- Is there an adequate network for distribution?
- Why should potential customers buy the product? What are the benefits that purchasers in the particular country will receive?

- Do customers need credit facilities?
- What is the profile of the DMU (decision making unit)?

3 POLITICAL

Assessing political criteria is in the main more qualitative than with the other five areas of screening.

- Is, for instance, the political system/regime stable and consistent in what it does?
- Does the government provide assistance to foreign companies considering establishing a production unit in its country?
- Is there a possibility that the present or future government will change attitudes to ventures by foreign companies within their borders or even nationalise a foreign company?
- Is there a possibility of an overthrow of government?
- Is there considerable corruption and bribery evident?
- What are the powers of local government officers in relation to the operation of businesses within their area?

4 ECONOMIC

- Is there planning of the economy by the government in which companies can establish a branch or division and plan for the future?
- Is there economic growth?
- How is wealth dispersed throughout the community through the tax system? What are the rates of income and sales and corporation tax? How may these aspects affect production and purchasing power?
- What raw material, processed material, service supplies and component parts can be purchased within the country?
- What are the labour costs for different levels of expertise?
- Do trade unions exist and if they do what is their role, structure and power?
- What do different sectors of the society tend to earn?

5 SOCIAL

- What are the society's attitudes, beliefs and behavioural patterns and are they changing?
- What are the socio-economic groupings in the society, the numbers in each group and their general behaviour habits?
- How many people constitute the society; adults, children, males, females and their dispersion and concentrations throughout the country?
- Is there a strong religious, militant, democratic attitude, etc.?
- What are the spending patterns – current and projected?
- Is the society ready to accept new ideas?
- What is the level of literacy? Many international companies use visual and/or oral advertising rather than written advertisements in countries where there is a low level of literacy.

6 TECHNOLOGICAL

- Do competent international advertising and marketing research agencies exist who can help in evaluating the criteria listed above, or will the company have to undertake its own market research and promotions?
- Is there sufficient expertise available for running a complex operation and for product development and marketing? If not, could people be trained?
- Is there an adequate transport system?
- Are there any suitable sources of information?
- Is there a formal credit system – lease, HP, credit cards – available that may be vital for the company to be able to make sales?
- Are there test market facilities and regions?
- What costs would be involved in supplying the market in the manner and at the quantities envisaged by the company?
- What is the quality of importing/shipping agencies?

Many multinationals who use a checklist like the one above will select areas essential to their business and then award each marks to determine the value of operating in each country under consideration.

■ 3 DIFFERENCES BETWEEN EXPORTING, EXPORT MARKETING AND INTERNATIONAL BUSINESS

There are three different approaches a company may adopt when considering expanding abroad:

1 exporting
2 export/international marketing
3 multinational/international business

1 Exporting

Kotler adopts a realistic approach when he defines the exporter's job as:

producing products and selling them abroad

In other words, producing them at home and then exporting them overseas.
We can look at exporting as the usual first step in the progress that culminates in the international company.
An exporter's marketing approach is virtually non-existent. He or she may

take any opportunity available without deep regard to market selection, market research, promotion or distribution. On the other hand, after some preliminary research he or she may have decided that marketing abroad was for the moment too risky, too costly or too time consuming.

The exporter's involvement will be minimal. There are very limited organisational changes required as the export task will be regarded as an additional function of the existing sales department. Salespeople may make overseas visits to major outlets or – as is more usually the case – the exporter will use an agent in the overseas country who in turn will market the product within the country.

In many cases, however, companies gain immensely out of exporting and subsequently become very committed to overseas markets and move into the sphere of export/international marketing.

2 Export/international marketing

Quite simply the difference between **exporting** and **export (international) marketing** is that the latter involves marketing abroad rather than simply selling. This may involve the use of branch offices within a country or possibly the setting up of a franchising network (aspects which will be considered later in this chapter).

The difference in the meaning of the words *selling* and *marketing* is fundamental to the orientation and success of the firm operating in the international environment.

There is no doubt that any company that markets abroad in several countries will meet problems such as having to cross political frontiers; dealing with foreign governments and legislation; quoting in foreign currencies; changes in duties; tariffs and quotas; transportation difficulties associated with vast distances; a multiplicity of languages and cultures; and various standards of weights and measures. To the intrepid exporter these differences could be regarded as formidable problems. To the committed international or export marketer, all the aforementioned differences do not essentially change the process of applying the marketing concept to export markets; it merely means that the export marketer must be more alert and knowledgeable about the environment to deal with these complications.

3 Multinational/international business

An international business may have manufacturing and marketing subsidiaries in many countries throughout the world. Hence the objective of the international business is to ensure that the rate of return on its capital invested is maximised on a global basis. This will involve the chief executive of an international company viewing the business in global terms and channelling excess financial resources of the business into the most promising countries or regions.

To summarise, there are three basic types of export operations:

(a) Exporting – which simply represents selling overseas.
(b) Export/international marketing – which refers to marketing overseas.
(c) International business – which implies manufacturing and marketing in different areas of the world.

It is worth noting however, that companies may have production units in some countries, market only in others and simply sell in or use a national agent for other countries. In other words a combination of (a), (b) and (c) may be used.

■ 4 METHODS OF ENTERING OVERSEAS MARKETS

Assuming that a decision to enter overseas markets has been finalised and assuming the actual country to be entered has been selected, there is a need now to examine the different ways in which a company can enter the market. All the methods offer marketers a series of advantages which can prove ideal for certain situations, but they all suffer from a series of limitations. The aim of this section is to highlight the positive and negative aspects of the different methods, so that comparisons of the methods can be facilitated.

The six most common methods of entering overseas markets are:

1 direct exporting to overseas customers
2 use of agents
3 use of branch offices overseas
4 use of manufacturing unit/company
5 joint ventures
6 franchising

The first two tend to relate to exporting, the fourth to international business and the rest to marketing internationally, though they may be mixed, e.g. a manufacturing/marketing unit may be established in an overseas country from which a franchising system is set up.

1 Direct exporting

Direct exporting can be defined as 'selling to customers overseas from your home base'.

This method of entry does not involve any major financial risks. It helps a company in generating additional funds through extra sales to overseas customers and can also be seen as a way of testing the popularity of a product in international markets.

These likely advantages disguise three serious marketing limitations which can be associated with this method.

(a) There is no control over the use, or even abuse, of the products sold to overseas customers. If a product is applied wrongly or is promoted inadequately to overseas consumers by the importing companies which have bought it, a poor reputation may develop for the product. If at a later stage the exporting company decides to commit itself to the overseas market and attempts to market the product on a large scale, adverse reactions by the consumers may prove extremely problematic.

(b) Product imitation by overseas manufacturers may occur. When a product is sold to somebody overseas, there is a transfer of technology taking place. Somebody may buy it, examine it, test it, evaluate it, understand its technology and applications and imitate it. When we refer to imitation we do not imply a blatant copy of the product (same name, colour, shape, etc.), we imply imitation of the concept. Highly technical products may not be easily imitated but certain convenience or shopping goods may prove extremely easy to copy. Of course imitation may take place under many conditions but the exporter has little knowledge of imitations when they do take place as he or she is not operating in the market and, therefore, may be too late with any counter measures.

(c) There is no reputation build up for the exporter. Imagine that a specialist machine has been exported to a manufacturer overseas which improves the overall production capabilities of that company. This advantage will be a closely kept secret from the buyer's competitors, and therefore, there will be limited awareness among the rest of the market of the true qualities of the machine. The exporter may have gained a sale but there is no communication about the product: its functions, its origin, etc.

Likewise, if products are purchased only on the understanding that they are under the brand decided by the importer, then the importer's reputation will develop but not that of the exporter who supplied the product.

The limitations of this method of entry can be overcome through a more committed marketing approach which will involve one of the following five more direct methods of entry.

2 Use of overseas agents

The appointment of an agent represents the creation of a legal relationship which enables a company to sell within another country through the efforts of an agent resident in the country. A specialist company/agency in a particular area of business may be selected to act as a representative of the company so that they can bring about vital contacts and sales, in return for a pre-agreed sales commission. There are many sorts of agents but the following are the most regularly used.

COMMISSION AGENTS

These negotiate the sale of products with customers and place the orders with the manufacturer who in turn supplies the products ordered. A commission is received based on the value of the sales achieved by the agent, and they, therefore, seek to maximise sales in order to obtain the highest possible commission.

STOCKING AGENTS
These agents offer the services of a commission agent, but they also provide additional facilities of storing the exporter's products in their own premises. They can supply customers from stock, thus reducing delays in delivery which are inevitable when supplying overseas markets from a home base. They receive commission on sales achieved but may also charge an additional fee for the storage and distribution of the products.

REPAIR AND SERVICE AGENTS
Many products offered to overseas markets – such as cars, domestic appliances and small industrial machinery – require regular servicing and the availability of spare parts. Repair and service agents offer a further extension to the two previous types of agency by additionally holding stocks of spare parts and by providing repair and general maintenance services. Fees for these services are of course charged to customers, unless they are part of a guarantee.

DEL CREDERE AGENTS
When dealing with orders from overseas customers, there is always the risk of not receiving full payment for products supplied, or receiving payments late or even an overseas customer defaulting due to liquidation. The last is a particular problem where each item is very expensive, e.g. industrial equipment. Del credere agents are agents who in addition to the previously discussed services are willing to accept the risk associated with payments by overseas customers. This involves a separate contractual arrangement which an overseas agent may be willing to undertake due to familiarity with the overseas market and customers and the level of commission the agent will receive for accepting the risk.

Irrespective of the type of agent used for entering into an overseas market, certain advantages and disadvantages must be considered in relation to this approach before it is adopted.

Advantages
- Acquisition of expertise overseas through the experience of the agent.
- The agent's operations and existing business contacts can ease the introduction of a new product from overseas.
- The approach involves minimal investment and it is subsequently very attractive to small companies lacking the resources required for a more committed market entry.
- The popularity of products can be measured in a very inexpensive way. Lack of success may cause the exporter to withdraw from the market, without suffering extensive losses. Success on the other hand may offer the necessary encouragement to invest heavily into an overseas market.

Disadvantages

- Agents tend to deal in a variety of related or even unrelated products. One cannot expect an agent to concentrate solely on a recently introduced product, so many opportunities may be lost due to the agent's inability to explore all likely options.
- Agents may insist on a sole agency contract and then not obtain any sales, with the result that the exporting company cannot enter the market itself or appoint another agent, and yet it has lost sales opportunities.
- As already indicated, agents receive commission on all sales achieved. The products with the highest percentage of total commission will obviously attract the attention and efforts of the agent and any slow moving product lines offering limited or irregular commission may be neglected or even totally ignored after a certain period of time.
- Agents are unlikely to be able to exploit the potential of overseas markets fully, due to the nature and limitations of their operations.
- The activities of agents may not be totally ethical or marketing orientated. Marketing organisations may seek a long term relationship with a group of customers, while agents may settle for one-off commissions. Any adverse reactions from the purchasers or users of the products may have an adverse long term effect on the reputation of the products which could make future growth extremely problematic if not impossible.

Agents have to be evaluated very carefully before they are appointed and the following screening criteria are strongly recommended.

- (a) *Agent's human and physical resources*: particularly important where the agent must use a salesforce and physically distribute the product.
- (b) *Years of experience*: in a particular industry or with particular products.
- (c) *Agent's overall reputation*.
- (d) *Financial stability*.
- (e) *Proven performance*: and/or evidence of contacts.

Never appoint a sole agency unless the agency is guaranteeing some success within a specific period or is willing to market in a manner agreed in writing. Never sign an agency agreement that does not clearly indicate the way in which the exporting company (the principal) and agency will settle disagreements between them.

Evaluate how much commission the agent may reasonably expect over a year and then determine if your company could obtain more customers through sending salespeople abroad or by advertising in the country, e.g. colleges often advertise abroad with students applying direct to the college for a prospectus and subsequent admission.

3 Use of branch offices

This method of entry represents a more direct approach to international marketing. The company invests in the overseas market by setting up its own office, service company or unit which actually represents them overseas. The type of office will be dependent on the product or nature of operations sought and the likely options may include repair centres, sales offices, distribution centres, retail outlets, marketing units, complaints centres, etc. It may be that a manufacturer in the country is also used to manufacture the product under the strict guidance and to the detailed specifications of the marketing branch to reduce costs and dispense with transportation and importation of the product from the parent company.

Advantages

- The costs associated with other methods of entry could be higher than the investment and costs associated with a branch office. As sales grow, the total commission of an agent could be extremely high, which makes a more direct method of entry financially attractive.
- Branch offices offer a greater degree of marketing control because they represent a corporate extension of the company. Policies, objectives, strategies and tactics selected can be more consistent and more easily controlled.
- Through this direct representation overseas, the marketing philosophy can be implemented and pursued more effectively. Market information can be collected, customer complaints can be handled more efficiently, business contacts can be developed, overseas customers can be made to feel more secure and the overall reputation of the company can be cultivated.

Disadvantages

- As already indicated, it may make financial sense to actually set up a branch office, but unfortunately there is a need for some initial investment which may be beyond the means of a small exporting company.
- Setting up branch offices creates additional control burdens for the organisation. Controlling operating units in one country is much easier than seeking control of the operations of business units dispersed in many different countries.
- The major decision makers in branch offices overseas may have to be personnel of the parent company, relocated to overseas markets. Such relocation may cause problems because people are not always willing to move or stay overseas for a long time and may not speak the language adequately. Frequent changes of personnel may cause continuity problems because different people may be pursuing the accomplishment of objectives differently. In addition, changes of personnel may not allow customer and employee relationships to blossom overseas and the efficiency of the operations may suffer. Finally the operations of the company in the home market may also suffer because experienced personnel are transferred to overseas units.

- Branch offices overseas can rarely be staffed solely with people of the parent company. Local skills will have to be recruited and this could prove problematic in terms of costs and training.
- Employment laws, personnel motivation and employee expectations vary quite distinctly from country to country and as a result it is often very difficult to keep the peace within overseas units due to the differences in nationality, customs, language and expectations.

4 Establishing a manufacturing, marketing and service unit

Here a complete company is established – usually by a multinational – because cost may then be reduced or expertise acquired and marketing opportunities maximised. Advantages and disadvantages are similar to those of branch offices. Two extra advantages, however, are that the company has complete control and obtains all profits, and it may be possible to export from the unit to other countries at lower costs than supplying from the home production unit. Further disadvantages relate to the addition of one more production unit to control in a culture and possibly language that is foreign.

5 Joint ventures

Joint ventures are basically a form of international partnership between two or more companies from different countries. The partnership is set up in order to enable companies to operate within specific countries or in order to combine resources.

Advantages

- A joint venture with a competent company operating in the market the exporter wishes to enter will provide the partnership with knowledge of the market which will facilitate entry and consumer satisfaction.
- Risks associated with this form of market entry and the actual costs faced may be shared.
- Many overseas governments do not allow foreign companies to invest directly into their countries and they will only permit market entry if a joint venture is set up. In other words, this method of entry could be the only way of operating in otherwise closed countries.
- The combination of resources of two or more companies may actually remove some operational weaknesses which the individual companies may have. A local firm, for instance, may have manufacturing, marketing, selling and research resources which are currently under utilised while the foreign company wishing to enter may provide new ideas, products or services which could prove profitable. A resulting combination in the form of a joint venture may create a formidable force within the market.
- Political uncertainty or general hostility towards foreign companies or companies from one particular market can be overcome due to the presence of

a local firm. Consumers may trust the product more and local business contacts can be cultivated further.

Disadvantages

- All forms of partnerships face problems arising from disagreements between the partners. It is difficult to find two companies with different expectations, origins, history, structure and procedures which can always operate harmoniously on a permanent basis. The actual areas of conflict will vary from joint venture to joint venture and every effort will have to be made to remove the problems through clearly established objectives, regular meetings, review of procedures, positive management attitudes, clear and frequent communications and willingness to listen, to adapt and to compromise.
- As already indicated, risks and costs are shared but profits are also divided between the companies involved, thus reducing the returns to the exporter.
- The overseas partner may accumulate the necessary expertise through the joint venture and become a direct competitor if and when the agreement is terminated.

6 Franchising

The term **franchising** refers to the selling of a licence which allows a company to use somebody else's name, product or service in return for a pre-agreed premium payment (initial payment) and annual commission/royalty fee. Franchise agreements involve the organisation that will provide its name, products, promotional support and expertise (the **franchisor**) and the person/company who is willing to pay a premium and commission (the **franchisee**) for the right to operate with the help and under the name of the franchisor.

For example, Colonel Sanders had the idea for Kentucky Fried Chicken, determined how the product could best be prepared, marketed and sold. He retained control over how this was done, but left the operation of the majority of individual retail outlets to the self-employed proprietor of the premises. The franchisor becomes in part a partner with every franchisee operating and owning an outlet.

The franchisor remains a service organisation, without the massive overheads and complicated controlling systems needed for operating regional branches, retail staff and outlets while receiving on-going payments from the franchisee.

The franchisee, on the other hand, can purchase a ready made business, with all the backup of a large and experienced organisation, but the business essentially remains his or her own. The major part of the profits generated remain with the franchisee.

To assess a successful franchising operation it is essential to evaluate the benefits to the franchisee, to ensure that what is offered as a marketable possibility appears attractive and worthwhile to the people who have to operate in the market place.

Advantages to the franchisee

- Business ownership with limited risk and financial outlay.
- Training in product knowledge, and in the running of the business.
- Established image. The business starts from a position of strength with a well known name and reputation, backed up by large scale promotions and advertising – usually in the national media – normally beyond a sole proprietor's pocket.
- Professional help is provided in raising finance, recruiting and training staff, finding premises and advising on-going operations.
- Purchasing benefits through the bulk buying power of the franchisor and consistency of quality.
- Reduced business risks, as the franchisor's problem solving team is on hand and is likely to have encountered similar situations before.
- Market research and product development is usually beyond the small business operation, so the franchisor will keep the franchisee up to date with relevant, recent and future developments that will help the business.

Disadvantages to franchisee

- Franchisor's control, essential to the successful operation, can prove constraining or rigid at times.
- Resentment of the on-going commission payments may build up after a while, especially if the franchisee senses any lack of value for money.
- Poor support. Things may not turn up as expected or indeed as promised. The franchisee may not get the back-up needed or the original idea may not have been sound.
- Freedom to sell the business may well be restricted by the franchisor.
- Dependence; if the franchisee becomes too dependent on the franchisor's support, some of the motivation and incentives associated with running one's own business may well be removed.

Having considered the franchisee we can now look at the advantages and disadvantages to the franchisor who may be franchising overseas as part of his international marketing strategy.

Advantages to franchisor

- The image of the franchisor's operation is maintained through strict control over the operations of the franchisee.
- Little to no financial outlay may be involved when adding one more franchisee to the current list. In fact, the franchisor may make a profit just in providing the franchise licence.
- Useful where there is a widely dispersed consumer market with geographical concentrations as operations throughout the market place become possible.
- The method ensures motivation by the franchisee as the franchisee wants to earn as much as possible.

Disadvantages to franchisor

- The franchisor must have a perfectly planned idea and preferably be already operating some units to reassure potential franchisees that their investment will be a success.
- The franchisor never owns the outlets and therefore does not enjoy all the profits.
- There can be great difficulty in convincing potential franchisees to part with a premium payment and also difficulty in finding franchisees who will most probably succeed and, therefore, keep up the good name of the franchise operation.
- The franchisor must be aggressively marketing orientated and remain that way if he or she is to retain the support of the franchisees and expand the operation.

PAST SUCCESSES
There is no doubt that franchising, which has been extensively used and stimulated by many American companies – though not exclusively – will continue to expand in the foreseeable future. Indeed, it is estimated that currently over 20 per cent of shops in the USA's high/main streets are in a franchise arrangement. The list in Table 9.1 identifies some major franchise operations in the UK although many of the franchisors are not resident in the UK.

Table 9.1 List of franchise operations

Catering, hotels, food	Automotives	Personal
Burger King	British School of Motoring	Badgeman
Holiday Inns	Budget Rent-a-Car	Pronupia & Youngs (hire)
Kentucky Fried Chicken	Home Tune	Steiner Hairdressing
Pizza Express	TI/Midas	
Strikes Restaurants		**Household**
Wimpy	**General Business**	Apollo Window Blinds
	City Link Transport	Colour Counsellors
	Kall-Kwik Printing	Kitchen Reject Shop
	PIP Printing	Dyno-Rod
	Prontaprint	

Before dismissing franchising or taking up a franchise, individuals are well advised to read books on the subject and if possible consult others who have or are in such operations. In several countries there are now franchising associations with their own publications who may be consulted on the values, limitations and pitfalls of such operations in their country.

■ CHECKLIST FOR COMPANIES CONSIDERING TRADING OVERSEAS

A series of practical questions that need to be answered when considering selling or operating abroad serve as a useful summary for us and an overall checklist for businesses of any size considering trading overseas to ensure that they have prepared themselves adequately.

1 What are your reasons for considering selling, marketing or operating abroad?
2 Is there a better alternative in the home market?
3 Have you formally investigated and screened possible overseas markets?
4 Will the product, brand, pack need changing?
5 What method do you plan to adopt in order to enter these markets?
6 How do you intend to

    (a) price
    (b) sell
    (c) promote
    (d) package
    (e) transport
    (f) distribute
    (g) finance

7 Have you drawn up forecasts of realistic sales in the target markets that relate to the amount you wish to – or can – produce and sell?
8 Do you have the right human and physical resources for servicing the market?
9 Have you carefully assessed the profits you may expect at various levels of sales?
10 What will your actions be if things don't go as well as you expect or there is a complete down-turn in sales?

If you take another glance at the list you may note that while the procedure involved may be a little more complex, the questions that you should consider are basically the same as those for a home market.

■ STUDY AND EXAM TIPS

1 Remember that the basic principles of marketing in a home market apply equally well to international marketing. The rules do not change, only the environments and the required marketing responses to such environments change.
2 Distinguish clearly between exporting and export/international marketing.

3 Familiarise yourselves with the basic methods of entry and be prepared to evaluate each one of them.

4 Concentrate on the environmental issues which form the basic differences between the home market and the overseas market(s) a company wishes to enter by remembering: **The legal, market PEST**.

5 International marketing can help a company grow, increase profitability and provide prestige, but at the same time it can be costly and risky. Be prepared to discuss the reasons for and the main advantages and disadvantages of going international and do not hesitate to draw on the knowledge you have gained from reading all of this manual when answering questions regarding exporting or marketing internationally.

6 Do not confuse the way companies may expand into overseas operations with how a company may enter an overseas market.

■ SELF ASSESSMENT QUESTIONS

Answer the following questions without reference to the text and then refer to the answers given at the end of the manual to determine your score. Award yourself 1 mark for each complete question that you answer correctly. If you score 7 or more you are reading efficiently. Where you answered wrongly check back in the chapter to see what the answer should have been.

1 Complete the sentence.

All people tend to see things from their own viewpoint based upon a particular cultural background. This is known as the self _____

2 Complete the sentence.

The legal, market _____

3 Two of the criteria or checks when screening countries as a possibility for sales are legal and market aspects. Name four more.

    (a) _____

    (b) _____

    (c) _____

    (d) _____

4 Two reasons for trading overseas are because of saturation of the home market and because there are more profits possible from selling overseas. Name three more reasons.

    (a) _____

    (b) _____

    (c) _____

5 There are three ways by which companies may expand abroad. One is the creation of a multinational business. Name two more.

(a) _____

(b) _____

6 Two ways of entering a market that exists in another country are to export direct and to use an agent. Name four more.

(a) _____

(b) _____

(c) _____

(d) _____

7 One sort of agent is a commission agent. Name three more.

(a) _____

(b) _____

(c) _____

8 Complete the sentences.

The company that offers a franchise is known as the _____

The person or company that takes up a franchise is known as the _____

9 Name three franchising companies mentioned in the chapter other than Wimpy.

(a) _____

(b) _____

(c) _____

10 In the text of this chapter it was suggested that marketing abroad is very different from marketing in a home based market.

☐ TRUE   ☐ FALSE (tick appropriate box)

■ EXAMINATION QUESTIONS

The Institute of Marketing

1 Your company is considering exporting for the first time. As the newly appointed Marketing Manager, prepare a brief report outlining the relative merits and potential problems of this course of action.

2 Explain the factors which an Export Manager should take into account when deciding the forms of representation and distribution to employ in each of his overseas markets.

The Association of Business Executives

3 For a product of your choice, identify the factors you would need to take into account before deciding if the product was suitable for an overseas market.

4 In the development of international marketing, one of the problems facing a company is deciding how to enter a selected foreign market. There are a number of ways of doing this, including exporting. Identify the major ways and indicate which circumstances would be appropriate to each.

5 As the export director of a company manufacturing industrial machinery, you are responsible for the appointment of sales agents in an overseas market which is new to your company. What characteristics would you investigate in a prospective agent?

10 The marketing plan

A plan defines where we wish to be at some time in the future and how to get there!

Understanding each of the 4 Ps of the marketing mix and marketing research is essential, but so too is knowing how to blend them together to meet future marketing challenges in a way that all major staff involved appreciate their role in achieving future objectives as defined in the marketing plan. To do this involves analysing the **past** and **present** marketing position of the company and setting measurable and attainable marketing objectives for a **forthcoming period**. Details of how to achieve future objectives and what it will cost to achieve them will be written into the marketing plan. The plan may be long term, i.e. cover five years or more, medium term, i.e. one to five years, or, as is more usually the case, cover one year. In large companies plans will usually exist, with the annual plan reflecting and helping to achieve the objectives of the other plans.

■ 1 CONTENTS OF THE PLAN

The plan is a written document containing

- **A statement of the marketing objectives** for the forthcoming period, for current as well as new products the company may introduce and for new as well as current markets.
- **Details of the strategies and tactics** to be used to achieve the objectives.
- **An operating plan** for the period defining the role of each department and major section and activities to be undertaken to put the strategies into operation.
- **Details of the resources** – staff, equipment and finances – that exist and those that will be needed to operate the plan.
- **A financial budget** detailing the monthly cost of achieving each aspect of the plan as well as the normal running costs of the marketing department.

Of course companies are not forced to plan, they can just wait for events to occur and hope that they can make the changes necessary in time to survive. They can just carry on as they have always done and hope that they are enjoying the same levels of sales and profits as their competitors. They may also hope that investors and banks will lend them money solely on promises (which is very doubtful) and that staff will understand what they should do and what performance is expected of them. The case for *not* planning does not make much business sense!

■ 2 THE ADVANTAGES OF PLANNING

Compiling a plan is not simply the writing down of ideas. A plan calls for logical marketing, thinking and evaluation which in turn requires consideration of what has and is happening and what will or could happen. Therefore, the activity of planning:

- Provokes managers into analysing what is happening and what should happen.
- Encourages better management, e.g. setting of targets for individuals, co-ordination, control, measurement and assessment of what takes place.
- Causes the company to re-evaluate its policies.
- Helps to prepare staff for possible unexpected changes in trading conditions.
- Encourages staff to feel that the efforts of the company are integrated, that management has planned and is prepared for the future.
- A well thought out plan enables banks and investors to feel more confident when lending or buying shares.
- Affords management the opportunity to assess if the necessary returns on investment will be achieved.
- Provides senior management with a control document to refer to in order to check what should be taking place against what is taking place.
- Helps keep monthly expenditure under control relating to planned costs and the revenue being generated.

The list could go on but enough advantages have been expressed for any serious marketer to realise the value of planning and the writing of a plan.

The approach

As already mentioned, planning requires analysing the past to evaluate the previous objectives and what actually occurred internally as well as externally to the company. This will require an audit (marketing audit/record) of the micro, meso and macro environmental factors that affected the company over the previous period: the sort of factors that we considered in Chapter 1, and then again when we used legal, market, political, economic, social and technological criteria to evaluate potential in an overseas market in Chapter 9. When analysing the internal operations and external environmental factors we should be concentrating on determining the **strengths** and **weaknesses** of the company in relation to marketing **opportunities** that the company may be able to realise and the **threats** it may have to face over the future period. These four considerations are often referred to as **SWOT** (Strengths, Weaknesses, Opportunities and

Threats) analysis and should relate directly to each product and market, e.g. the strength a company has in a segment of the market, the weaknesses of a product in satisfying changing needs of a market, etc.

■ 3 ASSUMPTIONS

The next step will be to make assumptions about the future in relation to the marketing audit and findings of the SWOT analysis. This will provide some idea of what is achievable in the future given the current strengths and weaknesses of the company. From this base we may then estimate what would happen if changes to current strategies were made. For example, if given current conditions we expected the future year's sales to be £10 million for a particular product, what would happen if we added ten extra salespeople as suggested by the sales manager?

However, to have a starting point from which to make assumptions, we need to predict what will happen in the future given our current mode and efficiency of operations, which will involve sales forecasting. There are a number of ways in which this may be achieved but five in particular – **salesforce estimations, buyers' estimates, time series, correlation** and **model building** – tend to be the most common.

1 SALESFORCE ESTIMATIONS

This is a forecast based on the collated individual estimates of what each salesperson hopes to sell over the forthcoming period. It is useful in that salespeople, particularly those visiting industrial or reseller customers, often have a good idea of what is happening in their sector of the market. A salesperson will often consult with the customers to determine their estimates before submitting his or her own figure. The estimates the salespeople put forward they also have to achieve personally, so there is a good chance of reaching the overall target. Obviously salespeople will often tend to underestimate so that they can easily reach and exceed the targets set, and this will have to be considered when determining the final forecast. The salesperson's lack of knowledge of the total market situation is understandably a drawback to this method. However, in small companies where there is inadequate past sales data to project into the future, or where sales are erratic, this method may be a first choice.

2 CHECKING BUYERS' ESTIMATES

This method involves asking a representative sample of all buyers in the market their estimate for the forthcoming year. Advantages are that the company is not depending solely on the opinions of its own salesforce or buyers who purchase its product and a more unbiased estimate may be obtained. The disadvantages are that collection of their opinions has to take place long before the plan is to be written in order to collate and present the findings. Therefore, any recent changes cannot always be accommodated. Buyers cannot always be interviewed in depth to discover if they are falsifying claims. Continuous research is needed to make worthwhile comparisons of changes over time which may involve marketing research expertise and make the process quite costly.

3 TIME SERIES

The use of time series rests on the relationship between sales and time and requires the employment of a statistical method. If we plot sales on a graph for each year, connect up the plottings we made and then draw a line straight through the plottings a year into the future we may arrive at a sales forecast for the next period as shown in Fig. 10.1. What we have done in the graph is draw a line straight through the middle (or trend) of the plottings and extend it forward to determine the average sales we can expect at the next point in time.

Fig. 10.1 *Forecasting sales with a straight line graph*

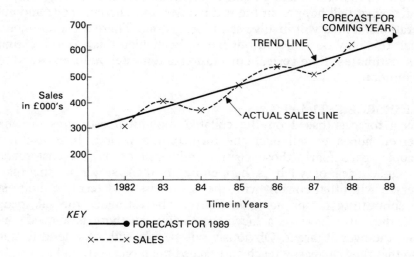

Methods for such forecasting are now available on computer and are sophisticated enough to take account of the most recent sales figures. In Fig. 10.2, for example, a straight line would give the wrong idea of where future sales are heading, but the second sales trend line (broken line) takes account of the most recent sales and represents the situation more correctly.

Several methods exist for forecasting in this way, among them **regression**, **moving averages** and **exponential smoothing**. They all rely on extrapolating (extending) in to the future previous sales performance.

The advantage of time series is that provided future performance is the same as previous performance they may be quite accurate. They also tend to eliminate human error and bias when forecasting. However, they do rely on having sufficient past figures to extrapolate which young companies may not have. They are also based on past performance rather than taking account of changes that may be taking place that will affect the future.

Fig. 10.2 *Forecasting sales with a curved line graph*

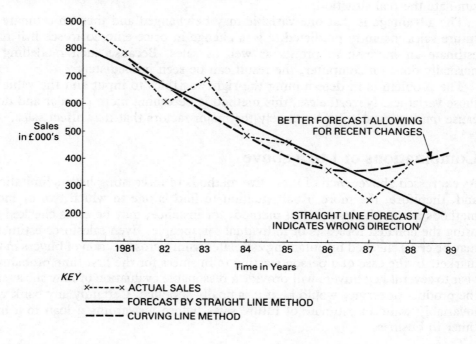

KEY

×------× ACTUAL SALES
———— FORECAST BY STRAIGHT LINE METHOD
- - - - CURVING LINE METHOD

4 CORRELATION

This is another statistical method that determines the degree of relationship between two activities or events. If there is a strong and useful relationship between a company's sales and some other activity or event we may be able to use this knowledge to forecast future sales.

For example, if historically an increase in the purchase of cars by 5 per cent has always meant an approximate increase in steel purchases from our car manufacturing customers of approximately 4 per cent we may assume that there is a strong correlation (relationship) between car sales and steel sales figures. The degree of strength of the relationship may be determined by a statistical formula and calculators and computers are likely to be used for this purpose. The method however, does rest on the assumption that there is a relationship between sales of our product and some other activity, and that the relationship is significant enough to be useful for forecasting. This may be the case with regard to sales resulting from advertising, i.e. as advertising increases so do sales, but it may be difficult to find other external factors that will correlate – or should – with the company's sales.

5 MODEL BUILDING

This again employs statistical methods but allows for the input of variables that are qualitative as well and quantitiative (provided they are given a number to represent their value). The object is to build a model of the major variables that affect sales such as price, seasonality, previous sales, etc. that attempts to simulate the real situation.

The advantage is that one variable may be changed and then an estimate of future sales instantly predicted, e.g. a change in price entered to see if it may estimate an increase in profits as well as sales. Because such modelling is normally done on computer, the result can be seen immediately.

The problem is in determining the right variables to input and the value of those variables. Nevertheless, this method is becoming more popular and does cause marketers to consider closely the major factors that may affect sales.

Combinations of 1 to 5 above

As expressed above, each of these five methods of forecasting has its limitations and, therefore, the more usual situation to find is one in which two or more methods are used. A statistical method, for instance, may be cross checked by using the collated forecasts of individual salespeople. Even salesforce estimates may be cross checked by obtaining estimates from a cross-section of buyers in the market. In the case of a person starting in business for the first time probably a visit to several key buyers will provide a reasonable evaluation of how successful the product or service would be if it is finally supplied. Certainly any bank will invariably want an estimate of future sales before forwarding a loan to a first timer in business.

■ . . . ASSUMPTIONS CONTINUED

Having completed a marketing audit, a SWOT analysis and forecasted what will happen if products, markets and the marketing effort does not change, we may continue to make assumptions: the, **What if . . . ?** aspects or questions of planning.

For example: What if we reduce the price of the product from £6.45 to £5.95? Would this generate more sales revenue than leaving the price at £6.45 and concentrating on promotions to generate sales?

What would happen if we start exporting instead of continuing to try to generate more profits or would it be better to diversify into another product line?

What would happen if we start exporting instead of continuing to try and obtain more of the home market?

These are just a few of the kinds of questions that would have to be answered before objectives and strategies may be finalised and entered in the plan. It is understandable therefore, that most companies undertaking planning seriously see it as a continuous process.

Having made assumptions a re-estimate/re-forecast of sales may be made, as well as a forecast of resources needed and profits that may result. Profits will need to be evaluated in terms of total profits for all products, for individual products, for contribution of individual products and in terms of return on capital employed.

■ 4 OBJECTIVES, STRATEGIES AND TACTICS

When the assumptions stage is complete objectives may be set and strategies for achieving the objectives must be selected. The objectives will be in relation to the product(s) and market(s) whereas the strategies will be in relation to the 4 Ps and their individual roles in the overall strategy. Whatever objectives are finally selected they must be:

- attainable
- affordable
- understandable
- measurable

and must take account of **internal strengths** and **weaknesses** as well as **external opportunities** and **threats** to their achievement.

Whatever strategies are chosen they will have to be capable of being measured in order to determine how successful they have been. The detailed planning and logistics of every effort involved in the strategy must be completed in order that major elements may be entered in the plan and represented in the budget and staff may be provided with an understanding of their personal role and the targets they have to achieve.

In fact, few stages of the development of a plan should be undertaken without full consultation with staff at all levels to ensure that a variety of ideas have been considered and some consensus of agreement has been reached. Tactics on the other hand represent decisions on the elements of the marketing mix which can best serve the achievement of objectives and strategies selected. Table 10.1 illustrates a selection of tactics which might be chosen to achieve a stated objective and strategy.

Table 10.1

Selected objective	Increase sales revenue by 15 per cent
Selected strategy	Introduce the company's products into two overseas markets
Selected tactics	Skimming pricing
	Intensive advertising campaigns in media reaching high socio-economic groups
	Intensive distribution involving wholesalers and retailers
	Use of consumer trial offers
	Trade promotions designed to maximise acceptance of the company's products by the trade
	Public relations concentrating on gaining favourable publicity for the new market entry
	Attractive packaging meeting local regulations and market expectations
	Use of expert salespeople who can contribute to the acceptance of the product by the market

■ THE MARKETING PLAN

Once a final decision has been taken the plan may be written and will (or should) include:

(a) A short analysis of internal strengths and weaknesses in relation to opportunities and threats from the environments.
(b) A preamble to the objectives justifying their selection and the strategies that will be used to achieve them.
(c) An operations plan, defining the role of the departments and their activities in fulfilling the strategies with timetables/schedules detailing prime events/activities.
(d) Resources that will be needed and when.
(e) A financial budget that will detail the areas of expenditure and amounts allocated for those areas so that checks may be made monthly on expenditure to see that efforts are remaining within the amounts allotted.

From the marketing plan individual plans will be determined for each department so that everyone in the department is clear as to their department's targets, workload and, possibly, expenditure in relation to the marketing plan of the company.

Figure 10.3 shows the sequence of stages in planning which are necessary to achieve the marketing plan.

People make a plan work

We have looked at marketing planning and plans in brief only and in skeleton form to provide the student or newcomer to marketing with an introduction to the subject. In the real life situation a much deeper analysis of the subject would be needed before an attempt at a detailed plan for a company could be safely undertaken.

Whatever the plan, however, it must take into account one overriding factor which is *people*, for the finest plan is only as good as the people who have to make it work. Therefore, always make certain when compiling a plan that you have consulted other staff and considered how they will be organised, directed, co-ordinated, controlled and above all motivated into performing their best in a satisfying but stimulating working environment.

Fig. 10.3 *Shows the sequence of stages in planning which are necessary to achieve the marketing plan*

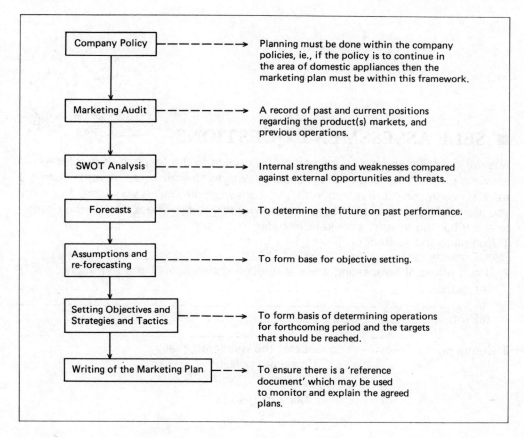

Company Policy	Planning must be done within the company policies, ie., if the policy is to continue in the area of domestic appliances then the marketing plan must be within this framework.
Marketing Audit	A record of past and current positions regarding the product(s) markets, and previous operations.
SWOT Analysis	Internal strengths and weaknesses compared against external opportunities and threats.
Forecasts	To determine the future on past performance.
Assumptions and re-forecasting	To form base for objective setting.
Setting Objectives and Strategies and Tactics	To form basis of determining operations for forthcoming period and the targets that should be reached.
Writing of the Marketing Plan	To ensure there is a 'reference document' which may be used to monitor and explain the agreed plans.

■ STUDY AND EXAM TIPS

1 When answering questions on marketing plans bear in mind that the question is often more concerned with the planning element than the actual plan, so read the question very carefully.

2 When answering questions on planning that appear to be beyond the coverage of the topic at a fundamentals level be prepared to draw on the knowledge you have gained on the individual areas of the marketing activity.

3 If you are at all concerned about a question on planning choose another question to answer. Planning is really a major part of corporate policy which students at a fundamentals level sometimes have difficulty in appreciating.

4 Remember in particular, the sequence of planning, the contents of the plan and forecasting and objective setting.

■ SELF ASSESSMENT QUESTIONS

Answer the following questions without reference to the text and then refer to the answers given at the end of the manual to determine your score. Award yourself 1 mark for each complete question that you answer correctly. If you score 4 or more you are reading efficiently. Where you answered wrongly check back in the chapter to see what the answer should have been.

1 Complete the sentence.

SWOT stands for strengths _____

2 One method of forecasting sales is through correlation. Name four more.

(a) _____

(b) _____

(c) _____

(d) _____

3 Complete the following sequence of the marketing plan.

Corporate policies
↓
Marketing audit
↓

_____

↓

_____

↓

_____

↓

_____

↓

_____

4 Complete the sentence.

A plan defines where you wish to be at some time in the future and _____

_____

5 Which of the following should not be in the list (tick the appropriate box).
A marketing plan contains

☐ a statement of the marketing objectives.
☐ details of the methods/strategies to be used.
☐ an operating plan.
☐ a marketing research analysis.
☐ details of resources needed.
☐ a financial budget.

■ EXAMINATION QUESTIONS

The Association of Business Executives

1 For effective budgeting and control it is essential for the enterprise to produce realistic annual forecasts of sales.
   Describe the main features and applications of at least FOUR methods which could be used to arrive at an annual forecast of sales.

2 A key element in a marketing plan is the formulation of objectives.
(a) Explain the significance of objectives giving examples of objectives that are commonly included, and,
(b) identify what factors could inhibit or prevent a company realising the objectives set out in its marketing plan.

■ NEXT IN THIS MARKETING SERIES

If you have enjoyed reading this book you may be pleased to learn that the follow on book *Marketing in Practice* has now been published by Stanley Thornes. It is written by the same authors to cover the 'Practice of Marketing' syllabus of The Chartered Institute of Marketing but also touches on many topics that appear in the Marketing papers of The Association of Business Executives.

Leading on from the fundamentals level the book extends the reader's knowledge on many of the topics covered in this book and puts the knowledge the reader has gained into practice through handling real-life case studies. A must for students, marketing lecturers and practitioners alike.

Likewise the latest edition of *How to Pass Exams* written by W. G. Leader is available covering every major area of examinations with worked examples. Whether you are at school, college, university or a home-study student you are bound to find that this invaluable book will improve your exam performance.

A personal note

Hopefully you have now read this manual fully so we take this opportunity to wish you once again every success in your examinations and your future career.

Answers to self assessment questions

Chapter 1

1 (a) King
  (b) sovereignty
2 (a) product
  (b) sales
  (c) market
3 false
4 two
5 false
6 (c)
7 product, price, promotion, place
8 micro, meso, macro
9 (b)
10 (c)
11 marketing mix
12 marketing integrated
13 refer to part 3 of chapter
14 refer to part 3 of chapter
15 product, market, combination/combined

Chapter 2

1 user
2 (b)
3 See page 50
4 reseller
5 See page 33
6 See page 33
7 durability
8 shopping goods, speciality goods
9 Decision Making Unit
10 user, influencer, decider
11 demographically, by buyer behaviour, psychographically, by benefits purchasers receive
12 A, B, C2, D, E
13 accessibility, substantiality
14 differentiated, concentrated
15 benefits

Chapter 3

1 yes
2 yes
3 desk research
4 field (primary) research
5 qualitative
6 stratified, systematic, multistage, cluster, quota
7 dichotomous, multichoice, semantic differential scales, open ended
8 telephone, postal, observation
9 non random
10 ad hoc

Chapter 4

1 (e)
2 re-purchase
3 interest, evaluation, trial, adoption
4 innovators, early adoptors, early majority, late majority
5 growth, maturity, saturation, decline
6 package
7 for convenience, reduce distribution costs, promote the product, distinguish the product, establish product group identity
8 See page 107
9 family brand name, individual brand name
10 break even

Chapter 5

1 no
2 price, ask
3 monetary, product
4 target pricing
5 channels of distribution
6 product line/range
7 cost plus/mark up pricing
8 going rate, negotiated
9 trade, quantity, seasonal
10 See part 3 in the chapter
11 contribution, losses
12 cost orientated, competition
13 failure

Chapter 6

1 See part 1
2 wholesalers and retailers
3 direct (personal) selling
4 two
5 provision of information, payment, title to goods
6 to the right place at the right time
7 direct (personal) selling, direct mail/mail drops, direct response advertising
8 street traders, vending machines, mobile shops, street stands, catalogue selling, personal selling, direct mail, direct response advertising

9 the market, competitor methods, financial position, the economy, seasonal factors, availability of an adequate network, marketing objectives, distributor resistance, legal restrictions
10 exclusive distribution, selective distribution

Chapter 7

1 improving performance of salespeople, ensure recruitment, selection and training, efficient administration and co-ordination of the sales office, co-ordinate post sales service
2 customer, product groups, region, combination of two or more other methods (compound)
3 customer type, customer size, product group, area, combination of two or more other methods.
4 See part 2
5 makers
6 prospecting and pre-approach, the approach, the presentation, the close (closing the sale)
7 means, authority
8 prepare job description, specification/profile, making the position

known, issuing application forms
9 initial interview, final interview
10 individual training needed (training gap)

Chapter 8

1 See part 1
2 TV, radio, the Press, cinema
3 line
4 fairs
5 target audience, impact, repetition
6 See part 2
7 See part 2
8 personal selling
9 stocks, store layout, store promotions
10 derived demand method
11 potential customers in order to improve sales
12 the media
13 opportunity to see

Chapter 9

1 self reference criterion
2 PEST
3 political, economic, social, technical
4 ferocity of competition, risk reduction, legal restraints, market acceptance
5 export, export marketing
6 branches, manufacturing unit/company, joint ventures, franchising

7 stocking, repair and service, del credere
8 franchisor, franchisee
9 see end of part 4
10 false

Chapter 10

1 weaknesses, opportunities, threats
2 time series, model building, salesforce estimates, buyer estimates
3 SWOT analysis, sales forecasts, assumptions and re-forecasting, setting objectives, strategies, and tactics, writing of the marketing plan
4 how to get there
5 a marketing research analysis

Index